THE JAMES BOND FILMS

The trick Aston Martin DB-5 with modifications
that saved James Bond's life in GOLDFINGER and
THUNDERBALL.

THE JAMES BOND FILMS

A BEHIND THE SCENES HISTORY

STEVEN JAY RUBIN

Arlington House, Inc.

For my father, Joseph S. Rubin,
with whom I first shared the wonder
of James Bond, Secret Agent 007.

ACKNOWLEDGMENTS

For consenting to interviews in both London and Los Angeles, I would like to thank the following individuals: Peter Hunt, Richard Maibaum, Tom Mankiewicz, Jane Seymour, Harry Saltzman, Kevin McClory, Terence Young, William Cartlidge, Lewis Gilbert, Roald Dahl, Ken Adam, Syd Cain, Peter Murton, George Leech, Chris Webb, Derek Meddings, John Stears, John Glen, Rick Sylvester, John Barry, Bob Fenn, David Middlemas, Derek Crachnell, Richard Jenkins, Maurice Patchett, Christopher Lee, Martine Beswick, Bernard Lee, Eunice Gayson, George Lazenby, Lamar Boren, Rik Van Nutter, Luciana Paluzzi, Maud Adams, Gloria Hendry, and Bill Hill.

I would particularly like to thank Messrs. Hunt, Maibaum, and Mankiewicz, and Miss Seymour, who continually made themselves accessible to me for further research questions. Without their patience, much of the information in this book would not have been available.

For their additional contributions to the manuscript, I would like to thank Jeff Kalmick, Robert Short, Kent Schoknecht, Whitney Bain, Richard Meyers, Buddy Weiss, Steve Swires, Steve Mitchell, Jerry Ohlinger, Ted Bohus, Tom Rogers, Frederick Clarke, and *Cinefantastique* magazine, and the staffs of the Academy of Motion Picture Arts and Science in Los Angeles and the British Film Institute in London.

For photographic materials, I owe a debt of gratitude to Danny Biederman, Don Griffin of Perry Oceanographics in Miami, Tom Sciacca, Ernest Burns of Cinemabilia, Pam Kerr of Life Photo Service, Denise Dilanni of Gamma Liaison, Bill Fitzgerald of Wide World Photos, Angelo at United Press International, and Bill Malone. For additional photographic materials, many thanks to Rick Sylvester, The Glastron Boat Company, Universal Pictures, NBC, NASA, Columbia Pictures, Charles Sherman, American International, and 20th Century-Fox.

Finally, I would like to thank Bob Enos of Arlington House for his support and enthusiasm for the project, Kevin Gough-Yates of Talisman Books, London, for his perseverance and massive creative input, Richard Schenkman of the James Bond Fan Club for his support on all fronts, and my mother, Evelyn Rubin, who is always there. Thanks, everybody, we made it.

First published in Great Britain, 1981/by Visorbond, Ltd.

Published in the United States by Arlington House, Inc.
Distributed by Crown Publishers, Inc., 225 Park Avenue South, New York, New York 10003

Rubin, Steven Jay, 1951-
    The James Bond films.

    Includes index.
    1. James Bond films—History and criticism.
I. Title.
PN1995.9.J3R8 1983   791.43'09'09351   83-11923
ISBN 0-517-55106-3
        0-517-55093-8 (pbk)

Manufactured in U.S.A.
Typesetting by Traditional Typesetters Ltd, Chesham, Bucks.

10 9 8 7 6 5

Revised Edition

CONTENTS

Where else would you find Sean Connery but in bed with the opposition? Here with lucky Lucianna Paluzzi from THUNDERBALL. *(Wide World)*

List of Abbreviations

PC Production Company
PROD Producer
DIR Director
SCR Scriptwriter

PH Director of Photography
ED Editor
PROD DES Production Designer
MUSIC Music composer

SP EFFECTS Special Effects
STUNT CO-ORD Stunt Co-ordinator

INTRODUCTION

It is now more than twenty-one years since production began at Palisadoes Airport in Kingston, Jamaica, on the very first James Bond film, *Dr. No*, in February 1962. The latest edition of this book is being written on the verge of 007's biggest year. The summer of 1983 may very well prove to be of historical significance if, indeed, Roger Moore and Sean Connery make their last appearances as Secret Agent James Bond. There is no doubt in my mind that both *Never Say Never Again* and *Octopussy* are going to be major box-office hits. You just can't keep a good man down.

Even if Sean and Roger do ride off in their twin Aston Martins into that 007 sunset, I am confident that a new James Bond will take their place. He's already waiting in the wings — in his youthful thirties, dark-haired, handsome, athletic, suave, and English — a man who will carry on the exploits of the world's most famous secret agent. One thing is certain — it isn't James Brolin.

Since I first started research on *The James Bond Films* in London in early 1977, I have had the opportunity to meet a great number of fascinating individuals, who have continued to tell me interesting stories about the world of James Bond. Screenwriter Richard Maibaum, who, with *Octopussy*, continues to be the literary soul of 007, has been a continual inspiration. He definitely belongs to the A-team — a creative group of people who have made the best Bond films — a team that includes director Terence Young, director/editor Peter Hunt, writer Tom Mankiewicz, stunt chiefs Bob Simmons and George Leech, composer John Barry, and of course the godfather himself — Albert R. "Cubby" Broccoli.

I also would like to take some time to congratulate those young upstarts: director John Glen and executive producer and Bond heir apparent Michael G. Wilson who have purposefully avoided the mindlessness of *Moonraker* in their last two efforts.

Since 1981 I have seen the *Casino Royale* 1954 television show, which featured Barry Nelson as 007 (nicknamed "Card Sense Jimmy Bond"), and I keep bumping into people with new stories. Cinematographer Frank Tidy, with whom I recently worked on the new 3-D adventure film *Spacehunter: Adventures in the Forbidden Zone*, told me he broke into the business working with Robert Brownjohn and Trevor Bond on the title sequence for *From Russia with Love*. Remember the titles on the undulating body of the belly dancer? The inspiration came when Brownjohn's wife walked in front of a slide show he was projecting. Since Brownjohn and Bond were cinematographers, the in-joke on that movie was projecting Ted Moore's credit on the girl's posterior.

I've also discovered that Eon Productions stands for Everything or Nothing Productions, an appropriate tag.

I hope you enjoy the new information.

STEVE RUBIN
Summer 1983

1

IN THE BEGINNING WAS... IAN FLEMING

It was in *Casino Royale*, not *Dr. No*, that James Bond made his first screen appearance. The first Bond film was transmitted on American live television on October 21st 1954. *Casino Royale* was the third episode in CBS's *Climax Mystery Theater*, an anthology of suspense stories presented by actor William Lundigan. Veteran Broadway producer and film director Bretaigne Windust decided to give the drama an American perspective and cast Yankee, Barry Nelson to portray the British agent. Peter Lorre played the evil Le Chiffre, a Russian agent who controls the resources of the world's largest and most famous casino, whilst Linda Christian became the first Bond girl.

Filmed mainly on a casino set built at Television City in Hollywood, *Casino Royale* lacked all the adventure and dazzling locations associated with 007. It was, essentially, a simple duel between Le Chiffre and Bond, with a baccarat table between them. Not surprisingly, Bond's first screen appearance passed almost unnoticed by the critics.

James Bond was born a decade earlier in 1944, when Ian Fleming spent some weeks in Jamaica on wartime business. Before returning to London, he asked his friend, American millionaire Ivar Bryce, to purchase some Jamaican beach property for him.

Two years later, Fleming was hired by newspaper magnate Lord Kemsley, to manage the foreign news section of a large group of English papers. He took the job on condition that his contract included a two month holiday each year.

The father of world Bonddom, Ian Lancaster Fleming, and his wife Anne Rothermere, ca. 1962. (*Wide World*)

With his beach house completed, Fleming began a routine that was to continue until the end of his life and which produced thirteen James Bond thrillers. Although he had toyed with the idea of writing for nearly six years, it was not until a few weeks before his marriage in 1952 that he decided to write a novel. Fleming took the name of his main character from the author of a book that always graced his coffee table – *Birds of the West Indies* by the ornithologist James Bond.

As he planned this first novel, Fleming drew upon his experiences as a journalist. In 1933, when he was working for Reuter, the 25 year old Fleming had been sent to Moscow to cover the scandalous trial of a group of Metro-Vickers engineers who were being accused of sabotage by the Soviet government. In despatches which won him the respect of his fellow journalists, he carefully avoided a mundane, blow by blow account of the trial and concentrated instead on the atmosphere surrounding the event and the strange personalities of the men who were making the news.

If he needed help on a story, he was not above asking someone with the proper expertise to collaborate. When he wrote the James Bond novels, he found himself particularly weak in automobile technology and ballistics. To rectify this he called in qualified experts. Like many journalists, Fleming had friends in every field: wine stewards, gunsmiths, diamond brokers, bankers, gourmet cooks, under-water explorers, and mechanics. The James Bond novels were as much a part of their combined experience as they were a part of Fleming's recollections.

The possibility of turning the James Bond

Goldeneye, Fleming's house in Jamaica, as it looked in 1962. (Wide World)

novels into dramatic scripts had interested Ian Fleming early on. He had many friends in the entertainment business, including actor David Niven and Alexander Korda, the well known producer. Korda had asked to see an advance copy of *Live and Let Die*, Fleming's second novel and, out of the blue, CBS offered a thousand dollars for the television rights to *Casino Royale*. Despite the good reviews of *Moonraker*, however, the only project to go forward was the feeble American television drama. Alexander Korda returned the advance copy of *Live and Let Die* with a polite note.

Desperate for hard cash, Fleming sold the movie rights of *Casino Royale* to film director Gregory Ratoff, for six thousand dollars outright. Ratoff in turn, was later to sell them to Charles K. Feldman who produced *Casino Royale* as a spoof in 1967.

A few months after Fleming had completed

From Russia with Love, in 1956, the actor Ian Hunter expressed interest in *Moonraker*. Fleming agreed to sell an option to Hunter who was working for the Rank Organisation but he would only accept an advance option of a thousand pounds, and ten thousand for the film rights. Shortly after this deal, he received an interesting offer from the American multi-millionaire Henry Morgenthau III who was working as a television producer for NBC. Morgenthau was planning a a half hour adventure series tentatively entitled *Commander Jamaica*, to be filmed on location, and wanted Fleming to collaborate on it.

Fleming's plot outline for this involved a main character, James Gunn. The base of operations was a thirty foot yacht moored at Morgan's Harbour, Jamaica. A crusty old admiral who speaks through the yacht's hidden speaker was outlined as Gunn's superior. The plot-line hinged on Gunn's investigations into the activities on an uninhabited island of a gang, thought to be behind a plot to deflect the course of American missiles from Cape Canaveral. When NBC did not pick up the series, Fleming retrieved this outline on which he based his sixth novel, *Dr. No.*

One year later, CBS entered the option game once more. In exchange for a liberal advance they asked Fleming if he would like to write a series of thirty two Bond episodes for television. He agreed, but yet again, a television deal fell flat. Fleming used six of the plot outlines he had written to form the basis for a collection of short stories entitled *For Your Eyes Only.*

Talk of a feature film deal resumed in the winter of 1958, when Fleming's friend Ivar Bryce arrived in London and introduced him to Kevin McClory, a thirty three year old Irish film director whom Bryce was backing in his first feature film venture. Fleming was quite willing to associate himself with Bryce and McClory and their new film company, Xanadu Productions. If the new project was filmed in the Bahamas, Xanadu could benefit from the Eady Subsidy Plan which allowed certain productions filmed within the "Commonwealth" to have part of their costs underwritten.

Fleming's new agent, Laurence Evans of MCA, told him plainly that young, inexperienced directors did not attract big name stars. Since Fleming wanted either James Stewart, Richard Burton or David Niven (with James Mason as a fourth choice) to play Bond, he advised him to consider another director for the project. Although Fleming took the point Evans was making, plans went ahead with McClory. Rather than use one of the existing James Bond novels as a basis for a script, it was decided to create an entirely new adventure that would feature plot and production values geared to a film audience.

In May 1959, Bryce, Ernst Cuneo, and McClory outlined a possible Bond adventure. In this treatment, a Russian agent poses as a US army sergeant working on board a USO airliner, loaded with celebrities, which is constantly flying to top secret US bases. Bond discovers that the Russians plan to detonate atomic bombs on these same bases.

When the sergeant transfers to the Caribbean USO, Bond follows, disguised as a British entertainer. In Nassau, he discovers that a mysterious power has ordered a fleet of Bahaman fishing boats, all of which are equipped with water-tight underwater hatches, just like those used by the Italian Navy during World War II. Atomic bombs

are to be delivered by Russian submarines to these fishing boats and hoisted through their water tight trap doors by frogmen. Cuneo concluded the outline by detailing an underwater battle between the enemy frogmen and Bond's unit which takes place during an outdoor USO concert in Nassau.

Fleming's main objections to Cuneo's outline concerned the lack of a Bond heroine and the use of the Russians as the principal villains. In place of the Russians, Fleming created SPECTRE,

Barry Nelson, the very first James Bond. He appeared on American television in CASINO ROYALE.

which, in his imagination, stood for: Special Executive for Terrorism, Revolution and Espionage, and which was an immensely powerful, privately owned organisation, manned by ex-members of Smersh, the Gestapo, the Mafia and the Black Tong of Peking. Fleming's idea was that this sinister organisation was placing the atomic bombs on NATO bases, with the object of blackmailing the Western Powers for one hundred million pounds.

"M" was to have had a double agent in SPECTRE for some time, a beautiful female agent called Fatima Blush, the stewardess on the USO plane assisting the baggage sergeant. From her, Bond gradually finds out the details of the plan which otherwise would be difficult to penetrate.

"In the final underwater scene", wrote Fleming, "Fatima Blush is, of course, with the enemy and her appearance in tight fitting black rubber suiting will make the audiences swoon. But as the fight progresses, the baggage sergeant finds her cutting a hole in his underwater suit and realises she is a double agent. In the ensuing

A 1952 publicity still of actress Linda Christian. She was to play the first Bond girl in CASINO ROYALE, the CBS television production that introduced Bond to the screen.

Veteran villain Peter Lorre became the first Bond nemesis in CBS's "Climax Mystery Theater" television production of CASINO ROYALE.

shemozzel, Bond kills the baggage sergeant just as he is turning off the valve on Fatima's oxygen tanks, and the curtain goes down as Bond and Fatima kiss through their snorkels."

In Fleming's first screen treatment, he actually abandoned SPECTRE and created a purely Mafia conceived conspiracy, headed by a Capo Mafioso named Cuneo, whose principal lieutenant is a huge bear of a man named Largo. Largo was to be played by American actor Burl Ives, who was already interested in the project. Largo and his hand-picked team break into an American atom base in Britain and steal an atomic bomb. They transfer the bomb to a helicopter which transports it to a tramp steamer anchored in the English channel. It is then passed on to a Sunderland flying boat which speeds across the Atlantic

Thomas Sean Connery, a proud Scotsman who became an international superstar as 007. *(Wide World)*

and deposits its cargo in the water near Largo's huge yacht *The Virginia*, where a complement of divers transfers it through the yacht's watertight underwater hatch.

Much of the early action in Fleming's treatment takes place at a public house in the British countryside, to which Bond tracks Largo. Here he meets a British agent named Domino Smith who has infiltrated the Mafia gang.

Rather than leave certain elements of the story to the viewer's imagination, Fleming sometimes allowed Bond to lapse into narration, during which he talked about his background. For instance, there is a sequence in which Bond is sitting in his office waiting for a call from "M" which will send him to Nassau. During this pensive moment, Bond begins to describe himself:

My name is James Bond. I am agent 007 in the Secret Service. The double o means that I have licence to kill in the execution of my duties. That means that

Over a decade before he became 007's stern superior, "M," Bernard Lee was a dashing young actor in his own right, here in *The Third Man*. Lee died in January 1981. *(Selznick Pictures)*

I get the dirty jobs – the jobs you never read about in the newspapers, the ones even the Government would rather know nothing about.

Bond follows the Sunderland flying boat to Nassau where he once more meets Largo who is now posing as the head of the Italian American Garment Workers Union, now convening in the islands. Meanwhile, the Mafia demand a hundred million pounds in gold bullion in return for the missing atomic bomb. Bond, with Felix Leiter of the CIA helping him, establishes that Largo is actually an American gangster. After a few encounters with Bond, Domino Smith, who is still with Largo, agrees to take a geiger counter aboard *The Virginia*. She is discovered and tied to her bunk. Bond and Leiter shadow *The Virginia* in a US submarine which leads to the finale, an underwater battle off Miami where Largo's men have placed the bomb. Bond is about to be killed by Largo when he, instead, is speared by Domino who has managed to escape the yacht and join the fight. The film ends as the Navy recovers the bomb, while Bond, rather than kiss Domino through her snorkel, lifts off her mask, takes her to a nearby beach and begins kissing her passionately.

Fleming's associates liked the treatment but they felt that someone with screenwriting experience was needed on the job. Eventually, Jack Whittingham was chosen who considered that the method by which the Mafia grab the Atomic bomb was unbelievable. Instead, he suggested that the Mafia hijack a NATO bomber with atom bombs aboard. They could crash land the plane in the Bahamas where the bombs could still be transferred aboard the Mafia yacht via frogmen.

Whittingham pointed out that Fleming's story was told too much in dialogue and that there were not enough visuals to carry the story along. He did not like Domino Smith's easy penetration of the Mafia gang, nor the counter espionage plot in which the Secret Service sends only two men and a girl to Nassau. Whittingham also felt that the Mafia should steal two bombs. The first could be detonated if the NATO powers failed to deliver the ransom.

He eliminated all passages where Fleming had stopped the action with a Bond narration, cut out the public house interlude as pointless and erased

Bond's description of the Mafia. Plans were made to introduce the villains visually.

He decided to begin the script with a Mafia agent named Martelli who journeys to Nassau to tell Largo that a NATO observer named Joe Petacchi is now under their control. Largo is pleased, offers him a fee of ten thousand dollars and then promptly has one of his bodyguards shoot Martelli in the back. After this, his body is thrown to the sharks.

Petacchi hijacks the plane but not before Allied Intelligence is able to get a faint trace of it in mid-Atlantic. Bond is informed by "M" that this faint trace is in Longitude 78 West and that is where Bond is sent. The longitude 78 West location became the working title of the script, until Fleming and McClory changed it to *Thunderball*, which was the code name for the Anglo-American Intelligence operation.

Whittingham's script followed the basic Fleming outline once Bond and Leiter arrive in Nassau. They lead the investigation on the island where they come across Largo and his convention of Mafia types. He added a scene where Bond fights it out with an underwater sentry while searching the hull of Largo's yacht (now named *The Sorrento*). A British gunboat (replacing Fleming's submarine) shadows *The Sorrento* until the final underwater battle which, this time, takes place off the Grand Bahama missile base.

Whittingham's ending has Largo flying off in a seaplane with the other atomic bomb, unaware the detonator has been reset. As Bond and a wounded Leiter observe, the plane is obliterated.

In the middle of 1958, everything looked promising for the new film. Two years later, everything had changed. Although Bryce was excited about the Whittingham script, he was no longer capable of financing the Bond film on his own. McClory and Bryce were pleased with the Whittingham treatment and continued to submit the script to potential backers. Little did they know that Fleming was using the very same Whittingham, McClory material as the basis for his eighth Bond novel which he was calling *Thunderball*.

Fleming went back to SPECTRE as the principal villain and the architect of the A-bomb

Warner Brothers contract player Lois Maxwell, who went on to become the forever frustrated Miss Moneypenny, is now the only surviving veteran of all twelve James Bond movies. *(Warner Brothers)*

hijacking. He also created an opening interlude in which Bond meets a SPECTRE agent at a country health clinic called Shrublands. Fleming had no idea that he had done something offensive until the following Spring when his book was about to be published.

No sooner did McClory read an advance copy of *Thunderball* than he and Whittingham petitioned the High Court of London for an injunction to hold up publication. In their legal plea, they claimed that Fleming had infringed their joint copyright by publishing a book based on the script, without their consent. Unfortunately for everyone concerned, no clear agreements had been signed during the pre-production phase on

Thunderball. What should have been a two week trial turned into a three year running court battle.

On April 12th 1961, just a few days after the summons, Fleming suffered a major heart attack. While he recuperated in the London Clinic, he received a kindly note from a Canadian film producer named Harry Saltzman whom he had met the year before. Saltzman wished the author well and explained that preparations were being made to take a James Bond package to United Artists. He had recently purchased options on all available Bond books and was confident that he could get a film deal off the ground. Despite all the setbacks, James Bond was to be born again.

An English journalist once described Harry Saltzman as a "tiny, tubby man with a larger than life attitude." The description is an apt one for the co-producer of the first eight Bond films who had made his name on the vaudeville circuits as early as 1928.

Saltzman's film career got under way in England in 1956 when he formed Woodfall Productions, an independent production company, with playwright John Osborne and director Tony Richardson. In a 1961 interview, Saltzman summarised his company's achievements as one flop (*Look Back in Anger*), one break even enterprise (*The Entertainer*), and one blockbuster (*Saturday Night and Sunday Morning*).

A disagreement in the latter half of 1960 led to his resignation from Woodfall. Shortly afterwards, Saltzman's lawyer, Brian Lewis, introduced him to Ian Fleming. They met in the winter of 1960. By now, Fleming, who was anxious to to set up a trust fund for his wife and son, was under pressure from Lewis, who was also his lawyer, to make a quick film deal. Failure to do this meant that the trust value of his books would have to be based on the 1954 outright sale of *Casino Royale* to Gregory Ratoff for the modest six thousand dollars. It was now that Lewis advised Saltzman to put in a bid for the Bond books.

At their meeting, Saltzman indicated that he might be able to scrape together fifty thousand dollars for a six month option and if the project was picked up by a major studio, he would try to get Fleming one hundred thousand dollars a picture, plus a percentage. Fleming agreed in principle, arranging for Saltzman to meet his film

Director Terence Young, the epitome of action-film directors, whose panache and general enthusiasm for the Bond character elevated 007 to the upper ranks of film history.

agent Bob Fenn of MCA to work out the deal on paper.

Fenn, MCA president Jules Stein's right hand man in London, had spent the previous two years consolidating Fleming's affairs. He had bought back Rank's unused option on *Moonraker* and tried hard to buy out Charles Feldman's rights to *Casino Royale*. Fenn offered Saltzman the seven available books plus future options on any other Bond novel.

For five months, Saltzman tried unsuccessfully to sell the studios the idea of a series of James Bond films. It was the old story. The studios would not touch the project without the commitment of a major star, and a major star would not commit himself to more than a couple of films. At last, with only 28 days left on the option, Saltzman received an important call from his writer friend Wolf Mankowitz who told him that London based producer Cubby Broccoli was interested in the Bond project.

Richard Maibaum, whose clever screenwriting was one of the key factors in the success of the Bond series.

Cubby Broccoli was a former coffin salesman (the inspiration for the flaming hearse in *Dr. No,* the funeral parlour of Nathan Slumber in *Diamonds Are Forever,* and the graveyard world of Baron Samedi in *Live and Let Die* comes from this experience). His career in films began when he became an assistant to Howard Hawks on *The Outlaw.* After war service in World War II, Broccoli returned to Hollywood where he became a successful agent working for none other than Charles Feldman. His interest in becoming a producer gained impetus when he renewed his friendship with director Irving Allen with whom he later formed a company. Because of the lack of opportunity for independents in Hollywood,

Broccoli and Allen moved to London where they founded Warwick Pictures and hired Alan Ladd on a three picture contract. Terence Young, a former screenwriter, was chosen to direct the first of these, *The Red Beret.* Warwick's personnel included cinematographer Ted Moore who started as a camera operator on *The Red Beret,* script writer Richard Maibaum who wrote *The Red Beret* and the extremely successful *Cockleshell Heroes,* art director Ken Adam, who designed the Warwick feature *The Trials of Oscar Wilde,* and of course Terence Young.

Two years before Harry Saltzman met Fleming, Albert Broccoli was given the opportunity to start a James Bond project, but, whilst he himself was keen, Irving Allen rejected the idea outright. This incident contributed to the disintegration of their partnership and the final collapse of Warwick Films in 1960. Alone, but extremely wealthy and resourceful, Broccoli began to search for a new project. Dubious about making any deals with Fleming after the earlier fiasco, he nevertheless agreed to meet Mankowitz's producer friend in 1961. The two men eventually decided to form a partnership, the slightly reluctant Saltzman accepting a fifty-fifty deal.

Broccoli took the Fleming option to Columbia Pictures but their eventual answer was negative. He then decided to offer the project to United Artists and on June 20th 1961, he and Saltzman flew into New York City for a meeting with United Artists president Arthur Krim. Fortunately for the future of James Bond, United Artists was ready to deal. On the recommendations of David Picker, who was a Bond fan and UA London Chief, Bud Orenstein, Krim decided to go for the project. When Broccoli and Saltzman entered his office they found, to their surprise, the entire UA Board of Directors waiting for them. Within minutes, as Broccoli remembers, they had agreed to a six picture deal.

John Derek captures his wife, Ursula Andress, in the mire of the Falmouth Swamps of Jamaica during the filming of DR. NO in 1962. *(UPI)*

2

"MR CONNERY, THE DOCTOR WILL SEE YOU NOW"

Dr. No, the book on which the first Bond film was based, was one of Ian Fleming's most consistently exciting novels. Like all the 007 thrillers, *Dr. No* was based, to some extent, on Fleming's own experiences. In this case, the story originated in a journey he made in March 1956, after receiving a telegram from Ivar Bryce inviting him to join the first scientific expedition since 1916 to visit the flamingo colony on the tiny island of Inagua in the Bahamas.

On the island, Fleming lived with a game warden, sleeping in a tent, watching out for mammoth centipedes and listening intently to the naturalists as they talked about various bird species. These included the fertilising guano birds which occasionally flew in from South America to drop their precious cargo. Fleming found it surprising that guano, or bird dung, was worth so much as a commercial fertiliser and began recording the pertinent facts. He also noted the unusual "marsh buggy" in which they travelled around the island. It looked like a jeep but was equipped with huge balloon tires. A year later, his experience on this short holiday paid off, as he transformed Inagua into the mystery shrouded Crab Key, fortress home of the evil oriental Dr. No.

The six foot six inch bald headed Doctor was Ian Fleming's tribute to Sax Rohmer's Fu Manchu stories which he had read at Eton. In the novel, Dr. No escapes to Crab Key with the million dollar treasury of a Chinese Tong Society. There he is working for the Russians and his island, disguised as a thriving guano factory, is actually a maze of sophisticated electronics hardware set up to confuse the guidance systems

DR. NO (1962) PC. Eon Productions – A United Artists Release 105 mins Col. **PROD.** Albert R. Broccoli and Harry Saltzman **DIR.** Terence Young **SCR.** Richard Maibaum, Joanna Harwood and Berkely Mather from the novel by Ian Fleming **PH.** Ted Moore **ED.** Peter Hunt **PROD DES.** Ken Adam **MUSIC.** Monty Norman – Bond theme John Barry **SP EFFECTS.** Frank George **CAST.** Sean Connery (James Bond), Ursula Andress (Honey Ryder), Joseph Wiseman (Dr. No), Jack Lord (Felix Leiter), Bernard Lee ("M"), Anthony Dawson (Professor Dent), John Kitzmiller (Quarrel), Zena Marshall (Miss Taro), Eunice Gayson (Sylvia Trench), Lois Maxwell (Miss Moneypenny), Lester Prendergast (Puss-Feller), Tim Moxon (John Strangways), Margaret LeWars (Girl Photographer), Reggie Carter (Mr. Jones), Peter Burton (Major Boothroyd), William Foster-Davies (Duff), Louis Blaazer (Pleydell-Smith), Michele Mok (Sister Rose), Yvonne Shima (Sister Lily), Dolores Keator (Mary), The Byron Lee Band (Themselves).

of American missiles. Crab Key, once a bird refuge which Dr. No destroyed with his flame-throwing "dragon" tank, is protected by a group of black Chinese thugs who extend their network of spies and assassins to Jamaica.

When Dr. No orders the death of the snooping Secret Service Chief, John Strangways, and his pretty assistant, James Bond is called into the case. He teams up with a useful Cayman Islander named Quarrel, foils several attempts on his own life and lands on Crab Key. There he meets a female Tarzan named Honeychile Ryder, evades a pack of dogs and the island's guards, loses Quarrel to the dragon tank, gets captured, meets Dr. No and survives the tunnel of death, rescues Honeychile and buries the Doctor in a mountain of bird dung. The novel was extremely fast-paced and was perhaps the closest to an American Mickey Spillane adventure that Fleming ever came.

Late in the summer of 1961, screenwriters Richard Maibaum and Wolf Mankowitz began working on Fleming's novel. Although they planned to retain nearly the entire plot, neither of

A wardrobe mistress repairs a break in Ursula Andress's skintight pants. *(UPI)*

them could stomach the title character, Dr. No. With his two hooks for hands (his fellow Tong members had cut them off) and his bald head, they thought him too gross a caricature for any film. Since Broccoli had early indicated the need for humour in the script, the writers wrote a first draft in which there was no person named Dr. No. The name was given instead to the villain's little spider monkey who sat on his shoulder, an amusing touch but one which infuriated Broccoli. To avoid further embarrassment, Wolf Mankowitz bowed out, leaving Maibaum to write the next draft of *Dr. No* alone.

The second draft still continued to follow the book but made several important additions. Since this was the first in a series, Maubaum wrote a dramatic introduction to the world of James Bond, set in a London casino. The opening also allowed Maibaum to introduce some early love interest and get the film off on the right foot. The novel was nearly half over before Bond met Honeychile Ryder, but the producers were not going to take any chances with the film.

Bond's first conquest became fetching Sylvia Trench whose line, "I admire your good luck, Mr. . . . ?" served to introduce James Bond in the film. The "gimmick" planned to run throughout the Bond series, was that Bond was always in too much of a hurry to make love to Sylvia. Terence Young signed his friend Eunice Gayson to play the frustrated woman; however, when he was replaced by Guy Hamilton on the third film, Eunice lost her part and the Sylvia Trench character disappeared.

Maibaum also embellished the role of Principal Secretary Pleydell-Smith's assistant, Miss Taro, the beautiful Oriental girl who lures Bond to certain death in the Blue Mountains of Jamaica. When planning the female roles in future Bond films, Broccoli and Saltzman always created a number of fresh parts.

From Fleming's *Thunderball* novel, Maibaum also introduced SPECTRE, as Dr. No's backers, an independent operation that conveniently sidestepped the political issues of the day. Fleming's reference to Dr. No's financial backers, the Russians, was removed. SPECTRE, as it does in Fleming's novel *Thunderball*, now stood for "Special Executor for Counter-intelligence, Terrorism, Revenge and Extortion."

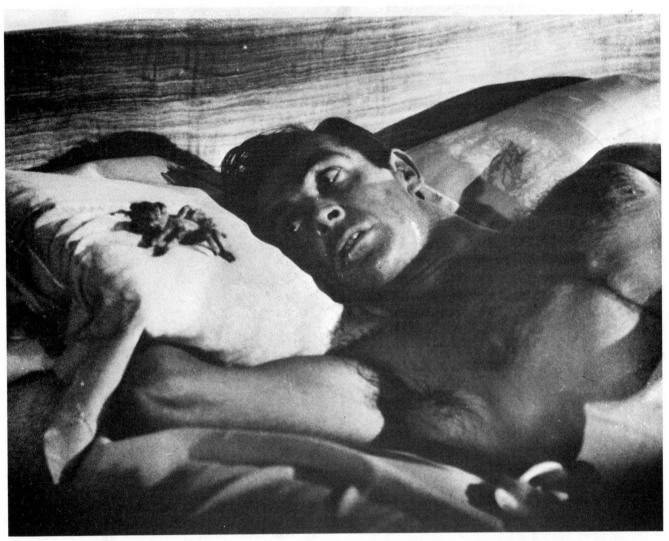

Talk about strange bedfellows! Here Rosie the tarantula approaches a perspiring Sean Connery. Note: In the film, stuntman Bob Simmons replaced Connery during the sequence in which the spider crawls along Bond's torso. *(UPI)*

Rather than end the film in the Doctor's guano works, as Fleming had, with thugs racing about in the dark, and Bond and Honey escaping in the dragon tank, Maibaum created the magnificent "reactor room" where Dr. No plans his destruction of American missiles. The room's boiling pool became a much more suitable final resting place for the evil Doctor than Fleming's mountain of guano dust.

Broccoli and Saltzman anticipated censorship difficulties in England and America. After a careful evaluation of the book's sex and violence content, they decided to take Fleming's cue and avoid explicit sex scenes whilst toning down the violence. To this end, Maibaum added a great deal of humour to the script, aiming to put the film in a class beyond that of the run of the mill spy adventure and to pre-empt any attempts by rivals to copy the film or to send up Bond. From the beginning, it was decided to abandon a straight dramatisation of the Fleming novels and to add a tongue-in-cheek element.

It was felt that the hero, James Bond, had to be lightened in character to survive in a film series, otherwise the action would become too repetitious. Unintentionally, a formula developed in the writing. A scene would build up to an incredibly suspenseful climax, leaving the audience on the edge of its seat, and then, after the horrible moment was over, Bond would throw away a funny play on words to make the audience laugh.

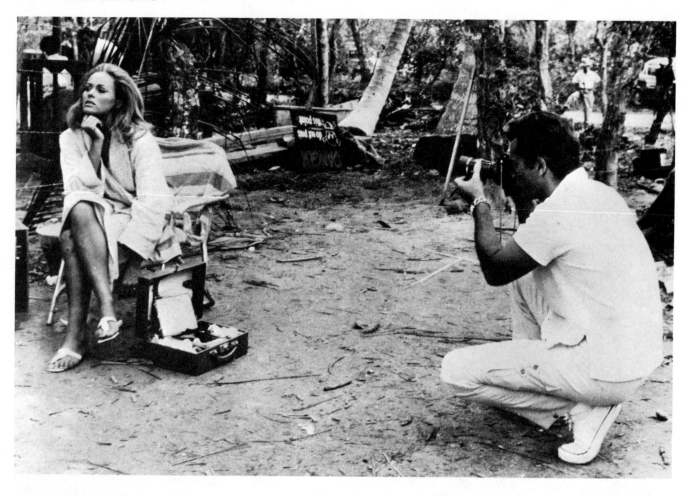

John Derek with Ursula Andress. Note upside-down warning sign in the background. *(UPI)*

The search for an unknown actor to play Bond began in earnest. Broccoli wanted Bond to be a rugged Englishman good with his fists – a commodity he could sell to American audiences who were used to the two-fisted handiwork of Mike Hammer and Sam Spade. Above all, Bond had to have powerful sex appeal; he must be a real lady killer.

In October 1961, the film editor Peter Hunt, who happened to know the producer of the comedy *On the Fiddle* suggested to Saltzman that this film's co-star, a dark haired Scot named Sean Connery, might well be suited to play Bond. Saltzman decided to run some footage of *On the Fiddle* to see for himself. Meanwhile, by an interesting coincidence, Cubby Broccoli, in Hollywood at the time, had also "discovered" Connery while viewing a print of *Darby O'Gill and the Little People*, a Walt Disney fantasy. Broccoli

liked the actor's thick Scottish accent, whilst his wife thought Connery was extraordinarily attractive. He decided to arrange a meeting back in London.

Connery's competition at that time included a number of promising young actors. One was Patrick McGoohan, a good looking stage actor whom Broccoli had introduced in a Warwick feature entitled *Zarak*. McGoohan considered the role but is said to have rejected it on moral grounds. Another potential Bond was the rugged looking Richard Johnson, an up and coming British actor. Johnson, however, was not willing to submit to a multi-picture contract. Ironically, both McGoohan and Johnson were subsequently to play in 007 spinoffs, the former doing *Danger Man* for six years on British television, the latter

Ursula Andress finds the cold water a bit surprising. Her limited wardrobe of a wet shirt and skimpy bikini contributed immensely to DR. NO's international popularity. *(UPI)*

It was Sean Connery's appearance opposite British comedian Alfie Lynch in the 1961 film *"On the Fiddle"* (also entitled *"Operation Snafu"*) that impressed producer Harry Saltzman and prompted him to interview Connery for the role of Bond.

portraying Bulldog Drummond in the 1966 film *Deadlier than the Male*.

British actor Roger Moore, then starring in American television, who could have been another possible, was not considered enough of a "he-man" to play the part. It was also doubtful whether Moore could pull out from his television commitments to do a series of Bond films. In a few months, he was to begin playing "The Saint" on British television.

Connery now had the inside track, but he was not a polished actor and Saltzman was afraid the Scottish accent would blur the film. After a series of meetings with him it was finally decided that, since the film was mostly action, with perhaps twenty or thirty minutes at the most of dialogue time, Connery could manage. Moreover, he was amenable to signing a long term contract. He would agree to play Bond, but on a non-exclusive basis, allowing him to take on other roles in between.

Connery came from a tough Scottish working class background. The son of a long-haul truck driver, he was born in 1930 in the slum-like Fountainridge sector of Edinburgh, Scotland. He started working to help support himself at the

Connery's two-fisted "Irish" machismo appealed to producer Cubby Broccoli when he and his wife Dana viewed a print of *Darby O'Gill* in 1960.

age of nine, later shuffling between school and a seven days a week milk delivery job. In 1946, he joined the Navy but was given a medical discharge after three years. In 1952, Connery was the Scottish representative in a "Mr. Universe" contest which indirectly led to his being offered a small part in *South Pacific* which was then on tour. He went on to act on the stage in London and, in the mid fifties, on television. His portrait of boxer Mountain McLintock in the BBC adaptation of *Requiem for a Heavyweight* won him a contract with Twentieth Century Fox. Fox, however, made no use of him and he was loaned out to other production companies such as MGM in *Action of the Tiger*, Paramount in *Tarzan's Greatest Adventure*, and Disney.

While Connery tested with a series of young actresses seeking parts in *Dr. No*, the director, Terence Young, was approached by Cubby Broccoli to direct the film. Young was not Broccoli's first choice. The producers had offered the project to a number of respected British directors, including Guy Hamilton and Guy Green, but each time, they were turned down cold. Broccoli was a little wary of Young because of the director's uneven track record. Time was running out, however, and Broccoli went ahead to secure the approval of United Artists, who agreed provided Broccoli and Saltzman guaranteed the film's budget with a completion bond. If the film went over, the money would come out of their own pockets, but, knowing Young's earlier work, both producers were willing to take this risk.

Tall, well-dressed and exquisitely mannered, Terence Young had all the panache of Ian Fleming's James Bond. He was also an avid reader of the novels and was in favour of retaining as much of Fleming's writing for the film version of *Dr. No* as possible. Young knew Sean Connery and was one of the few directors who had worked with him. Five years earlier, he had directed him in *Action of the Tiger* which had not been a success although Young and Connery had had a good relationship. With *Dr. No* in mind, Young immediately went to work on Connery. He realised first that the actor must appear to be comfortable in the role of Bond. If Connery was going to order a bottle of Dom Pérignon and some Beluga caviar, he had to do it with conviction. He also had to dress the part. Young escorted Connery to his own personal tailor and purchased the actor's sports shirts, leather sandals, an elegant dinner jacket and the finest ties. Gone were Connery's sweat shirts and jeans. Physically he *was* James Bond, Secret Agent.

With six weeks of location filming in Jamaica planned for January 1962, Young began to go over Maibaum's script. During one polishing session, the director was finding difficulty over a passage where Bond visits the quarters of Dr. No and discovers stolen art objects and other booty collected by SPECTRE. To give the film a contemporary edge, it had originally been decided to include in the treasure hoard a stolen Picasso from the recent robbery of the Aix en Provence Museum in France. His script girl Joanna Harwood, however, suggested using the Goya portrait of Wellington which had been stolen just a few months earlier, a nice touch since everyone in England would immediately recognise it. Young agreed at once.

To match the script to actual locations in Jamaica, he visited the island in the winter of

1961, together with Broccoli and Saltzman, production manager L. C. Rudkin and art directors Ken Adam and Syd Cain. They discovered at once that there was no need to look for an island to duplicate Crab Key. Jamaica itself, with its varied terrain and beaches could easily be Dr. No's devil's garden. The beach sequences could be filmed at Laughing Water, the hideaway estate of Mrs. Minnie Simpson, a perennial recluse who also happened to be a Bond fan. The mangrove swamp where Dr. No's dragon tank captures Bond and Honey was duplicated at Falmouth, a tropical quagmire on Jamaica's north shore about twenty miles east of Montego Bay. Syd Cain considered this location ideal, with its sickly white trees sticking out of the mud. To accommodate the studio-built "dragon" he built an underwater ramp that would allow the vehicle to move through the swampy area.

Other locations picked on this trip included the Palisadoes Airport at Kingston, where Bond arrives from London; Morgan's Harbour, where Bond first visits Quarrel; Kinsale Street which was the site of John Strangways's cottage; the Afro-Chinese section of Kingston, through which the three blind beggars come marching; a bauxite mine near Port Royal which duplicated Dr. No's bauxite mine on Crab Key; the waterfalls outside Ocho Rios, which doubled for the beautiful shoreline of Crab Key; Queen's Club which is the site of Strangways's weekly bridge game; Government House, where Bond first meets the Colonial Secretary; and the foothill country of the Blue Mountains, which was to become the home of Dr. No's agent, Miss Taro.

All the Jamaican exteriors were the responsibility of Syd Cain, a former RAF fighter pilot who had joined Broccoli's Warwick company as a designer on *Zarak* and *A Prize of Gold*. While Cain worked with the location crew, production designer, Ken Adam, another Warwick veteran, was working at Pinewood Studios, where he was in charge of the film's interior designs. The German born Adam was known for his stylised sets. His interiors for the film – the big nuclear reactor room, Dr. No's living area and the other assorted anterooms of the Crab Key fortress – contributed the fantasy element, a decor that reflected the ambitions of the fanatical Doctor.

If there was one scene in the book that con-

vinced Broccoli and Saltzman that *Dr. No* was ripe for a screen treatment, it was the first meeting of Bond and Honeychile Ryder. Bond is awakened on Crab Key's beach by the voice of a girl singing a Jamaican love ballad; he soon encounters an almost naked woman wearing only a leather belt and a hunting knife in a leather sheath, whom Fleming likens to "Botticelli's Venus seen from behind". It only remained to cast the girl.

Eventually, Broccoli spotted a picture of a girl wearing a man's T-shirt. She was soaked to the skin and the nipples on her breasts were prominent whilst her face was extraordinarily beautiful. The actress was Ursula Andress. In spite of objections from various quarters that she could not act and that she talked like "a Dutch comic", Broccoli insisted on signing her up at a thousand a week, even before he had met her. Swiss born Ursula Andress had been acting in Italian films until Paramount offered her a Hollywood contract in 1956. Her reluctance to work at her English and drama training led to her being dropped from the payroll. She acted in a couple of minor films and television dramas but remained essentially unambitious. It was her husband, actor John Derek, who persuaded her to accept the part in *Dr. No*.

With casting completed, shooting began in Jamaica on Tuesday January 16th, 1962. Sean Connery was especially good on the first day of shooting, particularly in the late afternoon, when he appeared in the key "phone booth" sequence in which Bond discovers that the chauffeur from Government House is actually an enemy agent. Terence Young did several takes of the scene and finally caught Connery glaring at actor Reggie Carter in a vivid close-up. It was such a good shot and displayed so much of Connery's magnetism as 007, that Young would always recall it as the beginning of Bond. The total screen time completed on the first day of shooting was one minute and fifty six seconds but the ice had been broken.

Composer Monty Norman was with the crew during those first few weeks of shooting, and had discovered some highly rhythmic Calypso ballads to incorporate into the film's score. These included the romantic, "Underneath the Mango Tree", the animated "Jump Up Jamaica", and a calypso version of "Three Blind Mice", which was chosen to open the film and also served to introduce the three "blind" beggars. The producers had signed Byron Lee's all Chinese band to play the songs.

Thirty minutes of film were in the can when Young took his crew to Jamaica's north shore to begin filming the "Crab Key" beach sequences. Joining Connery on the beach were John Kitzmiller, who was playing Quarrel, and the newly arrived Ursula Andress.

Trudging through virtual jungle to get to Mrs. Simpson's Laughing Water estate was no easy task. The roads were not good and the unit's equipment – the heavy generators, arc lights and reflectors – had to be hauled on to the beach by work gangs who sweated in the Jamaican sunlight and fought mosquitoes. Working in the jungle

The premiere of DR. NO with Sean Connery, Phyllis Newman, and Leonard Bernstein. *(Wide World)*

locations was quite dangerous and there were a number of minor accidents as well as constant cases of sunburn and dysentery. Filming on location had its drawbacks but the footage was extremely valuable. Near the end of the location shooting, the crew actually used the exterior of their own hotel, the Sans Souci in Ocho Rios, as the exterior of Miss Taro's Blue Mountain cottage. Additionally, Jamaica's primary bauxite mine, located on the coast near the Ocho Rios, was well suited to become Dr. No's Crab Key installation. Special effects expert, John Stears, was later to create a miniature bauxite mine equipped with a motorized radar dish with which Dr. No "topples" American missiles.

On February 19th, Young was out on the bauxite dock filming the arrival of Professor Dent in a small launch. Dent, played by British character actor, Anthony Dawson, was another of screenwriter Richard Maibaum's improvements

on the original Fleming novel. Dent is the chief agent of Dr. No in Kingston and it is he who plans the numerous assassination attempts on Bond. Most of Dawson's work was to be completed in London. His only location scenes called for him to play bridge with Strangways during the film's opening at the Queen's Club, and then to pilot a launch to the bauxite dock where Dr. No's gun-toting guards escort him into the island fortress. In reality, when Dawson crosses the dock, he is walking from sunny Jamaica into London, where Ken Adam had already created the superb interiors of Dr. No's quarters.

Location shooting was completed on February 21st 1962 and Young and his crew left for London. Joining them in England was a new team of actors whose parts were completed entirely under the sound stage spotlights. They included Bernard Lee as "M", head of M.I.7 and Lois Maxwell as Moneypenny, Bond's most ardent admirer. These actors went on to appear in eleven consecutive James Bond films, the only two performers to accomplish such a feat.

Filling the shoes of the dreaded Dr. No was a difficult casting chore. It was not surprising that Maibaum and Mankowitz had thought of giving the part to a monkey. In the book, the evil Doctor glides along the floor like an immense worm, clutching objects with his hooks and glaring at people with jet black eyes. Originally, it was thought to ask Ian Fleming's neighbour, Noel Coward, to portray Dr. No. He lived on the spot in Jamaica and could have appeared on location at no extra charge to the production. Coward, then an old man, however, received Fleming's cable and invitation and immediately wired back "Dear Ian, the answer to Dr. No is No, No, No, No!"

Harry Saltzman eventually chose Joseph Wiseman to play the part, a New York stage and film actor whom Saltzman had enjoyed in a number of films, including *Detective Story*. If Wiseman did not look like Fleming's worm, he certainly sounded like him. His frightening monotone was so effective for the "voice of doom" lectures that the producers later offered Wiseman the voice-over part of Ernst Stavro Blofeld in the fourth James Bond film, *Thunderball*. To avoid the comic book caricature element, Wiseman was given a pair

of plastic gloves to replace the unwieldy and comical hooks, a wardrobe of smart looking military style kimono jackets and a rather conservative make-up job that gave him the essential Chinese look.

Filming on the Pinewood lot began in late February 1962, with the first interior sequence set in "M" 's office, where Bond is called late at night to hear the news about Strangways's disappearance. Shooting Maibaum's introduction of 007 at the gaming tables in London, Terence Young did a take off of the entrance made by Paul Muni in the 1939 film, *Juarez*, in which Muni plays the whole first scene with his back to the camera and only turns round when someone asks him his name. "Juarez", he sneers. Young planned James Bond's introduction in the same way. His camera faces Sean Connery's back until that precisely worked out moment when Sylvia Trench addresses him, and he is seen for the first time lighting his cigarette and announcing himself as "Bond . . . James Bond".

John Derek and Ursula Andress. It was Derek who convinced Andress to play Fleming's voluptuous heroine Honey Ryder. *(UPI)*

It worked well on paper but when the time came to shoot the sequence, something went wrong. When Connery put the cigarette to his lips, flicked the gunmetal lighter and then intoned, "Bond . . . James Bond," Young could not help seeing a certain humour in the moment. LIGHTER . . . FLICK . . . NAME . . . It had a comical edge to it, almost as if the flame in the lighter was spotlighting the moment and Young wanted nothing of the sort. It was Connery who suggested a solution. He would hold the cigarette to his lips, flick the lighter and then wait a beat before he threw out his name to Sylvia. The first shot of Bond would hold on that last beat, after the lighter had operated. Connery would appear in a cloud of cigarette smoke, uttering his name, with no distraction. Twenty minutes later, the scene played beautifully and was no longer funny.

Production designer Ken Adam's handiwork was spread all over the sprawling Pinewood lot. Stage D was crammed with a number of collapsable sets, and each day, Terence Young worked in a different one. On February 26th, he he was in "M" 's office; two days later he was in Professor Dent's laboratory. On March 1st, the stage hands broke down the smaller sets and created the Secret Service communications room. At the end of that day, the communications room was broken down and Terence Young began filming the Sylvia Trench seduction sequence in Bond's London flat.

At various times in March, Stage D became Colonial Secretary Pleydell-Smith's office in Jamaica, the interior of the elevator in Dr. No's underground apartment, the gaming room where Bond first meets Sylvia, and the long series of tunnels that were part of the Doctor's fiendish obstacle course. Maibaum had "cleaned up" the latter quite a bit. Gone were Fleming's tarantulas and the man-eating squid at the end of the tunnel.

Ken Adam's best work could be viewed on Stage A where he constructed the Doctor's marvellously inventive reactor room. Adam was lucky to have a construction manager named Ronnie Udell as his right hand man. Udell and the other craftsmen at Pinewood encouraged him to try out new materials and techniques. With a limited set budget of fourteen thousand pounds, (*Dr. No's* total budget was only nine hundred thousand dollars) it was a wonder that Adam could create the magnificent reactor room at all, with its multi-coloured levels, terraced superstructures and phosphorescent atomic pool. It is fair to say that Adam received a great deal of support from Broccoli and Saltzman and, when he asked for an additional eight thousand pounds to complete the sets, they both agreed, even though the film would be over budget.

Principal photography on *Dr. No* was completed on Friday, March 30th 1962. The crew had spent a total of fifty eight days on the project.

Although Monty Norman is credited as the music composer on *Dr. No*, it was John Barry who created the striking James Bond theme that became the instant trade mark of the series. Broccoli and Saltzman had been dissatisfied with the theme Norman had offered them. Barry, who had formed his own jazz oriented group in 1956, The John Barry Seven, had worked on the scores of three other films, *The Amorous Prawn*, *The L-Shaped Room* and *Never Let Go*. He was asked to produce a quick workable theme for *Dr. No* as soon as possible, and indeed, he completed the job without ever having seen the film. He was simply handed a timing sheet and told to come up with a two and a half minute theme that could fit conveniently into the title track. Although he composed the piece from scratch, it was not entirely original. He borrowed from his own instrumental repertoire, in particular, from a little tune entitled, "Bea's Knees" which featured that same distinct plucked guitar. Initially, no one realised how popular those two and a half minutes were to become. Barry's fee for the James Bond theme was a mere two hundred pounds, less than five hundred dollars!

With a tiny budget, Broccoli and Saltzman had pooled their ingenuity and were coming up with some extraordinary talent. This was an English picture that played to American values and which was to make its mark on the American film industry.

Ian Fleming visits the Istanbul location of FROM
RUSSIA WITH LOVE. *(Wide World)*

3
MURDER ON THE ORIENT EXPRESS

Dr. No received its premiere at the London Pavilion on October 6th 1962. The opening had been planned for London for good reasons. If *Dr. No* could pass the keen London critics who knew of Bond, then United Artists could send the film into the American market with confidence. The prevailing mood, however, was "if it failed in England, then let it die a European death." Despite the confidence of Broccoli and Saltzman, United Artists were already planning to banish the film to the US drive-in circuit in Texas and the Midwest. There was no scheduled world premiere in New York or Hollywood.

Fortunately, there were some good omens. Peter Hunt's final cut of the film had passed the censor without problems; he granted *Dr. No* an "A" certificate, which meant that it was suitable for virtually all audiences.

For Harry Saltzman and Albert Broccoli, the first Tuesday in October 1962 was to be a major event. In a rare show of splendour, the entire range of English filmdom turned out for the opening of the first James Bond film. They were joined by such social stalwarts as J. Paul Getty and Ian Fleming himself.

The press reviews ended any of the producers' misgivings. Derek Hill, in *London Scene* noted that, "Terence Young is hardly a name that leaps immediately to mind when one compiles a list of our most efficient technicians, yet *Dr. No* has the kind of rock hard competence more usually associated with Hollywood."

FROM RUSSIA WITH LOVE (1963)
PC. Eon Productions – A United Artists Release 105 mins Col. **PROD.** Albert R. Broccoli and Harry Saltzman **DIR.** Terence Young **SCR.** Richard Maibaum, Joanna Harwood based on the novel by Ian Fleming **PH.** Ted Moore **ED.** Peter Hunt **PROD DES.** Syd Cain **MUSIC.** John Barry **SP EFFECTS.** Frank George, John Stears
CAST. Sean Connery (James Bond), Daniela Bianchi (Tatiana Romanova), Pedro Armendariz (Ali Kerim Bey), Lotte Lenya (Rosa Klebb), Robert Shaw (Red Grant), Bernard Lee ("M"), Eunice Gayson (Sylvia Trench), Walter Gotell (Morzeny), Francis de Wolff (Vavra), George Pastell (Train Conductor), Nadja Regin (Kerim's Girl), Lois Maxwell (Miss Moneypenny), Aliza Gur (Vida), Martine Beswick (Zora), Vladek Sheybal (Kronsteen), Leila (Belly Dancer), Hasan Ceylan (Bulgarian Agent), Fred Haggerty (Krilencu), Neville Jason (Rolls Chauffeur), Peter Bayliss (Benz), Mushet Auaer (Mehmet), Peter Brayham (Rhoda the flower truck driver), Desmond Llewelyn (Boothroyd), Jan Williams (Baltic Masseuse), Peter Madden (McAdams), Anthony Dawson (No. 1 – uncredited), Eric Pohlman (voice of No. 1 – uncredited).

Pedro Armendariz, who carried on in the part of Turkish agent Kerim Bey despite having a fatal illness.

The News of the World correspondent called *Dr. No* "magnificent mayhem, with Sean Connery fitting Fleming's hero like a Savile Row suit". Hard-hitting critic Penelope Gilliatt, known for her stinging pen, noted the snobbish and brutal character of Ian Fleming's hero but spotted, with approval, the element of self mockery in the film.

The positive critical reaction was topical enough for *Time Magazine* to devote a pre-American release review to it which included Ian Fleming's own reaction to the film. Fleming wrote: "Those who've read the book are likely to be disappointed, but those who haven't will find it a wonderful movie. Audiences laugh in all the right places."

The critical and commercial success of *Dr. No* guaranteed the continuation of a James Bond series of films. To reinforce this, the producers had included a brief note at the end of their first film. It read, truthfully: "The End of *Dr. No* but James Bond will return in *From Russia with Love*."

When Harry Saltzman and Albert Broccoli formed Eon Productions in 1960, their immediate future was devoted entirely to the creation of the first James Bond film. Despite their differences, both men respected each other, a factor that was to carry them through twelve stormy years of film making. Cubby Broccoli took his role in the creation of the James Bond films more seriously than Harry Saltzman. For Broccoli, the Bond films became his sole interest in the film business. When Ian Fleming died of a heart attack in 1964, shortly before the release of *Goldfinger*, the future of James Bond fell into Broccoli's lap.

Saltzman whistled a different tune. Almost from the beginning, he had other interests. He was a gambler, and when a table cooled off, Saltzman was ready to move on to new action. No sooner was Bond off and running, than the international wheeler-dealer was searching for new projects. Later in the series, he became a super consultant, operating a worldwide watch for unusual talent, the type of heart beat stopping "act" that would contribute to the world of 007. In 1963 with United Artists' financial backing and Broccoli's support, Saltzman began to court new projects that would add to the coffers of Eon Productions.

With his next project, *Call Me Bwana*, Saltzman hoped to produce a real money maker for Eon Productions but these hopes were not realised. This Bob Hope vehicle merely recovered its costs and Saltzman and Broccoli settled down to make the second James Bond film which was now in pre-production.

Even the staunchest Bond critic cannot deny the effectiveness of *From Russia with Love*. It also works superbly as a straight spy adventure, although it was the last of the serious Bonds. As Secret Agent 007, Sean Connery still depends on his wits and raw courage to get out of impossible situations. Although, in the end, the gadget-rigged briefcase supplied by industrious "Q" Branch saves his life, it is James Bond who manipulates its arsenal of weapons. It was the last time such an order of events would prevail.

Richard Maibaum, who was once again hired to write the script, loved this Fleming novel with its fascinating characters. They were already larger than life, especially the three Russian master spies: Klebb, the evil Head of Operations for Smersh; Grant, the assassin and Kronsteen, the master planner. Such three dimensional characterisations, combined with the fantastic blackmail plot and the exotic locale of Istanbul made the story immediately cinematic. However, as was to be the case in all the Bond screenplays, Maibaum was ordered to make changes. Broccoli and Saltzman had decided that the Russians could no longer be the heavies in the film since it was

The celebrated gypsy fight in the ice-cold Pinewood paddock. The sexy contenders: Martine Beswick and Aliza Gur. *(UPI)*

felt strongly that Bond should never get involved in politics. His enemies once more became SPECTRE.

Having lost their operative Dr. No, in the first film, it was only logical to offer them another shot at Bond. Maibaum also felt it made the story even more interesting. Instead of the Russians using a decoding machine and a beautiful female agent as bait to trap and murder 007, SPECTRE would utilise the same plan to play off the Russians against the British, extracting their own revenge on everyone concerned. To explain SPECTRE's complicated strategy conveniently, Maibaum created the symbolic analogy of the Siamese Fighting Fish, a wily creature who watches as two fellow creatures fight to the death, only to pounce on the victor "who is too exhausted to defend himself."

Meanwhile, Broccoli and Saltzman began testing actresses for the part of the charming Tatiana Romanova, the pawn in SPECTRE's blackmail scene. On *Dr. No*, they had long searched for a young woman to play a latter-day Botticelli Venus. Their new task was no easier, for Ian Fleming had termed Romanova "a young Greta Garbo".

The producers, according to Terence Young, spent almost as much on the tests for *From Russia with Love* as they had done on the whole *Dr. No* film. Their first choice for the role was a French actress, Elga Andersson, but their minds were changed by a top United Artists executive who also happened to be a disgruntled admirer of the actress. He suggested, untruly, that her reputation made it impossible for them to cast her in the film, and they turned, instead, to their second choice, Daniela Bianchi, an Italian who had been the runner-up in the 1960 Miss Universe pageant.

From amongst the girls who were tested for the part, Young picked out Martine Beswick, a Jamaican who had been turned down for *Dr. No*, to be one of the fiery gypsy girls whose fight to the death over a common lover is interrupted by a Russian commando raid.

Since Fleming had created such masterful villains in Klebb, Grant and Kronsteen, a search began for actors to match their literary counterparts. Harry Saltzman prompted the most offbeat casting of the three when he suggested Lotte Lenya for the Rosa Klebb part which had been

Fleming observes the train sequence in FROM RUSSIA WITH LOVE. He died one year later, in 1964. *(Wide World)*

toned down considerably from Fleming's original conception. Lenya was hardly the type of actress one would instinctively cast to play the most hideous role in the film. Widow of composer Kurt Weill, she had acted on the German stage during the Twenties and Thirties. A member of the famous Berliner Ensemble, she had also appeared in films, most notably in Pabst's *Dreigroschenoper*. Now in her late sixties, Lenya's most recent role had been in *The Roman Spring of Mrs. Stone*.

Robert Shaw was offered the part of Red Grant and advised by Terence Young to build up his body before shooting began. Shaw went directly into a body building programme to produce a physique capable of withstanding a direct blow to the solar plexus from Colonel Klebb's knuckle duster.

Completing the SPECTRE triumvirate was Vladek Sheybal, a thirty four year old, sleepy-eyed, Polish born actor and director who was to portray Kronsteen, the master planner who treats life like a chess game, with considerable panache.

By eliminating the Russians as Bond's principal enemies and substituting SPECTRE, Maibaum had automatically thrown out the entire first half of Fleming's novel which deals with the Moscow plan to murder 007. The problem now was how to introduce the SPECTRE group. Fleming had chosen to open his book with Grant, lying by a pool on a Russian estate in the Baltic Provinces, being massaged by a bosomy peasant girl. The film opens differently.

The "teaser", a pre-title sequence that not only introduces Grant but gives the new Bond film a powerful send off, was Harry Saltzman's bright idea. Saltzman's original concept called for an 007 double to be tracked through a SPECTRE training area, beset by an arsenal of weapons which he evades, only to be expertly strangled by Red Grant. In this way, the film would begin with Bond being killed; only it would not be Bond.

Young changed the setting when he saw the newly released Alan Resnais film *Last Year at Marienbad*, in which there was some evocative night shooting in a garden surrounded by Greek statues. Instead of having Bond's double running through the SPECTRE obstacle course, Young and Maibaum devised the strange moonlit garden setting with Bond being tracked to the tune of

Connery with lovely Daniela Bianchi, whose sensuous Tatiana Romanova was a high point of FROM RUSSIA WITH LOVE. *(Wide World)*

chirping crickets, snapping wood, and rippling fountains. The teaser was immediately followed by the inventive title sequence in which the credits were projected onto the undulating body of a Turkish belly dancer, thanks to Robert Brownjohn and Trevor Bond.

The film proper opens on an indoor set at Pinewood where Kronsteen is playing in an international chess tournament with a Canadian opponent. Maibaum moved the match from Fleming's Moscow setting to Venice where the atmosphere was considerably more lavish. With Venice as the setting, it was convenient to pencil in a SPECTRE yacht, moored on one of the canals, where Kronsteen and Klebb explain their plot to kill Bond and capture a brand new Russian Lector decoding machine.

The Lector was Maibaum's new name for Fleming's "Spektor", a machine that held the coding key to all of Moscow's top secret diplomatic traffic. Fleming had based his concept for the Spektor on Enigma, a British decoding machine of World War II, which was part of the extremely secretive Ultra Network that had broken the Nazi diplomatic code in 1939.

The truth about the Ultra organisation and Fleming's part in its activities was not revealed until 1975, when British wartime secrets were first declassified. Sir William Stevenson, the head of Ultra and a close friend of Fleming, revealed the secrets of Fleming's contributions in a book entitled *A Man Called Intrepid*. This concise history of British Intelligence activities was later to explain a great deal of the source material, upon which Fleming based his James Bond novels.

The Russians were not the only ones with gadgets. Working directly from Fleming's description, art director Syd Cain and special effects expert John Stears, created the first Bond "toy", a black attaché case that Bond carries with him to Istanbul. This played an important part on the first day of shooting. Joining Connery, Bernard Lee and Lois Maxwell on April 1st 1963, playing the six foot two and half inch head of "Q" Branch, was Desmond Llewelyn. In addition to the fifty gold sovereigns, the throwing knife and the .25 calibre ammunition, Cain and Stears had added to the case the folding sniper's rifle, actually an Armalite Survival Gun, equipped with a telescopic infra-red lens, and the trick canister of tear gas disguised as a tin of talcum powder.

Llewelyn, with his peculiar tone of British authority, tells Bond, "Normally, to open a case like that, you move the catches to the side. If you do, the cartridge will explode in your face. Now, to stop the cartridge exploding, turn the catches horizontally like that and open normally." By describing the attaché case in such a manner, Maibaum had reflected Fleming's penchant for lecturing his readers. The weapons lecture was always to be a standard feature of subsequent James Bond films.

Daniela Bianchi's first sequence as Tatiana Romanova occurs in the special bridal suite set, constructed by Syd Cain on ice cold Stage D. Behind the mirror above the king sized bed, Cain had skilfully captured the *cabinet de voyeur* where the SPECTRE camera unit was filming Bond's love making for the elaborate blackmail scheme. The producers had been advised by the British Board of Film Censors to keep the "sweating" cameraman in the shadows, otherwise the entire sequence would have to be eliminated as too suggestive. Miss Bianchi, with a black ribbon tied round her neck, and protected by a flesh coloured body stocking played the scene quite well despite her nervousness. To accommodate her, Young closed the set to all but a few technicians, allowing his two key actors to "wrestle" in peace throughout the afternoon. Connery himself spent the day in a towel.

Two days later, Young was working with Vladek Sheybal aboard Ernst Blofeld's yacht. To simulate a boat moored in Venice's Grand Canal, Syd Cain had added a number of effects to the set of Stage D. These included the porthole lights which were gently rocked from side to side during the shooting, and the camera which was also placed on a gentle rocker, moving in rhythm with the lights. Aboard the SPECTRE yacht that day, was Anthony Dawson, portraying Ernst Stavro Blofeld. He had made a big impression the previous year as the evil Professor Dent in *Dr. No*. Dawson's part, which was uncredited, simply called for him to sit in the chair (back to camera), stroke a white cat, press a remote button summoning Morzeny (Walter Gotell), and take the dead

Siamese fighting fish out of its aquarium and feed it to the cat. His voice was later dubbed by British actor Eric Pohlman.

Much of *From Russia with Love* was filmed in the park-like grounds of Pinewood Studios. The main studio administration building became the mansion-like SPECTRE headquarters, in front of which a helicopter bearing Colonel Klebb first lands. This very same area became the setting for the teaser which was first shot on the night of April 12th 1963. Dubbed the "Renaissance Garden" exterior, this was designed by Syd Cain, complete with statues, little outdoor stairways, ornamental plants, a fountain, and back lighting that simulated a moonlit night in the Adriatic.

Shooting began at 7.00 p.m. each night and continued into the early morning. A dinner break was scheduled for midnight. The only problem

with the sequence occurred when Gotell peeled the Sean Connery mask off the victim. When Terence Young saw the sequence in rushes the next day, he realised that the extra looked too much like Connery. To an audience that might still be unfamiliar with Connery, this would create confusion. He decided to reshoot the sequence with the double wearing a moustache.

On April 22nd 1963, interior location shooting in Istanbul began inside Saint Sophia, one of the most beautiful and historic mosques in the world. A production convoy left the Hilton Hotel at 7.30 a.m. and headed west, twenty eight vehicles in all. Half the convoy was loaded with lighting equipment that would help illuminate the blackness of the mosque. Shooting began in the late afternoon when the Turkish guide Muhammat Kohen took his group of tourist extras through the mosque.

While Kohen conducted the lecture in the background, Young put his principal actors to work – Connery, Daniela Bianchi, Robert Shaw and a character actor, Hasan Ceylan, who was portraying the pock-faced Bulgar. Shooting continued at Saint Sophia until 6.20 p.m. with a twenty minute delay in the late afternoon when the museum was overrun by an influx of real tourists. The Turkish Ministry of Information had graciously allowed the British film crew into Saint Sophia, but the filming could not disrupt the normal tourist flow.

On April 30th Young divided his forces. A second unit camera crew, headed by his assistant director David Anderson, travelled by train to the Greek border, shooting background plates for the Orient Express sequence. This footage would be used by the optical effects crew back at Pinewood for the train interiors planned for the studio.

Young stayed in Istanbul to prepare for another series of night shots. In an industrial section of the city, Syd Cain had built a special exterior for the Russian Agent Krilencu's apartment which consisted of a billboard and a trap door. The billboard in Fleming's novel had advertised the 20th Century Fox film *Niagara* featuring Marilyn

Connery and his wife Diane Cilento arrive in London after location shooting on FROM RUSSIA WITH LOVE. *(Wide World)*

Monroe, with the trap door built into her mouth. Broccoli and Saltzman substituted their own product, *Call Me Bwana*, and Anita Ekberg replaced Marilyn Monroe.

To escape from Istanbul, Bond and Tanya leave on the world famous Simplon Orient Express, which leaves Istanbul and travels through Thessalonika, Belgrade, Venice and Lausanne, until it arrives in Paris, four days and five nights later. After Bond kills Grant, he and Tanya leave the train at the Yugoslav border, steal Grant's getaway truck and capture a motor boat that will take them to Venice. Before this happens, the script called for nearly twenty minutes aboard the train, as it passed through three stations. One of these, St. Sophia, was in Istanbul and would be shot in daylight. The other two, simulating Belgrade and Zagreb, were targeted for night shooting.

Working with the Turkish unions in Istanbul's Sirkeci Station was a nightmare for production manager Bill Hill. He recalls that cinematographer Ted Moore began his camera setup at 6.00 each night and by eleven, he was still directing the lighting. Generators were hauled aboard the crew's special train and instructions were given to the Turkish engineer. He was told to pull into the station and to stop at a special chalk mark. This would allow Robert Shaw to leave the train (in the Zagreb sequence) and dispose of the local British agent. Hill had problems with the driver who was unable to hit the chalk mark. He repeatedly slammed on his brakes, snapping the generator cables so that all the lights went out. The union officials stood passively by and it took hours to get right. Harried as he was, Hill acted in the film. He played the unfortunate British agent Nash who is taken into the Zagreb bathroom by Grant, and murdered.

If there was chaos filming the railroad sequences, the motor boat chase was worse. Everything went wrong at Pendik, a little coastal hamlet near the Greek border. The motor boat chase and Bond's fight with a SPECTRE helicopter were entirely original sequences that do not appear in Fleming's novel. It was felt that the film needed opening up after the long, claustrophobic sequence aboard the Orient Express. The best way to do this was to turn the last quarter of *From*

Bond is seduced by Tatiana in the bridal suite of an Istanbul hotel. Behind them: the *cabinet de voyeur* where SPECTRE agents are secretly filming the steamy proceedings. *(UPI)*

Russia with Love into a spectacular chase sequence where Bond must fight off wave after wave of revenge-seeking SPECTRE agents.

Once Bond shoots down the SPECTRE helicopter with a well aimed shot (in a sequence taken directly from Hitchcock's *North by Northwest*), he finds Grant's motor boat and heads for Venice by water. He is soon pursued by three SPECTRE speed boats, carrying men armed with machine guns and rifle genades. Bond eventually

wipes out his opposition by using a trick Maibaum had used in *The Red Beret*.

In that film, Alan Ladd's unit is trapped in a mine field. To escape, he has a comrade skip a bazooka rocket across the ground, touching off a path of lethal mines. In *From Russia with Love*, Maibaum merely changed the sequence to the sea. Bond dumps his punctured gasoline drums overboard, watches them float among the SPECTRE boats and then skilfully fires a flare at the gasoline. The skipping effect of the flare rocket touches off all the gasoline, engulfing the SPECTRE flotilla.

The complicated outdoor sequence was planned for the quiet seas off Pendik, an ideal spot picked by the reconnaissance team. Certain problems, though, were unforseen. The speed boats were anything but speedy. They were constantly breaking down. The Turkish production assistants had poured kerosene into the gasoline tanks causing further delays. To compound the technical problems, the sky became overcast.

Young's crew was spending thirteen hours on the water and getting less than thirty seconds of footage for its efforts. Daniela Bianchi was overcome with seasickness several times and the entire crew was grateful each night to return to dry land.

After a second straight day of zero footage, Young was ready to call it quits. Already three days behind schedule, he phoned Broccoli in London and advised that they shoot the boat sequences in the UK where they would have more control. He told them he could remember a number of isolated coves off the coast of Scotland that resembled the Gulf of Venice. Conscious of the delays and frustrations, Broccoli and Saltzman agreed to bring back the production crew. A small second unit crew was left behind to shoot a number of background shots for matching in Scotland.

In a film crowded with mysterious people, all with highy unusual mannerisms and personalities, it was Pedro Armendariz as the exuberant and yet deadly Kerim Bey, head of Station T-Turkey who came off best. Interestingly, Kerim Bey's most important sequence was cut from *From Russia with Love.* It occurs just before Bond meets Tanya on the Bosphorous ferry boat. In the scene, everywhere Bond went, he was followed by a Bulgarian with a big moustache, black beret and Citroen.

Bond is heading for the ferry to meet the girl, and he has to shake off his pursuer. In a taxi, followed by the Bulgarian, Bond suddenly leans across in front of the taxi driver and pumps the brakes. The taxi comes screeching to a halt, the Bulgarian piles in behind, and he, in turn, is struck by a third car.

Out of car number 1 steps James Bond; out of car number 2, steps the Bulgarian; and out of the third car steps Pedro Armendariz. Young shot ten takes. Armendariz wanted a long ash on the end of his cigar, and every time the Bulgarian expressed his shock the ash fell away from the cigar. On take ten, Armendariz comes out with his cigar with a long ash and the Bulgarian turns on him protesting. Armendariz leans across, takes his cigar from his mouth and taps it saying, "My friend, this is life." At that point, the big British Embassy Rolls Royce drives up, Bond gets in and drives away. With his car locked between bumpers, the Bulgarian cannot follow 007 to the ferry boat. It is a perfect deception and was certainly Armendariz's best scene.

At a private screening the week before the film came out, Terence Young's twelve year old son was the first to notice that the Bulgarian had already been "killed" by Robert Shaw in the Saint Sophia mosque. The scene had to be jettisoned.

Connery meets Daniela Bianchi at a reception held at London's Connaught Hotel in March of 1963. *(Wide World)*

Scriptwriter Richard Maibaum, Ian Fleming, and the Duchess of Bedford after the first day's shooting on FROM RUSSIA WITH LOVE. Maibaum's long association with Broccoli dates from his time at Warwick Films.

Terence Young recalls that when he later found out that Armendariz was dying of cancer, he went to his hotel and tried to say something dignified and meaningful but could only stare at the walls. Once more, Armendariz had a cigar in his mouth. He leaned across, looked Young right in the eye, tapped an ash on the carpet and said: "That, my friend, is life."

It was Terence Young, who, on his return from Istanbul, had discovered that Armendariz had a fatal illness. The actor, who had managed to work successfully on *Captain Sinbad* in Germany had hoped to be fit for the duration of the Bond film. He was anxious to be able to leave some money to his wife. However, his health had failed more rapidly than he had anticipated.

Apart from anything else, the producers were faced with the dilemma of whether to try and finish the film without Armendariz, or whether to re-cast the role of Kerim Bey. Armendariz was desperate to complete the film for his wife's sake. Young, who felt he could not do the film without

Armendariz, convinced the producers that he could shoot all the Pinewood sequences with Kerim Bey in one lump. A meeting was quickly called and art director Syd Cain and his assistant, Michael White, were told to begin construction immediately on everything that would require Armendariz, including the sprawling gypsy camp.

Young, with cinematographer Ted Moore, planned to shoot all of the Armendariz closeups in a two week period, shooting on to the actor over a stand-in's shoulder. Weeks later, Connery was to finish his scenes with Terence Young, himself, playing Kerim Bey.

The atmosphere was heavy at Pinewood Studios during those last weeks of May 1963. On Sunday, June 9th 1963, Terence Young held a going away party for Armendariz at his London town house. Most of the production crew were there and Ian Fleming, himself seriously ill, arrived in the late afternoon. The two stricken men had met for the first time in Istanbul and taken a considerable liking to one another. They spent much of the afternoon on a couch in Young's living room discussing Armendariz's good friend, the late Ernest Hemingway, who had committed suicide rather than submit to a lengthy terminal illness.

A month later, Pedro Armendariz, lying deathly ill in a hospital bed in Los Angeles, took a pistol from under his pillow and killed himself. Ian Fleming was not to last much longer, himself.

Production had to continue, and with the crew due to leave shortly for Scotland and the exteriors on the motor boat and helicopter chases, Young tightened up the schedule, working everyone around the clock.

Syd Cain had finished his gypsy camp in time to shoot the battle with the Bulgarians. Now it was time for the other principal actors to begin their assignments in the sprawling exterior of the Pinewood paddock. Two of these were Terence Young's gypsy girls, Martine Beswick and Aliza Gur. Beswick had a secret admirer in Young and this did not go down too well with Miss Gur, who was fresh from Hollywood and used to all the attention. An off-screen rivalry began to develop between the two and this spilled over into the delicious fight sequence cooked up by master chef Ian Fleming.

The best fight sequence in the film, the duel between Bond and Grant on The Orient Express is usually cut in television versions of *From Russia with Love*. It is a pity because it is one of the most bloodthirsty examples of hand to hand combat ever filmed. With Maibaum's script linked to Peter Perkins's choreography, it was James Bond at his best.

Maibaum had to rework Fleming's original fight. In the novel, Bond places his cigarette case inside a book lying on his lap and when Grant fires his gun, the bullet is deflected by the case. When Grant steps over the sprawled body of Bond, 007 takes a throwing knife out of the tip of his briefcase and rips through Grant's groin. The fight is over in a minute.

In the script, Maibaum dragged out the fight for nearly two minutes. All the gadgets that "Q" branch had created were put into play, especially the tear gas cartridge hidden in Bond's briefcase. Grant is staggered by the gas when he mistakenly opens up the briefcase without adjusting the catches, is stabbed by Bond with the flat-bladed throwing knife, and then is garrotted with the same strangler's watch that had killed the phony Bond in the pre-title sequence. In between, both men trade a dozen punches, tearing apart the tiny train compartment.

All this was filmed on two of Pinewood's main stages where Syd Cain had built the interior of the Orient Express. Peter Perkins was stunt co-ordinator with Bob Simmons returning as Sean Connery's double, and Jack Cooper doubling Robert Shaw.

At first, Young intended to use only two stationary cameras to catch the action, one on a dolly, tracking down into the compartment, and one on ground level. Peter Hunt suggested that a free third camera also be used. It was a good suggestion and Young put it into play. Hunt's free camera later picked up some excellent shots of Bond and Grant spilling on to Tanya's sleeping form.

Ever since the disastrous location shooting in the Bay of Pendik, Young had been waiting to get another crack at the motor boat chase. He had originally planned to shoot the sequence along with the helicopter chase somewhere in Scotland. His chance came in early July, when a main unit headed north to Lochgilphead to begin work on the helicopter sequence while a second unit went over to Crinan on the west coast of Scotland to test the new motor boats.

For the climactic motor boat chase, the plan was to film the actual chase off Crinan, in the ocean, while the destruction of the SPECTRE flotilla by Bond's skipping flare would be staged in the Pinewood tank, a water filled soundstage where gas explosions and special effects could be triggered safely.

Five swift motor boats were ordered from Fairey Marine in Glasgow, loaded on to trucks and taken to Crinan overland where they were deposited on an estuary and then motored out into the Atlantic. The operation of the boats, no longer in the hands of the fumbling Turks, was assigned to Fairey Marine's own Peter Twiss, a former Air Force pilot who was credited as the first Englishman to break the sound barrier.

Since the weather was uncertain, the crew shuttled between the helicopter chase at Lochgilphead and the coastline boat chase, completing one scene at a time.

On July 6th, at Crinan, art director Syd Cain suggested to Terence Young that they have a closer look at a particularly interesting cove which he had seen the day before. Young agreed, left Cain on the dock and with assistant art director, Michael White, climbed into the helicopter with their pilot, Captain Cyril Sweetman of Film Aviation Services. However, no sooner was Sweetman airborne than he ran into a tiny wind pocket that flipped the Hiller on to its side, right into the water. Cain and the support crew could do nothing as the helicopter smashed into the sea, its perspex passenger compartment going completely underwater, while its rotor whipped up the ocean around it. Terence Young found himself ten feet under water in only a few seconds and confesses that he was lucky to be alive.

The crew quickly smashed the helicopter canopy and pulled the bleeding director from the wreck. Sweetman's lap belt was severed by a switchblade, and he too came to the surface. White had popped out just as the helicopter hit the water and survived the accident with a bruised right elbow. Young suffered a cut right hand, cut legs and general bruising.

Despite the accident, he was back shooting the boat chase at 10.30 that morning, just over an hour after he had taken off on the ill-fated flight. A special camera crew was landed on a deserted island in the middle of the bay to catch some long shots of Bond's speedboat. The crew worked until 7.30 that night, after which Terence Young was treated at Lochgilphead hospital. As if the crash were the last hindrance, the chaotic motor boat sequences began to straighten themselves out and by July 16th, the exteriors at Crinan were completed.

In August, during the last few weeks of shooting, Young took a small crew to Madrid in search of wild rats. A key sequence in *From Russia with Love* occurs in the underground cistern after Kerim Bey has blown up the Russian consulate. To escape, Bond, Tanya and Kerim race through the cistern, followed by thousands of brown rats. The only problem was that English law forbade the use of wild rats in English film productions and Syd Cain had to find a substitute.

Initially, they tried to use tame white rats which were dipped in cocoa to give them the proper colour. But after the stage lights were fixed and the set dressed, they became drowsy and would not co-operate. All they would do was to lick the chocolate coating off each other's bodies. The crew ended up in Madrid where a Spanish rat catcher was hired who trapped two hundred brown rats for them. They then hired a garage and built a tiny part of the Byzantine cistern. Young shot the rats coming down the tunnel with a plate of glass in front of the camera protecting him from the rats. Finally, Syd Cain remembers, everyone ended up on chairs, including Cubby Broccoli who came over to watch, because all the rats escaped and nobody wanted to be bitten.

From Russia with Love finished shooting on August 23rd 1963. Two months later, it opened at the Odeon Theatre, Leicester Square. Once again Penelope Gilliatt of the *Evening Standard* was in the forefront of those in praise of Bond, commenting on the flippancy of the film which was to her, "a voice of the age, the voice of sick jokes about the bomb, and gruesomes about Belsen." The general critical response was good. Happiness at Eon Productions in the autumn of 1963 was not only because of this, or indeed, because of the film's amazing box office success (it was making its cost back, in England alone), but also because of the gratis publicity it was receiving. *From Russia with Love* was actually on the reading list of American President, John F. Kennedy. What political writer Hugh Sidey had cooked up as an interesting example of what a President might read, was actually a windfall for the Bond people.

With encouragement from the White House, paperback publishers began to spread Ian Fleming's novels across America and sales began to rise spectacularly.

"Hands up, Mr. Bond." The deadly ladies of GOLDFINGER. Left to right: Shirley Eaton, Honor Blackman, Tania Mallet. (*Life Picture Service*)

4
ODDJOBS AND HARD KNOX

By the middle of 1964, Harry Saltzman and Albert Broccoli were reasonably satisfied with the performance of James Bond. Their first two films had become extremely successful in England with *From Russia with Love* the top moneymaker of the year, and business was picking up in the States. Nevertheless, United Artists was still hedging its bets on Bond in the U.S. film market, hesitating to give the series the proper fanfare, unsure of the product.

Saltzman continued to point to the book sales figures that were coming in daily. If the first two films had whetted the American appetite, the books were creating a massive interest in the British Secret Service agent. When, in the summer of 1964, United Artists was confronted with the script for the third Bond film, *Goldfinger*, it began to take a more positive interest and initiated an important promotional campaign for this film.

Fort Knox, Kentucky, houses the United States Army's Armor Center but it is hardly known for its military purposes. It is the bullion depository that lies within the Fort Knox base that has gained world renown as the storage place for all America's gold reserves.

In the new screenplay of *Goldfinger* the master criminal Auric Goldfinger plans to break into the gold depository, detonate a small atomic bomb and therefore contaminate the entire gold supply of the United States. Since Goldfinger already possesses sixty million dollars in stolen gold bullion, the value of his own gold will increase spectacularly.

Bond meets Goldfinger in Miami Beach where the criminal is cheating a Mr. Simmons at gin. After foiling Goldfinger's plans and stealing his girlfriend Jill Masterson, who dies soon afterwards when her entire body is painted gold, Bond

---

GOLDFINGER (1964) PC. Eon Productions – A United Artists Release 109 mins Col. **PROD.** Albert R. Broccoli and Harry Saltzman **DIR.** Guy Hamilton **SCR.** Richard Maibaum, Paul Dehn from the novel by Ian Fleming **PH.** Ted Moore **ED.** Peter Hunt **PROD DES.** Ken Adam **MUSIC.** John Barry **SP EFFECTS.** John Stears, Frank George (assistant) **CAST** Sean Connery (James Bond), Honor Blackman (Pussy Galore), Gert Frobe (Goldfinger), Shirley Eaton (Jill Masterson), Tania Mallet (Tilly Masterson), Harold Sakata (Oddjob) Bernard Lee ("M"), Martin Benson (Mr. Solo), Cec Linder (Felix Leiter), Austin Willis (Simmons), Lois Maxwell (Miss Moneypenny), Bill Nagy (Midnight), Alf Joint (Capungo), Nadja Regin (Bonita the Flamenco Dancer), Raymond Young (Sierra), Richard Vernon (Colonel Smithers), Denis Cowles (Brunskill), Michael Mellinger (Kisch), Desmond Llewelyn ("Q").

Production designer Ken Adam on the GOLDFINGER set. Adam's artistic genius continued to dazzle audiences with the most imaginative vault ever, a mythic interior of Fort Knox, Kentucky. *(Life Picture Service)*

returns to London. On a directive from "M" who is working with the Bank of England, Bond is sent to investigate Goldfinger's illicit activities, a journey that takes him from the Alps in Switzerland to the blue grass country of Kentucky.

To film Goldfinger's raid on the gold depository, at Fort Knox, the producers received co-operation from the United States Army which always maintains a large armoured force in the area. The script called for ground and aerial shots of the base, plus close-ups of large numbers of troops being put to sleep by Pussy Galore's

"This Bond epic is the best yet," as the lines of moviegoers testify.

private air force, which expels a deadly nerve gas into the atmosphere above the sprawling base. As for filming inside the actual depository, Broccoli and Saltzman had already received a polite "no" from the US Treasury Department.

In February, Broccoli, his stepson Michael Wilson, the newly appointed director Guy Hamilton, Ken Adam, and about eighteen crew members travelled by plane from New York to Fort Knox. With Hamilton was a light camera crew headed by the Bond veteran, Ted Moore. They filmed all over Fort Knox, and with the aid of a retired Army Colonel named Charlie Rushon, who had connections with the Defence Department, they were allowed on to the base where they were given a large contingent of soldiers for doubles.

In fact, when the little Commanche monoplanes come flying in, Moore's cameras pan across the airfield where there is a large marquee on one of the hangars, saying: "Welcome General

Rushon", a private joke among the crew that is actually seen in the film.

During their stay, Hamilton's crew ended up shooting in the tank repair centre, along the parade ground and everywhere they could set up a number of troops.

To portray the flying circus, a group of voluptuous blondes led by Miss Pussy Galore, Broccoli hired a group of male pilots from a local Kentucky flying school, who were dressed up in black jump suits and blonde wigs and told to bring their Commanches over the Fort for aerial shots. A camera helicopter with Moore, Hamilton and Johnny Winbolt aboard, photographed the little planes winging over the Kentucky greenery and landing in a little rural aerodrome that was simulating Friendship Airport, Baltimore.

In his biography of Ian Fleming, John Pearson points out that after *From Russia with Love*, Flem-

"It seems I am too good for you," says actor Gert Frobe, who as GOLDFINGER was perhaps the best of all Bond villains. *(Life Picture Service)*

ing decided to abandon the thought of elevating the literary quality of 007 and instead returned to writing basically the same book over and over again, with only the settings changing.

On the verge of writing the script of *Goldfinger*, Richard Maibaum found himself in a similar predicament. *From Russia with Love* would always be his favourite Bond, but he knew instinctively that its semi-straight approach was not the direction in which Broccoli and Saltzman intended to take the series. It was not the plot or the setting that was going to make Bond unique. It was the presentation.

With *Goldfinger*, Maibaum and his co-writer Paul Dehn, who developed an early draft of the film, were to write what was to be the key script in the James Bond series and which later became the blueprint for all future Bond films. *Goldfinger* was the first of the stylized Bond thrillers where virtually every scene was planned with tongue deep in cheek. It was a romp but with a very important twist. The writers never forgot the one element that would expertly balance the comedy – danger. Without Bond falling into constant danger, the humour would upset the balance of the film.

The car chase became the perfect prototype. Bond is driving his trick Aston Martin, wiping out the opposition with machine guns, oil slicks and smoke screens. His passenger, Tilly Masterson, is enjoying the fun. Her smile reflects the audience's delight in the sequence. But then Bond is trapped. He runs out of road, stops his car, tells Tilly to run for cover, kills a few of her pursuers and then watches as Oddjob flings his razor sharp bowler. With one smack, Tilly is cut down and the audience is hushed to silence. John Barry's score suddenly turns ominous and James Bond is no longer having fun. This ability to switch from comedy to shock was a key ingredient in Bond's adventures. It was this careful approach to the action that made the Bond films superior to all their imitators.

Still with increased attention to style and pace, the writers began, for the first time, to lose sight of Fleming's Bond. If the novels had at times resembled comic strips, they still included their brief studies of a man undergoing extreme pressure. Fleming's Bond went through typical middle-age hangups. He had health problems, bouts of sexual melancholy, an obsession with drink and cigarettes and doubts about his own effectiveness as a human being. He was human and he fought against an inhuman world with his own wits and few surprises.

With *Goldfinger*, the Bond writers created a new agent, an indestructible man who would survive any situation. It was no longer a question of whether Bond would survive, it merely became a case of which button he would push, or what he would say.

In the middle of *Goldfinger*, Bond is about to be cut in half by a laser beam (Maibaum had replaced Fleming's buzz saw with a more modern torture device although it still smacked of *The Pit and the Pendulum*). It could have been a ridiculous sequence. The audience knows that Bond is not going to be castrated by a hot beam of light. The problem is how he will escape, spreadeagled on the table in full view of his guards, with the light inching towards him. The dialogue written for this sequence is masterly. Bond talks his way out of a horrible death. This was the type of sophisticated writing that would make otherwise unbelievable sequences credible.

The final script took some other interesting liberties with the 007 character. In the two previous films, Bond had never appeared funny. He simply courted laughter with his clever throwaway lines. The first sequence in the new Bond film carried the humour a long step further. Since the teaser in *From Russia with Love* had worked so well, it was decided to have another one. Fleming had opened his novel in a Miami airport lounge where Bond is contemplating the recent killing of a South American drug smuggler. This reference to the drug smuggler inspired Maibaum and provided the basis for the teaser. The three dots roll across the screen and reveal the moonlit waters of the Caribbean. A seabird is paddling through the water, past a shadowy dock and up to a deserted beach. The bird rises out of the water and we realise that it is a rubber decoy, perched on the head of James Bond.

It is said that on the night this sequence was shot in the big tank at Pinewood Studios, a number of crew members told Hamilton that they found it too silly. It is certainly the first time in the entire series that Bond courts direct laughter by his actions. The teaser goes on to show Bond

Connery before the golf match at Stoke Poges. *(Wide World)*

disposing of a beach guard and then running up to a huge storage tank where he pushes a hidden switch, opening a door into a secret room in the tank. Poppy plants are everywhere.

After depositing a quantity of plastic explosive on a drum of nitro-glycerin which will blow the drug-filled room to pieces, Bond walks outside, tosses away his frogman's wet suit and reveals a white dinner jacket, complete with carnation.

He then walks to a nearby nightclub where a flamenco dancer's gyrations are disturbed by the horrible explosion. After a friendly agent tells Bond to leave as soon as possible, Bond excuses himself and goes to meet the flamenco dancer who is taking a bath in the back room of the nightclub. She rises out of the bath and embraces Bond, who sees the approach of an assassin reflected in her eyes. At the very last moment, Bond jerks the girl in front of the man, who strikes her, full force, with a club.

Even 007 seems to be having a good time in the sequence. That is, until the assassin is thrown into a bathtub where he reaches for Bond's revolver, which raises the tension.

Bond reacts fast and throws an electric heater

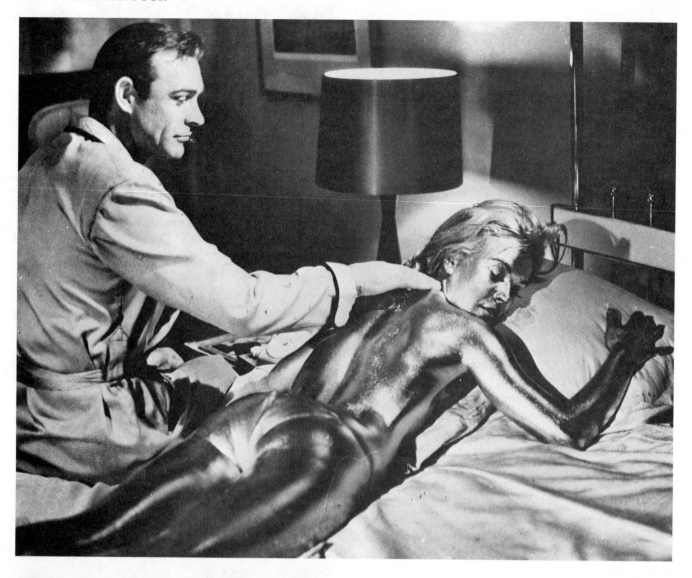

James Bond examines the corpse of Jill Masterton (Shirley Eaton), whose body "has been covered in gold paint." *(UPI)*

Connery and Eaton clowning on the set. *(Wide World)*

into the tub, frying the assassin. Capping the incident, Bond stares down at the groggy flamenco dancer and says: "Shocking, positively shocking." After this, we hear the first strains of Shirley Bassey singing "Goldfinger" and the titles begin to roll. If we compare the *Goldfinger* teaser with that of *From Russia with Love*, it is easy to see the change that had come over the world of James Bond.

Terence Young had started pre-production on *Goldfinger* but he wanted a percentage of the new

Bond film and Broccoli and Saltzman would not agree to it. Young went off to direct *The Amorous Adventures of Moll Flanders* and the producers hired Guy Hamilton. Hamilton was a forty two year old former assistant director for Paramount News and later, assistant to Sir Carol Reed and John Huston. He had directed his first film, *The Ringer,* in 1952 and had achieved considerable success, especially with *The Colditz Story,* four years later. Hamilton was particularly good at putting together action sequences involving armies of technicians and actors. It was, nevertheless, difficult for him to walk into the world of James Bond in mid-series. Terence Young had left behind a team used to a certain director's style.

Meanwhile in Berlin, the producers had found their "Goldfinger": Gert Frobe, a mountainous red-haired man who was at that time a well known German character actor. He had played a German sergeant on Omaha beach in *The Longest Day* – a film which also features Sean Connery as a British private. Although Frobe spoke English, his voice was entirely redubbed for the film.

Broccoli did not believe that well-known actresses added anything to the box office receipts. His policy in *Goldfinger*, as well as in the rest of the Bond films was to cast unknowns. To provide the necessary female interest for Bond, Maibaum wrote five actresses into the script. Shirley Eaton, a blonde British actress who had appeared in a long series of British comedies was cast as Jill Masterson, who dies of skin suffocation after she is covered with gold paint. She became the virtual symbol of the film.

Tania Mallet was signed to play Jill's revenge seeking sister, Tilly Masterson, a beautiful girl in a black cat suit for whom Oddjob takes his hat off. For Pussy Galore, Goldfinger's personal pilot, Honor Blackman was chosen. Broccoli admired her stylish appearances in the popular British television series *The Avengers* where she was especially renowned for the leather outfit she wore. Maibaum had changed the role considerably from Fleming's original Lesbian gangleader. In the film, Pussy is definitely butch but not sufficiently so to survive the charms of James Bond.

Margaret Nolan, who was tested to play Jill Masterson, ended up in the bit part of Dink, Bond's masseuse. Nadja Regin, who had starred in *From Russia with Love* as Kerim's girl, played Bonita in *Goldfinger*, the girl smacked in the teaser. Actress Mai Ling was signed to play the exotic stewardess on Goldfinger's private jet.

If Pedro Armendariz had stolen *From Russia with Love*, it was Harold Sakata, as Oddjob, who makes the strongest impression in *Goldfinger*. Sakata's only dialogue in the entire film is a series of grunts, but one look at his immense, sumo wrestler-like bulk made audiences shudder. In person, he was a kind, gentle man, who was always careful to avoid hurting his acting partners. In the film as a massive, indestructible "wicked oriental", stuffed into ridiculous formal wear and equipped with the razor sharp bowler, Oddjob became the prototypical Bond villain. After *Goldfinger*, the writers were always dreaming up Oddjob types to fight Bond.

Honor Blackman left television's "The Avengers" to play Goldfinger's tough pilot Pussy Galore, whose flight of Commanches put Operation Rockabye Baby to work. *(Life Picture Service)*

Despite the number of scenes in *Goldfinger* that take place in America, practically all the film's exterior sequences were shot in England. To give the film an American flavour, the producers brought back their old favourite Ken Adam who had experienced similar problems with Stanley Kubrick on the recent *Dr. Strangelove*. To absorb the proper background material for the *Goldfinger* sets, Adam joined the reconnaissance unit throughout the winter of 1963-1964, collecting still photographs of the Fort Knox installations, as well as the exterior of the Fontainbleau Hotel in Miami, where Bond first meets Goldfinger.

With both Sean Connery and Gert Froebe unavailable (Connery was then working on *Marnie* for Alfred Hitchcock) the plan was to shoot only exteriors in Miami, with doubles playing the part

Stuntman Bob Simmons, doubling Connery, shows Honor Blackman a few interesting judo moves. *(Life Picture Service)*

of Bond and Goldfinger. The only actors to journey to the Fontainbleau were Cec Linder, a Canadian actor who was playing Felix Leiter, and Austin Willis who became Mr. Simmons, Goldfinger's card opponent in the rigged gin game.

For the opening of the film, following the titles, Hamilton took a crew up in a helicopter to photograph an airplane trailing the "Welcome to Miami Beach" sign. He also took aerial shots of the hotel, including one long shot of springboard diver Al Coffey plunging into the Fontainbleau pool. A ground camera crew filmed around the cabana area where Leiter searches among the tanned bodies for his friend Bond.

When James Bond is found in the capable arms of Dink, he is no longer in Miami Beach but on Sound Stage D at Pinewood where an intricate lighting pattern was arranged to duplicate the intensity of the Florida sun.

If *Goldfinger* had a symbol other than gold-plated Shirley Eaton, it was the marvellous Aston-Martin DB V with modifications that "Q" Branch assigns to Bond. The silver sports car was then considered the best of its kind in England. Ian Fleming had been rather conservative in developing the Aston Martin DB III in the original novel. Apart from a number of concealed compartments and a homing device that allowed Bond to follow Goldfinger from long distances, the original DB III was practically a stock car. With money in the special effects bank, John Stears and Ken Adam became much more ambitious.

Late in 1963, they visited the Aston Martin plant in Newport Pagnall. The product of this interesting relationship between a film studio and a car manufacturer was an expensive sports car equipped with various capabilities that were either actually operational or which would give that impression when they were filmed with the help of special effects. The latter group included the front wing machine guns which were actually thin metal tubes activated by an electric motor connected to the car's distributor. Acetylene gas was discharged into the tubing to give the impression of guns firing.

In the film, Bond destroys the tires on Tilly Masterson's Mustang by activating a special "chariot scythe" which, like the fixture in Messala's chariot in *Ben Hur*, achieves murderous effect when it is spun into a moving target. On the

James Bond and Oddjob meet again!
11-inch action figures complete with fabric clothes

Secret Agent 007 actually swings out right arm to shoot cap-firing pistol . . . kicks out knife-wielding foot.

Oddjob throws his steel-rimmed top hat . . . executes a deadly karate stroke.

James Bond *plus* weapons attaché case
$6⁹⁹

Extra Outfits for James Bond
$2⁹⁹ to $3⁹⁹

Oddjob . . Goldfinger's fearsome handyman
$6⁹⁹

The merchandising bonanza had already begun with these toys advertised in a 1964 Sears catalog. *(UPI)*

DB V, the chariot scythe was really an enormous screw knife welded to a spare pair of the knock-on wheel nuts. The car had to be stopped to exchange these nuts, but Ted Moore's photography and Peter Hunt's editing showed them somehow gradually emerging from the hub centres whilst the car is moving.

Bond's radar scope which allows him to track Goldfinger was another non-working feature that appears as an insert shot. It shows the lighted map, its dialling feature, and the moving blip which indicates the position of the Goldfinger Rolls.

The ejector seat, Bond's ace in the hole, actually worked, but was more a prop than an actual part of the real Aston Martin. The ejector seat came from a fighter plane. It took up a lot of room and could only be mounted immediately prior to the shot where the Chinese guard is thrown through the roof. Just as it works in the air, the ejector seat in the Aston Martin was triggered by com-

pressed air cylinders. For close shots of the Aston Martin, the air force seat was replaced by an ordinary passenger seat.

The working features of the Aston Martin included the rotating licence plate which gave Bond three alternative registration numbers for his car and which was operated electrically. Bond's smoke screen worked, being operated by Army type smoke canisters which were discharged into the exhaust tailpipe. The bullet proof screen which was not really bullet proof was built into the car's boot and could be raised or lowered electrically. Into the car's rear light cluster, the special effects expert built two chambers which could be opened to reveal an oil injector that squirted oil on to the roadway and a supply of three point nails which were blown out on to the road by compressed air.

The car was completed on schedule in the Spring of 1964. According to Aston Martin, the reason that the nail ejection device was not used in the film was to avoid children being given the wrong sort of inspiration.

In March, the Aston Martin was sent out at night into the area of rural England where *Goldfinger* was being filmed. Bob Simmons (as Bond) was driving the car and a young stand-in named Phyllis Cornell (as Tilly) was doubling Tania Mallet. Nine Chinese actors piled into the twin black Mercedes 190's that were chasing Bond. Guy Hamilton, who was yet to work with his principal actors, was surrounded by a huge crew of special effects men, camera operators and assistants who were making the chase sequence one of the most spectacular ever. With the road work completed in a week, Hamilton took his crew onto the Pinewood lot which was simulating the alleyways of Auric Enterprises in Switzerland.

Here, along the narrow driveways, Ted Moore began cranking the high speed camera that would punch up the speed of both the Aston Martin and the Mercedes, giving the impression that the cars were literally, flying across the factory. All the stunt work was done without the services of Sean Connery who was not due to arrive until March 19th for the main shooting.

All over Pinewood, Ken Adam and art director Peter Murton were busy constructing the huge working sets that would double and triple the set budgets of the earlier Bond films. One of the most spectacular was the huge, gleaming interior

"You're not really that tough, are you?" says Sean Connery to Honor Blackman in a quiet moment between takes on GOLDFINGER. (UPI)

of Fort Knox, a multi-storied chamber of dazzling gold and chrome where Bond was to make his last stand against Oddjob.

Adam was never able to enter the real Fort Knox and therefore had to use his imagination. "The very nature of a gold depository is dull", comments Adam. "You can't stack gold very high because of weight problems and questions of transportation. The ingots would be stored in small chambers which would be situated along narrow tunnels. And there's simply no drama in a series of little rooms. In my case, I stacked gold bars forty feet high, under a gigantic roof. I had a whole crew of men polishing the metal work so that it would shine when we turned the lights on. And it was the perfect place to stage the last battle with Oddjob. It was like a golden arena and Bond was able to use gold bars as weapons."

Working from photographs taken during the winter, Adam also designed a full scale replica of the exterior of the Fort Knox depository, complete with metal loading gate, wire enclosure and a good mile of concrete driveway. It was one of the most expensive outdoor sets ever created at Pinewood, at a cost of well over one hundred thousand dollars.

Ken Adam was not only good at designing enormous sets full of detail and movement, he could make even the smallest sets brim with atmosphere. This was important as each Bond film featured a number of exotic sets that swept an audience round the world. *Goldfinger* was the first of the true globe-trotting Bonds.

In fact, the first set in the film, the interior of the El Scorpio nightclub somewhere in South America, is a good example of Adam's handiwork. It is here in this run down dingy bar on the edge of the jungle that James Bond appears in his white dinner jacket. This kind of small set had to look good and although it consisted of only a few bamboo crossbeams, a bar, some electric fans on the ceiling, fanning the smoke-filled air, the set worked.

Sean Connery began work on *Goldfinger* on Stage D on March 19th 1964. Here, fifty men and women acting as local South Americans were rehearsing under the choreographer Selina Wylie. Three dummy musicians, their music piped in electronically, were portraying a typical flamenco trio and on a small stage in the centre of the room, Nadja Regin was practising her erotic flamenco dance.

The Connery who donned the white dinner jacket and walked into the El Scorpio Nightclub was better prepared and more intuitive than before. After working with Hitchcock, *Goldfinger* was like a holiday. However, the first day's shooting was exhausting for Hamilton. The El Scorpio set was small and cramped; crowding sixty extras into it was difficult. Despite this, tempers were controlled, the extras stayed in line and the sweat on everyone's face contributed to the realism of the scene. Connery later told Hamilton that he was impressed with his handling of the crowd and the two men continued to work well together.

The best part of Fleming's novel is the description of a crucial game of golf between Goldfinger

features one exotic set after another, but this turns out to be one of the film's most interesting sequences. It works for a number of reasons. First, Maibaum cut Fleming's eighteen hole description to only two holes. Secondly, Guy Hamilton, a golfer himself, was familiar with the tension in a high stakes golf match and knew what he wanted. The golf sequence became a breath of fresh air in the film, one of those subtle, relaxing, moments that prepared the audience slowly for the roller coaster ride that was coming. Connery's development as an actor is evident in this sequence. He was given more to say, and the film benefitted from this.

By the beginning of July, Guy Hamilton had

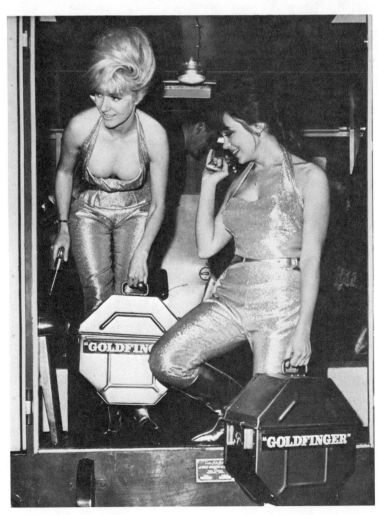

Golden girls Darlene Larson (left) and Diane Sandra guard the premiere print of GOLDFINGER, in New York which was delivered by armored truck. *(UPI)*

Sean Connery surrounded by the usual James Bond appreciation society. *(Wide World)*

and Bond which takes place at the Royal St. Marks Country Club, one of Fleming's own hangouts. Fleming was passionately fond of golf and his explanation of the game is superb. In the script, Bond has returned from Miami where Goldfinger has murdered Jill Masterson. He joins "M" and Colonel Smithers for dinner at the Bank of England and first learns about Goldfinger's alleged smuggling activities. He is ordered to make contact again with Goldfinger and discuss a possible business arrangement which might throw light on Goldfinger's operations. The bait is a single gold bar recovered from the Nazi hoard at the bottom of Lake Topliz in the Salz Kammergut. The next scene takes place at the Golf Club where Goldfinger challenges Bond to a winner take all game, the prize being the gold bar.

Something as mundane as a golf match might have looked ridiculous in *Goldfinger*, which

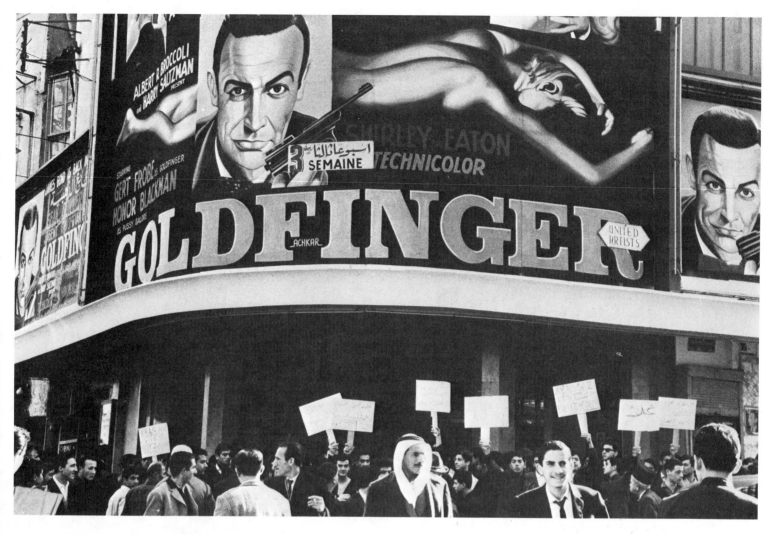

Lebanese students demonstrate for lower ticket prices at the box office during the 1964 release of GOLDFINGER. *(UPI)*

completed most of the film's interiors, including the bone-jarring fight between Bond and Oddjob in the Fort Knox set. On the 6th, the Bond crew left England for Switzerland and the film's principal European location. It was at Andermatt, in the Alps, that Bond's Aston Martin was to follow Goldfinger's Rolls Royce to the Auric Enterprises factory. This was also where Tilly Masterson's white Mustang convertable would make its first appearance.

The American car had arrived on the car ferry and was the first of its kind ever to be seen in Europe. It was provided free of charge by the Ford Motor Company. Exposure in a Bond film later sent many American companies into the Eon Productions camp to unveil their various devices. The Mustang was the first of these.

Maibaum and Dehn eliminated practically all Tilly Masterson's tedious drive across Europe as it appeared in Fleming's novel. They retained only the sequence where Bond meets her on the highway. The Swiss location sequences were short but added an international dimension to the picture with the chase along the beautiful Swiss highways with the Alps in the background. Location shooting was finally completed on July 11th.

Ever since January, Saltzman and Broccoli had been concerned about the Pussy Galore character which they felt might be eliminated by the censor. It seemed silly to consider an optional name for her but for several weeks Maibaum was set to change her name to Kitty Galore until Tom Carlisle, their publicity man, got them out of their dilemma. When shooting was finished, he escorted Honor Blackman to a charity dance where Prince Philip was scheduled to attend. During the course of the evening, Carlisle managed to have a photograph of Honor Blackman and the Prince taken together. He then gave an exclusive story to a newspaper on condition that they printed the caption : "Pussy and the Prince". When the paper appeared the next day, no one objected and the producers were emboldened to go ahead and use the name in the final cut of the film. The producers were, perhaps, hypersensitive to the possibility of hostile public reaction. Audiences were not offended and took it for the punning joke it was.

The underwater army of SPECTRE. *(Life Picture Service)*

5

SHARK TREATMENT

Cubby Broccoli was scouting locations in Portugal for *Goldfinger* in December 1963 when word reached him that the *Thunderball* case in London had finally come to an end. Two and a half years had passed since Ian Fleming had first appeared in court to fight Kevin McClory's injunction and other assorted grievances against his ninth Bond novel.

By 1963, Ian Fleming was seriously ill, and tired of the legal manoeuvrings. When his long-time friend and co-defendant Ivar Bryce decided to back down and end the long court case with a settlement, Fleming threw in the towel as well. According to the court verdict, *Thunderball* would remain a published Ian Fleming novel, but all future copies of the book were to include a reference stating that it was based on an original screen treatment created by Jack Whittingham, McClory and Fleming. The most important result of the trial was that McClory won the complete film and television rights to *Thunderball*. This was a blow to Broccoli and Saltzman who had felt confident that Fleming would eventually win back the rights to the contested book.

The production world of James Bond was now becoming increasingly crowded. Not only was Charles Feldman preparing to go into production on *Casino Royale* for Columbia Pictures, but in Hollywood, in the autumn of 1964 producer Norman Felton was launching another Ian Fleming inspired property for American television.

Felton, a Hollywood television producer and veteran of such series as *Dr. Kildare* and *The*

THUNDERBALL (1965) PC. Eon Productions – A United Artists Release 125 mins Col. **PROD.** Kevin McClory – Executive Producers Albert R. Broccoli and Harry Saltzman **DIR.** Terrence Young **SCR.** Richard Maibaum, John Hopkins based on the novel by Kevin McClory, Jack Whittingham and Ian Fleming **PH.** Ted Moore **ED.** Peter Hunt **PROD DES.** Ken Adam **MUSIC** John Barry **SP EFFECTS** John Stears, **UNDER-WATER PH.** Lamar Boren **CAST.** Sean Connery (James Bond), Claudine Auger (Domino), Adolfo Celi (Emilio Largo), Luciana Paluzzi (Fiona Volpe), Rik Van Nutter (Felix Leiter), Bernard Lee ("M"), Martine Beswick (Paula Caplan), Guy Doleman (Count Lippe), Molly Peters (Patricia Fearing), Desmond Llewelyn ("Q"), Lois Maxwell (Miss Moneypenny), Roland Culver (Foreign Secretary), Earl Cameron (Pinder), Paul Stassino (Derval), Rosa Alba (Madame Boivard), Philip Locke (Vargas), George Pravda (Kutee), Michael Brennan (Janni), Leonard Sachs (Group Captain), Edward Underdown (Air Vice Marshall), Reginald Beckwith (Kenniston), Evelyn Boren (Domino Double), Frank Cousins (Bond Double), Mitsouko (Mademoiselle La Porte).

"My condolences, Madame," says 007 as he belts SPECTRE agent Colonel Jacque Boivard in the THUNDERBALL teaser. *(Life Picture Service)*

Lieutenant, had met Ian Fleming in the spring of 1962 to discuss a possible television series for NBC that autumn. Felton planned a series around a "new" type of hero, an intelligent character who might be seen getting out of a taxi outside the United Nations, or steaming up the Bosphorus on a ferry boat. Fleming envisaged this hero as a man who smoked too much, who forgot to button his waistcoat and spent a lot of time travelling around the world. Felton came to suspect that he himself was the subject of Fleming's revelations. Preoccupied as he was with other matters, Flem-

French beauty Claudine Auger, who portrayed sensuous Domino in THUNDERBALL. *(UPI)*

ing would not commit himself to collaborating on the proposed script. Nevertheless, just before he left New York, he sent Felton a pad of Western Union telegram blanks, on the back of which he had written some ideas. Much of it was useless, but Felton did note the names Fleming gave to his two principal agents. They were Napoleon Solo and April Dancer.

Felton arrived back in Hollywood and with his associate, Sam Rolfe, developed a pilot script entitled *Solo,* about an international crime-fighting organisation named UNCLE and its various operatives, one of which, Napoleon Solo, was a secret agent like James Bond.

One year later, Felton tried again to get Fleming's interest in the venture, but this time, the author was advised to stay away from any television venture that involved secret agents. Already involved in the law suit over *Thunderball,*

Three actresses vie for the role of Domino: left to right, Yvonne Monlaur, Marisa Menzies, and Gloria Paul. They all lost to Claudine Auger. *(UPI)*

Fleming was advised not to get involved in another, especially since Broccoli and Saltzman were already hostile to the Felton project.

In January 1964, Eon Productions actually brought a suit against Felton's television company, claiming that by using the title *Solo* for their proposed series, they were, in effect, stealing an actual character name from *Goldfinger*, then in production at Pinewood. Felton pointed out that Mr. Solo in *Goldfinger*, a Mafia chieftain, was certainly not the same man as Napoleon Solo in their series, and after he brought MGM's best lawyer into the case, Eon Productions backed down, demanding only that Felton change the name of the series. Arena Productions agreed and *Solo* was changed to *The Man from UNCLE* which

first appeared on American television in the autumn of 1964.

Meanwhile, Kevin McClory was wasting no time in making his own preparations. In February 1964, he formed Branwell Productions in the Bahamas and scheduled *Thunderball* as his first film project, with a budget of two and a half million dollars. He then began searching for an actor to play James Bond. Sean Connery was immediately out of the question as a long-term contract kept him in the Eon stable until 1967. (Broccoli had ensured Connery's loyalty by offering him five percent of *Goldfinger*.) McClory had a real problem, since any actor he cast would have to compete against Connery and the reputation he had already established in the role.

Broccoli and Saltzman had their own plans. With *Thunderball* lost to McClory and *Goldfinger* already nearing completion, it was time to plan Eon's next Bond thriller. The producers chose the best of Fleming's later Bond stories, *On Her*

Sean Connery and French actress Mitsouko outside Chateau D'Anet, 40 miles west of Paris. *(Wide World)*

Majesty's Secret Service. Arrangements were made to return to Switzerland that winter to scout locations for the new film, which takes place almost entirely in the Alpine snows and involves Bond in a search for Ernest Stavro Blofeld, the missing head of SPECTRE.

Throughout the autumn of 1964, McClory kept his own production hopes alive, but with United Artists now backing *Goldfinger* with a high-powered pre-release publicity campaign, emphasising the merits of Sean Connery as Bond, it looked as if *Thunderball* was a doomed project. In view of this, McClory took the obvious step and contacted Broccoli and Saltzman with an offer. Since they had been so keen on *Thunderball* for their own series, perhaps they would be interested in going into the venture as partners. Broccoli was to purchase the screen rights to *Thunderball* from McClory who would be included in the deal as a producer with a percentage of the profits.

To Broccoli and Saltzman, the deal did not seem all that attractive. There were more than enough Bond books around. However, Broccoli decided not to pass up the offer, believing that if anyone else made *Thunderball*, it would have a damaging effect on their own series.

In view of this, plans for *On Her Majesty's Secret Service* were dropped and *Thunderball* became the next Bond production. McClory was delighted at the prospect of his film going into production during the height of the Bond fever. He personally had twenty per cent of the film's profits written into his contract but, in turn, he was to prove valuable to Eon Productions. During the past five years, he had rewritten his script a dozen times and had covered every foot of the Bahamas, searching for possible locations. He was an expert diver and underwater explorer and his expertise was invaluable on a film which emphasised underwater effects.

Goldfinger, the third James Bond film, appeared in the United States in December 1964 during a particularly lean period for the American film industry. Nevertheless, it attracted considerable attention and within weeks of its release, broke every box office record in New York and Los Angeles as well as London. Cinema owners were running the film round the clock and asking for the re-release of the first two Bond films as a double bill.

The long-awaited incursion into the American film market had been prepared with the precision of a SPECTRE plot. Since *Goldfinger* was such a prestige film, the producers were originally advised to send it into a road show release at selected cinemas only. Broccoli did not like this idea since it meant that returns would be slow.

"No well-dressed man should be without one," says Bond of the Bell jetpack, here operated by a member of the U.S. Army, doubling Connery. *(Life Picture Service)*

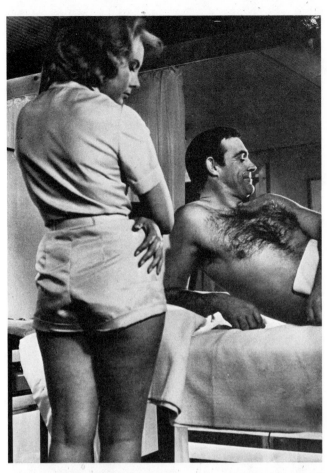

Molly Peters, as the alluring physical therapist Patricia Fearing, prepares to give Sean Connery a rubdown. *(Life Picture Service)*

The interest in Bond was worldwide and he wanted the film to open everywhere simultaneously.

Hollywood's major grossing films usually established their prestigious records over a period of years, in a number of carefully arranged pre-release engagements. *Goldfinger* set a new precedent and seemed to indicate that money could still be made quickly in the film industry with the right product.

In Europe, too, *Goldfinger* achieved a major success. The French were quick to introduce a merchandising tie-in that was to spread James Bond toiletries throughout the world. In Italy, Bond was nicknamed "Mr. Kiss Kiss Bang Bang"

Connery and Claudine Auger at a cocktail party announcing the start of filming on THUNDERBALL. *(UPI)*

Fiona's jet-equipped motorcycle. *(UPI)*

a clue that leads him to the pilot's sister, a beautiful girl named Domino who is the mistress of a mysterious man named Emilio Largo. Largo is in Nassau, posing as a millionaire adventurer. He is actually SPECTRE's number Two, head of the hijacking scheme.

In his search for the missing bomber, Bond meets and destroys several enemy agents, including chief assassin, Fiona Volpe. The story concludes in the water off Nassau, where Bond smashes the SPECTRE plan with the help of the US Air Force and the Coast Guard. To film this spectacular adventure, Eon Productions returned to Ian Fleming country, a lush tropical paradise, where sandy beaches, coral reefs and bikinis prevailed.

From the beginning, the emphasis on *Thunderball* was size. With money flowing in from *Gold-*

Adolfo Celi as tough SPECTRE No. 2, Emilio Largo, was not nearly as venomous as Fleming's other classic villains. *(MGM)*

and plans for Italian imitations were soon under way. Bond was now big business and Eon Productions was in a position to expand.

SPECTRE is featured for the third time in *Thunderball,* launching the most ambitious of all its criminal schemes. Plan Omega calls for an imposter named Angelo to infiltrate an English NATO base and hijack a Vulcan Vindicator bomber equipped with two nuclear bombs. SPECTRE then demands a ransom of two hundred and eighty million dollars from the NATO treaty powers for the plane's return. Otherwise, it will destroy a major city in England or the United States.

The story moves from England to the Bahamas where Angelo crash lands the captured bomber and where James Bond eventually goes to find it. Bond has already found the dead body of the original NATO pilot at an English health clinic, *finger*, the budget was raised to $5.6 million, six times the cost of *Dr. No*. Terence Young was returning to direct.

By the beginning of January 1965, Richard Maibaum was already re-writing the McClory/Whittingham screenplay. Ken Adam and Terence Young had taken a small crew to Nassau to scout locations. Harry Saltzman was in Paris, preparing a visit to the Chateau D'Arnet, where the *Thunderball* teaser was to be filmed.

Much of the action of *Thunderball* was to take place underwater. Here, in the waters off Nassau, a running battle takes place between James Bond, who once more commands an arsenal of lethal gadgets, and SPECTRE'S black-suited frogmen. At the film's climax 007 and a unit of US Air Force aquaparas engage SPECTRE in a full-blown underwater battle fought with CO_2 spear guns. A number of key sequences take place below the surface, including an underwater tryst between Bond and Largo's beautiful mistress Domino, a watery foray by Largo's henchmen who hide the stolen atomic bombs in an underwater cave, and an eery sequence in which Bond finds the hijacked bomber in fifty feet of water, covered with protective camouflage netting and guarded by a school of Golden Grotto sharks.

For this reason, Eon Productions hired one of the world's most experienced underwater cameramen, Lamar Boren of La Jolla, California, who had been photographing underwater films since the late Forties and had worked on the popular television series, *Seahunt*. He knew of *Thunderball* because Broccoli had originally contacted him in the Summer of 1961 when the film was being considered for the first Bond film.

Underwater photography had come a long way since 1914 when the photographer Ernie Williamson handcranked the original version of Jules Verne's *Twenty Thousand Leagues Under the Sea* off Nassau. In those days, Williamson worked on a specially built catamaran upon which a photosphere was balanced between two pontoons. The photosphere, a glass canopy in which Williamson placed himself and his camera, was then lowered into the water to photograph the various divers and props that had been assembled for the film.

Boren knew Williamson and he admired his techniques, but his own dream was to follow the underwater action physically with an airtight camera that could operate under its own power. In his early days at RKO, around 1950, Boren had designed a watertight stainless steel camera case for an old Eymo camera. For the power supply he was followed round the studio tank by a stage hand with a car battery. This worked well enough in the studio tank, but as he discovered, when working in the Caribbean on *Sea Hunt* something more practical was needed.

He did not want generator cords or battery cables to inhibit his progress underwater and he looked to an independent source of power. In 1957 he acquired some miniature silver cells from a friend which were part of the guidance system of an air to air missile and were being manufactured in limited quantities by the Yardney Company in New York.

Boren incorporated them into his Eymo and created one of the first independent underwater camera units. The quality of his work and the variety of his subject matter improved considerably and it was not long before a number of

Connery with a borrowed wig clowns around on the beach in Nassau during THUNDERBALL. *(UPI)*

Largo with his team of SPECTRE frogmen. *(Life Picture Service)*

producers were hiring him for underwater work. By the early 1960's, he had replaced the Eymo with a watertight Panavision camera. Two of these were to film all the underwater action in *Thunderball.*

While Boren assembled an underwater crew in Nassau that included over sixty professional divers and $85,000 worth of diving equipment, Ken Adam was busy designing the arsenal of weapons that would be featured throughout the underwater war sequences. On the SPECTRE side, there were to be some huge working props. These included the Disco Volante, a swift hydrofoil, camouflaged to look like an ordinary luxury yacht; a two man submarine sled for transporting

stolen atomic bombs from the hijacked bomber to an underwater cave; and a number of one man underwater scooters, equipped with the deadly CO_2 spear guns.

On the dock at Nassau, Adam personally supervised the construction of a full-scale mock-up of a Vulcan Vindicator bomber which was then lowered into the Caribbean by crane. The production team was joined by Jordan Klein, a Miami diving specialist who installed electric motors in all the underwater props, and assistant director Ricou Browning who choreographed the underwater sequence with Terence Young and Kevin McClory.

Despite its large budget, magnificent props and

Two members of Ivan Tors's crew move a huge tiger shark into camera range. *(UPI)*

exotic scenery, *Thunderball* was not to be one of the best of the James Bond series. Although the plot was built round a subject as simple as a NATO hijacking, there were major script problems. After *Goldfinger*, the characters in *Thunderball*, especially the villains, seem one dimensional. Bond himself now appeared more like a technician assigned to "Q" branch in charge of operating their plethora of gadgets than a flesh and blood secret agent. He even discovers the SPECTRE plot by luck rather than skill.

Thunderball, nevertheless, had elements to disguise the transformation of its principal character. The large scale production, the lavish locations, the outsized sets and the sense of world-wide alarm give the film a spectacular background. It was a playground so exquisitely fashioned that the defects in the development of the plot tended to be overlooked.

Just as exotic Jamaica had enlivened *Dr. No*, so, in *Thunderball* the ocean itself became a protagonist in the story. The underwater sequences were to take on an enchanting atmospheric quality, especially in the early sequence where Bond meets Domino in the sea off Nassau, swimming underwater amongst the brilliant tropical fish that inhabit the Caribbean coral. John Barry's mellow score is particularly effective here. The composer, who later went on to score *The Deep*, claims that it was on *Thunderball* that he learned not to slow up the action by using fast music.

Sean Connery worked well in the water. If the action sequences with Largo's henchmen seemed at times confusing, and the final underwater battle between the Air Force and the SPECTRE group repetitive, the moments between Bond and Domino were of a quality that gave the film a genuinely romantic atmosphere.

The problem with *Goldfinger* had been the short lifespans of its women. It was not a romantic film and there was little prolonged chemistry between Bond and his mates. In *Thunderball*, by contrast, Bond finds Domino early in the film and sticks by her despite the allure of others, including the voluptuous SPECTRE assassin Fiona Volpe. Casting Domino in *Thunderball* was more difficult than casting some of the other Bond heroines, since she was not only to be beautiful but was to have character as well. In *Thunderball*, Domino

spends a lot of time in the water with Bond and has to stand up to him.

With this in mind, Broccoli began his yearly chore of actress hunting, taking his cue from Fleming's own description of the girl, as someone sprung from peasant stock, wilful, hot tempered and sensual, not one to succumb easily to Bond's domination. In the autumn of 1964, he saw an actress on British television who interested him who had appeared in John Schlesinger's *Billy Liar* and was rapidly becoming established. She was blonde and wore her hair in the Brigitte Bardot fashion. Her name was Julie Christie. When she came to the office a few days later to see Young and Saltzman, she was dishevelled and nervous. She wore jeans and did not look at all like she had on television. Broccoli was disappointed but,

"Women taste rather good," quips 007 as he sucks the poisonous egg spine venom out of Domino's luscious foot. *(Life Picture Service)*

according to Terence Young, the deciding factor against casting her in a role where she would spend most of her time in a bikini was the smallness of her bust.

The next serious contender for the role was Raquel Welch whose photograph Saltzman had seen in the October 1964 issue of *Life* Magazine. At that time, she had made only one film, with Elvis Presley, but Broccoli and Saltzman signed her up on a visit to Hollywood. Back in London, Broccoli received a phone call from Richard Zanuck, the production chief of Twentieth Century Fox in Los Angeles, asking him, as a favour, to release Raquel Welch from her contract so that she could appear in the forthcoming *Fantastic Voyage;* Broccoli reluctantly agreed.

His third choice was Faye Dunaway whom he

After Bond spears Vargas, life returns to normal on Love Beach. *(Wide World)*

spotted in a Broadway play. Some negotiations took place, but eventually the actress was advised by her agent to accept an offer from Sam Spiegel to work on *The Happening* instead.

Broccoli continued his search in London, with a short list of three: Yvonne Monlaur, a Parisian beauty with several French film credits, Maria Buccella, a former Miss Italy and Miss Europe, and Claudine Auger, a former Miss France and a rising young actress in the French film world. Auger was finally chosen for the role for as well as an exquisite figure she had the style and could easily project a spoiled playgirl who meets her match in James Bond.

One of the main problems in transferring Fleming's *Thunderball* to the screen was the novel's lack of a major villain of the Goldfinger/Dr. No variety. Ernst Stavro Blofeld, Bond's future grand antagonist appears briefly in the first few scenes of the novel but he remained anonymous in the film, referred to simply as "Number One".

Blofeld's field commander is Emilio Largo, a tough Italian mafia type who leads the underwater hijacking in Nassau. However, Largo was a very average villain, and even though the Italian actor Adolfo Celi, replete with eye patch and muscular frame, looks convincing in the role, there was need for a more evil antagonist. With this in mind, Maibaum created Fiona Volpe, a female executioner who becomes Bond's chief nemesis in Nassau. Fiona is a real man killer who drives fast, kills fast and makes love like a tornado. As SPECTRE's top assassin, she uses her voluptuous Italian figure to finger the NATO officer François Derval (Paul Stassino) who is soon murdered and replaced by an exact duplicate.

When the SPECTRE operative Count Lippe (Guy Doleman) jeopardises the NATO hijacking by attacking James Bond at the Shrublands health clinic, it is Fiona, racing down the highway on a motorcycle who blasts Lippe's Ford apart with a barrage of rockets. In Nassau she becomes the perfect land adjutant to Largo, who spends much of his time in a wet suit directing the underwater operations.

To play Fiona, a lady who is comfortable in leather jackets as well as a negligée, the producers found Luciana Paluzzi, an experienced international actress who had appeared in a number of films as well as the American television series *Five*

Fingers, which was first shown in 1959. The success of the Fiona character depended on Miss Paluzzi's ability to project bloodthirsty sexuality.

Although the Bond series had its repetitive moments, even the least successful films have a powerful degree of fantasy and imagination. *Thunderball,* despite its length, and some sequences that lack clarity and suspense, had its own share of this. The original *Thunderball* teaser, as written by Maibaum, takes place in a Hong Kong "fan tan" parlour, where a beautiful girl, dressed from head to toe like a peacock, sits in a golden cage above the main ball room. Bond gives her the eye and later follows her into a dressing room, enters into a polite conversation and then slugs her in the mouth. Her peacock head comes off to reveal a man, the enemy agent Bond is searching for.

"We won't tell a soul, Sean." *(UPI)*

The sequence was subsequently considered too outlandish. Maibaum then suggested the idea of a funeral where Bond comes to offer his condolences to the widow. He follows her to a country house, somewhere in France, and gives her the same rough treatment as the "fan tan" dancer. The sequence was planned for the Château country where Harry Saltzman had found the original home of Diane de Poitiers.

On February 16th 1965, the principal photography on *Thunderball* began outside the chapel of this ancient residence. A crew of fifty eight left London on February 12th. Accompanying the convoy of covered trucks and passenger cars were Bond's silver Aston Martin, fresh from the *Goldfinger* campaign, and a special Lincoln Continental limousine which was flown over on the Air Ferry from London.

In the teaser, enemy agent Jack Boivard masquerades as a widow at his own funeral to elude British Intelligence. Bond is suspicious when he sees Madame Boivard open the car door of the Lincoln herself, instead of waiting to be helped. He follows the lady to her home and offers his peculiar form of condolence. In order to lend realism to Boivard's disguise, Rose Alba plays the widow up until the fight sequence, at which point stunt man Bob Simmons, takes over in drag. In the vicious fight, Harold Sanderson who was doubling Sean Connery receives some nasty swipes with a poker, before breaking Boivard's neck.

Standing guard over Bond's getaway Aston Martin is Japanese actress Mitsouko, who, as 007's French contact, waits for her partner to escape Boivard's bodyguards. 007 is soon soaring over the rooftops of the Chateau in a Bell one-man Rocket suit. The jet pack had been sent over to Eon productions by the United States Army, along with a qualified operator, who spent the afternoon of February 19th demonstrating the newest in Pentagon technological wonders.

Bond arrives back at his Aston Martin just as three bodyguards reach the driveway. He raises his rear bullet-proof screen and proceeds to drench his enemies in a long cascade of water

Connery listens to Terence Young's direction during a key bed sequence with Lucianna Paluzzi. *(UPI)*

from the Aston Martin's hidden tank. The water splashing on to the screen served to introduce the *Thunderball* titles.

As production commenced on the Pinewood lot, the rest of *Thunderball's* international actors arrived. These included Martine Beswick, returning to the series as Paula Caplan, Bond's contact in Nassau; Philip Locke and Michael Brennan, who portray Largo's two bodyguards, Vargas and Yanni; and Rik Van Nutter, who became the third and best actor to portray Bond's American CIA associate, Felix Leiter.

Big time gamblers themselves, Broccoli and Saltzman knew of Ian Fleming's fascination with card games. Nearly all his books make some reference to them. Le Chiffre in *Casino Royale*, Goldfinger, and Hugo Drax in *Moonraker* are each involved in elaborate card cheating schemes, all of which are defeated by Bond. For the duel at cards between Bond and Largo, Ken Adam brought out the old Chemin der Fer table used in the opening to *Dr. No*, and placed it in the exotic casino set at Nassau. Bond never loses at Chemin de Fer.

On March 24th 1965, the long-awaited underwater love sequence, probably the first ever shot for the cinema, was being filmed under the direction of Lamar Boren. It had been a long afternoon in the twenty feet of water off Clifton Pier. In the previous sequence, Boren's wife Evelyn had ridden a great sea turtle that had been captured that morning by members of the Miami Seaquarium. The turtle had been stubborn and it took hours before Mrs. Boren could hitch a ride on its shell. Evelyn Boren was standing in for Claudine Auger, Frank Cousins for Sean Connery. Both wore aqualungs over their swimsuits. Cousins wore a simple pair of swimming trunks while Mrs. Boren wore the Claudine Auger bikini which left very little to the imagination. Behind Boren, the actual stars, Connery and Auger, watched the whole scene with polite interest. They wore the same outfits and were available for closeups.

Behind Mrs. Boren were two diver's assistants, manning the Par-64 underwater floodlights, their long cords trailing off to the surface where their companion generator stood moored to a huge barge, the underwater crew's base of operations.

A propman, carrying with him a third duplicate of Claudine Auger's bathing suit dived down into the water and swam towards Boren. At a given moment, Sean Connery and Claudine Auger were to slip down behind the coral and the prop man would float the bathing garments to the surface. Even the gadget-bedecked Bond would never think of making love to Domino without taking her bathing suit off.

Receiving the "okay" signals from his crew, Boren twirled his hand in the "camera rolling" signal, picked up his huge Panavision camera and counted down from four. When he reached one, Connery and Auger swam over to the coral, embraced and drifted downward.

To adjust the level of his camera, Boren used his lungs like an elevator. To rise up he took in a deep breath of oxygen and to drop down, he exhaled. By controlling his breathing in this fashion, he could achieve a perfect balance, a factor that contributed to the steadiness of his camera and the clarity and effectiveness of the scene.

A few seconds after the stars drifted behind the coral, the prop man let go of Auger's bikini which promptly floated to the surface accompanied by a burst of bubbles from the two actors. The sequence went flawlessly, although months later Broccoli decided to eliminate the floating bikini as too suggestive. Bond and Domino were still seen to disappear behind the coral, but the long stream of bubbles replaced the offending bathing suit.

Two nights later, Terence Young's main crew began filming the exterior of the Café Martinique where Bond, having beaten Largo at cards, dances with Domino and discovers that she is leaving Nassau in two days time.

This short sequence was to be one of *Thunderball's* most romantic. The Café Martinique lies on Paradise Island, a two mile strip of sand and rock that forms the outer edge of Nassau Harbour. Here, every evening, the rich élite of Nassau society arrive in their motor launches to eat, drink and dance, and it is in this lush atmosphere that Domino begins to fall in love with James Bond.

With the help of Patty Turtle of the Nassau Tourist Board, and an offer to donate a sum of money to the local Red Cross, a group of Nassau's social élite were persuaded to portray themselves for the two all night parties during which Terence Young was to shoot his key sequence. Eon Productions also threw in a bucket of the finest caviar as well as several cases of Dom Pérignon champagne.

It was a glamorous scene, the women dressed in long revealing gowns and glowing jewels, the men resplendent in dinner jackets, everyone chattering about the latest arrivals, the weather and the plans for the coming week. The same group was later hired to attend the special Junkanoo parade which was organised especially for *Thunderball*.

Normally, the Junkanoo is held on Boxing Day, December 26th, but, with Broccoli and Saltzman offering a special prize for the most colourful costumes and floats, the residents and shop keepers of Nassau responded with their own Easter version of the colourful pageant.

To film the parade (a real one) where a wounded Bond eludes Fiona and her SPECTRE henchmen, Terence Young called a meeting of his assistant directors. Young planned to film around the parade as it moved through downtown Nassau. He instructed his assistant directors that whatever happened they must not try to stop it, or move it backwards. They must shoot around it doing the best they could. The parade was eventually two miles long travelling around in a large circle and there were forty companies co-sponsoring the event. To bring the whole thing to a halt might cause a disaster.

As it moved through Nassau, there was a constant rhythm of "Whistle whistle, boom boom". For two nights, that was all that was heard. The performers were wild and when their paper costumes began to loosen up, they would take them off and heat them over a flame to make them stiff again. "Several times our cameras picked up a crowd of people coming round a corner with nothing on", recalled Richard Jenkins, a third assistant.

Six hours into the second night, Young, in spite of his own instructions, called out that he had a headache and that the parade must stop for a while. Forty five thousand people were watching the parade, and although the assistants feared the worst, all went well and Young was able to realign some cameras and continue shooting.

In Nassau, *Thunderball* attracted unprecedented attention from journalists. Three magazines had their own "exclusive" articles on "The Girls of James Bond" and everyone wanted exclusive interviews with Sean Connery who was less than cooperative. Young was able to protect his stars from the press barrage by working them constantly. If an actress was not busy, she became an instant pin-up for the magazine photographers.

One of the later complaints about *Thunderball* was that the three principal actresses all looked alike, and that at key moments in the film it was difficult to tell them apart. The actresses wore their hair in the same way, and Claudine Auger and Martine Beswick were the same height. Certain slips in the film compounded the confusion. For instance, when Luciana Paluzzi picks up Bond in her Mustang and takes him "for a ride" to Nassau, and the audience finally has the opportunity to notice that she is the same red-haired girl who had ridden the motorcycle at the beginning of the film, Paluzzi's hair is concealed by a headscarf.

The Bond girls were not the only look-alikes in Nassau that year. Floating out in the harbour were two mammoth luxury yachts, both of which were dubbed the "Disco Volante". One was the special creation of art director Ken Adam. The Disco Volante was the gleaming super yacht of Emilio Largo, but hidden beneath Adam's calm 110 foot exterior lurked a hydrofoil boat, a craft that operated on hydraulic skis that lifted the entire hull out of the water, propelling it along at forty five miles per hour. Once the hydrofoil was loose, the cocoon portion of the Disco turned into a floating battleship, with enough armament to keep a Coast Guard flotilla at bay.

To build such a vessel, Ken Adam went to Puerto Rico in December 1964 to purchase "The Flying Fish", an old Rodriguez hydrofoil which had once carried passengers between Venezuela and Mexico. Rodriguez was the manufacturing firm in Messina, Sicily that had originally built hydrofoils for use in the Adriatic. The rusty craft was driven under its own power to a Miami shipyard for a complete overhaul. Its 1320 horsepower Mercedes Benz diesel was put into top condition to propel the extra fifty foot cocoon that Adam was constructing nearby.

Adam remembers that there were two slip

bolts holding the cocoon. He used a real pleasure yacht as the prototype for his own creation. Some naval experts thought it would not work but there was less trouble with the Disco than there was with any other gadget. The cocoon itself was about fifty feet long and was fitted out with a yellow smokestack. Once the hydrofoil slipped away it was planned to turn the cocoon into a floating arsenal.

Adam installed the type of armaments normally found on a destroyer, including an anti aircraft cannon, heavy machine guns and armour plating. Special effects expert, John Stears, later constructed a model of both the hydrofoil and the cocoon and both were blown apart in the Pinewood tank.

Luxury yachts and swift hydrofoils were not the only gadgets that merited attention: even the smallest prop on a Bond film had its moments. One of these, designed by Ken Adam, was a tiny rebreather that allows 007 to breathe underwater for four minutes at a time. It was a wonderful creation but only a prop. A few weeks after *Thunderball* was released in England assistant art director, Peter Lemont, received a telephone enquiry about the rebreather at his Pinewood office. It came from a Commander in the Royal Navy who had just seen *Thunderball*. It seemed that the Navy was working on a rebreathing device and was having no luck at all. It was not the first time that a simple prop in a Bond movie had interested the Ministry of Defence.

Midway through the location in Nassau, Sean Connery was called to Palmyra, Largo's land headquarters, which was actually the sprawling summer home of the Nicholas Sullivans of Philadelphia. Eon Productions had taken over the estate and, aided by the Miami Seaquarium, turned the Sullivans' Olympic size swimming pool into a haven for three huge tiger sharks. In *Thunderball*, Bond falls into this very pool where he fights a SPECTRE agent to the death.

It was a difficult sequence, because Bond is caught in the pool without a face-plate, prohibiting the use of a double. Reluctantly, Connery agreed to swim with the huge tiger sharks. Lamar Boren, who was part of the underwater crew assigned to protect Connery from any danger explained: "Those sharks weren't drugged, nor were their jaws wired. They were the real thing,

and Sean was depending on us to keep him out of trouble. But you really don't have to worry about sharks unless there's blood in the water or a lot of garbage. In that pool, the sharks were very sluggish. They ended up ignoring Sean and just swimming around."

The same tiger sharks (Maibaum changed their name to the Golden Grotto variety in the script) were later used in the eery sequence where Bond finds the Vulcan bomber, and one shark swims through the final battle between Largo's underwater army and the aquaparas. The final battle, the most ambitious of all the underwater sequences, was handled by the full Ivan Tors crew, forty divers strong, and filmed by Boren who, single-handed, paddled through the underwater battleground.

The battle was filmed in segments over a period of six days. One important sequence was filmed outside Nassau harbour around a sunken US Navy landing craft, where Bond lures two enemy frogmen to their deaths. The rest of the battle spread itself out along the Nassau seascape. Filming underwater was at times too realistic for comfort. In one sequence, Bond flicks a switch on his diving gear and fires an explosive spear at an enemy diver. In the filming, the SPECTRE diver was given an explosive squib that was ignited on his body by remote control but which backfired, giving the diver a severe burn and putting him in St. Margaret's hospital.

Bond's jet pack which gives him super underwater speed was actually a prop with a piano wire attached to a speed boat which pulled Bond's double, Frank Cousins, through the water. If Cousins had turned his face at any moment, the force of being dragged at such speed would have torn the diver's mask from his face.

Most of the battle took place in twenty feet of water off Clifton Pier. Into the battle the producers threw every piece of equipment in the *Thunderball* arsenal, including the SPECTRE bombsled, the scooters, and the scores of CO_2 guns that sprayed a lethal underwater rain of spears among the fighting ranks. With the free swimming orange-suited aquaparas attacking the enemy convoy, it was almost a return to the Indians versus Covered Wagon fights of the Old West.

Seemingly invincible behind their spear firing

sleds, Largo's frogmen are systematically over-whelmed in hand to hand combat by Bond and his Aquaparas. Terence Young, who became disenchanted with *Thunderball* during the final weeks of shooting, thought that apart from being repetitious, the underwater sequences, especially the final battle, went on too long and were confusing to the audience.

Young's disappointment with *Thunderball* was felt mostly by editor Peter Hunt, who in the autumn of 1965 found himself editing the huge picture virtually alone. As usual, the location crew had left a pile of insert shots to finish and many of these were causing problems. One, in particular, involves Bond's attempts to control the runaway Disco Volante after the dying Largo jams the controls. The window shots of the hydrofoil skimming the reefs were originally shot by helicopter. Hunt later sped up the film in the cutting room by frame cutting the footage. It turned out to be a confusing sequence because it seemed impossible that the Disco could negotiate the channel at such a speed.

Hunt had commented that the whole film does not bear watching too closely. There are many continuity slips. One of the most notorious is where Bond and Leiter are looking for the Vulcan from their helicopter and, in one shot, Rik Van Nutter is sitting there with a hat on whilst in another sequence he has on a completely different set of clothes. Both sequences are cut together and, in Hunt's opinion, work.

In another sequence, Bond rips a black mask off a SPECTRE frogman and then, in the next scene we see him wearing a blue mask from earlier in the film. Hunt takes a practical view of the problem: "There are times when you want to juxtapose certain bits of film and you can't. It's not possible. And that's how the gaps occur. It's better to have the speed of the film than to worry about continuity."

6

UNDER THE VOLCANO

It would be hard to over-estimate composer John Barry's contribution to the Bond series. Barry himself has said "The Bond music seems to convey the sentiment of the period of the sixties everywhere. The themes actually became nostalgia in their own lifetime." This was particularly true of Barry's score for the fifth James Bond film *You Only Live Twice*, one of his best, and undoubtedly the highlight of a film in which actor Donald Pleasance is totally miscast as Blofeld, Sean Connery sleep-walks through his role and the action sequences lack credibility at key moments. However, *You Only Live Twice* has an interesting story that, in part, explains its failures. Like the original novel which elicited its own unusual breed of suspense amid a travelogue

Sean Connery back in hot water in YOU ONLY LIVE TWICE, and as the trailers remarked, "Twice is the only way to live" for 007. *(UPI)*

format, the fifth James Bond has some high points amid the roughage. If Terence Young and Richard Maibaum were gone, their spirit was carried on in a new team that at least appeared enthusiastic, if not overly innovative.

You Only Live Twice takes place entirely in Japan. In the original novel, published in the Spring of 1964, James Bond is sent to the Orient to meet the head of the Japanese Secret Service and gain for England the secrets of Magic, a decoding apparatus that is systematically intercepting Russian diplomatic traffic. The chief of Japanese Intelligence is ex-Kamikaze pilot Tiger Tanaka, who offers Bond the Magic ciphers if he will assassinate the evil Dr. Shatterhand, a Swiss citizen who has created a lethal garden of poisonous plants and insects in the remains of an old castle in North Eastern Kyushu. There, hundreds of suicidal Japanese are finding a deadly salvation.

Shatterhand is none other than Ernst Stavro

YOU ONLY LIVE TWICE (1967)
PC. Eon Productions – A United Artists Release 116 mins. Col. **PROD.** Albert R. Broccoli and Harry Saltzman **DIR.** Lewis Gilbert **SCR.** Roald Dahl based on the novel by Ian Fleming **PH.** Freddie Young **ED.** Thelma Connell **PROD DES.** Ken Adam **MUSIC.** John Barry **2nd UNIT DIR.** Peter Hunt **SP EFFECTS.** John Stears **STUNT CO-ORD.** Bob Simmons assisted by George Leech
CAST. Sean Connery (James Bond),

Akiko Makabayashi (Aki), Tetsuro Tamba (Tiger Tanaka), Mie Hama (Kissy Suzuki), Teru Shimada (Osato), Karin Dor (Helga Brandt), Lois Maxwell (Miss Moneypenny), Donald Pleasence (Blofeld), Bernard Lee ("M"), Desmond Llewelyn ("Q"), Charles Gray (Dikko Henderson), Tsai Chin (Chinese Girl), Alexander Knox (American Leader), Robert Hutton (Leader's Aide).

Blofeld, who, after many years of evil-doing has come to Japan to retire. His peculiar form of gardening is destroying the flower of Japanese youth and Tanaka sees Bond as Japan's only hope.

In Fleming's previous book, *On Her Majesty's Secret Service*, Blofeld, once again foiled in his plans for world domination, spitefully murders Bond's bride Tracy in the last scene. Bond's thirst for revenge is satisfied in the final chapter of *You Only Live Twice* when he breaks into Blofeld's loathsome castle fortress and kills the ex-SPECTRE chieftain. The castle itself, with its volcanic fumaroles, deadly creeping plants and poisonous insects was the highlight of a book that was more of a travelogue than a James Bond adventure.

In March, 1966 after two weeks of general location hopping in the main Japanese islands, where Cubby Broccoli visited historic Himeji castle (where Tanaka's Ninja agents train), and the cities of Tokyo and Kobe, where he estab-

Actor Donald Pleasance was the first to portray SPECTRE chief Ernst Stavro Blofeld. This time the makeup department helped considerably. *(UPI)*

lished a good rapport with the Japanese government, the reconnaissance team headed south to Kyushu, the southernmost island in the Japanese chain. Here, Broccoli hoped to find a castle on the Japanese coastline that could be used as Blofeld's fortress. The team cruised up and down the Japanese coastline, along the Tsushima straits, searching in vain for the right ruins. There were no castles anywhere and Broccoli soon realised that Fleming's imagination had been working overtime on *You Only Live Twice*. The Japanese, Broccoli discovered, did not build castles on the coastline because the typhoons made it too dangerous. Any castles were built inland to defend strategic passes and valleys.

Before they returned to England, Broccoli's reconnaissance unit planned one last search across the island of Kyushu. One hour out of Kagoshima, the helicopters began to cross a stretch of desolate mountainous landscape set aside as a National Park and containing over twenty extinct volcanoes. Broccoli was excited about the find and he soon ordered his pilot to take a closer look at one of them in which he spotted a huge crater lake. In the background, the other volcanoes loomed ominously, and Broccoli decided that this setting was ideal for the next film. He planned to abandon Fleming's castle of death and to create a more interesting fortress, hidden inside a volcano cone. What Blofeld would be cooking up inside this strange environment would be determined by screenwriter Roald Dahl, who was already at work on the script in England.

Dahl, a tall, wiry ex-fighter pilot and friend of Ian Fleming, well known as a writer of grotesque and inventive short stories, was the first of a number of new people brought in to freshen up the series. He was not known as a screenwriter, and had only one script to his credit – a shelved World War One adventure entitled *Oh Death Where Is Thy Sting-a-Ling-a-Ling?* Before Dahl began his script, he attended several conferences where the established pattern of the Bond films was pointed out to him. He was told that each film had to have a pre-title teaser that would get the film off on the right footing. He was also told that there had to be at least three women in Bond's life.

In Dahl's script, Blofeld's castle was gone and with it the strange tale of mass suicide in southern

James Bond goes Japanese, here as an Ama Island fisherman. *(Wide World)*

Japan. In its place was a return to a *From Russia with Love* type plot in which Blofeld, backed by Red China, enters the space race by playing off the Russians and Americans. The agent of his plans is a specially designed Intruder rocket which captures spacecraft and returns them to Blofeld's secret volcano hideout.

By 1967, it was commercially attractive to send Bond into space. Practically the entire world was watching the heavens as American astronauts and their cosmonaut competitors were flung skyward in increasing numbers.

Dahl believed that *You Only Live Twice* was the only Fleming book that had virtually no semblance of a plot that could be made into a movie. He felt that the concept of Blofeld patrolling his garden of poisonous plants in a medieval suit of armour and lopping off the heads of half-blinded Japanese was ridiculous. When he began the script, he felt able to retain only four or five story ideas from the original novel – the Japanese setting, Blofeld and Tiger Tanaka, Bond's pearl diving girlfriend Kissy Suzuki and the Ninjas, those masters of oriental martial arts who use their talents to raid Blofeld's hideout.

Broccoli's idea of transferring Blofeld's hideout to the volcano fitted neatly into Dahl's space story. Inside the volcano, Dahl placed a rocket base, complete with launching pad and bogus crater lake, a helicopter landing port, numerous blockhouses and enough sophisticated electronic hardware to compete with Cape Canaveral.

Starting with *You Only Live Twice*, the Bond story ideas began to develop from the latest newspaper headlines. Dahl read the American papers daily which were describing NASA's new Gemini programme and the orbiting two man space craft which was sending men out for "walks in space". This material was useful for the teaser in which a recently launched US space craft is captured by Blofeld's intruder ship.

Coincidentally, a month after Dahl began his script, a United States Air Force B-52 Stratofortress was lost off the coast of Spain with two atomic bombs on board. The mystery that surrounded that catastrophe produced a number of books, magazine articles and television specials and served to give the newly released *Thunderball* a helpful push towards a fifty million dollar world wide gross. It also proved to any still doubting critics that if Bond's films appeared funny at times, the humour did not obscure an astute realism.

Dahl's finished script featured some of the most spectacular action material of the series, including three car chases, huge sparkling sets that only Ken Adam could design, and more ingenious gadgets to wipe out the opposition even more quickly than usual. True to formula, Dahl created three women in Bond's life – Aki and Helga who are sacrificed, and sexy Kissy who ends up in Bond's arms. Unfortunately, James Bond seems to be noticeably absent from the film for the producers were content to let Dahl concentrate on making their product bigger and more spectacular. It no longer mattered who James Bond was, as long as he went through the required tricks.

This time, the tricks did not sit too well with Sean Connery who was rapidly tiring of his commitment to Bond. His original contract, signed in 1961, called for him to do one Bond film a year until 1967. By the time *Thunderball* was completed, Connery was near the end of his tether. The rumbles began in October 1965 when he demanded that the producers shorten the shooting schedule on the next film to twelve weeks. Nine months later, Eon Productions released Connery from his six picture contract and signed him to do *You Only Live Twice* on a one picture commitment only, hoping that he would be wooed back to another Bond film if the price were right.

However, in an interview in the *Los Angeles Times,* Connery made it clear that he did not plan to make a sixth Bond film and that he was "bored to tears talking about the James Bond image." In another interview, he complained that Saltzman and Broccoli had not made him a partner in the Bond enterprise. Broccoli counter-

attacked, pointing out that Connery had become a wealthy man because of the Bond films and that he had begun to "attribute his success to himself, rather than to anyone else" and to make impossible demands.

It was Lewis Gilbert who directed the tiring Connery in *You Only Live Twice.* Gilbert at first declined the offer but was won over by the idea of making a film for a guaranteed mass audience. His last film had been the popular comedy *Alfie,* starring Michael Caine, an actor who was under personal contract to Harry Saltzman and whom Gilbert had borrowed for the film. New personnel on *You Only Live Twice* included cameraman Freddie Young, who had just won an Academy Award for his work on *Dr. Zhivago,* and who had worked with Gilbert on *The Seventh*

Japanese actors Tetsuro Tamba (as Tanaka, left) and lovely Mie Hama (center) join Connery on Ama Island. *(Wide World)*

Dawn, and Thelma Connell, who replaced Peter Hunt as principal film editor.

After *Thunderball,* Peter Hunt had been anxious to direct the next James Bond film himself. When he was turned down, he offered his resignation, but was persuaded to take on the second unit direction with the promise of directing the next Bond film.

In London, casting was completed when Czech actor Jan Werich was signed to play Ernst Stavro Blofeld, appearing for the first time on camera. The other two important European parts were given to Karin Dor who became Helga Brandt, another of Blofeld's sultry assassins, and Charles

Ken Adam's magnificent missile silo is unveiled to a horde of international journalists. *(Wide World)*

Gray, who, as Dikko Henderson, introduces Bond to Japan. The rest of the film's primary characters were all Japanese actors and actresses signed during the second trip to Japan in May 1966.

Apart from Kissy Suzuki, the Ama islander who helps Bond prepare for his assault on Blofeld's castle, all the girls in Fleming's original novel were cardboard cut-outs. To accommodate 007's lusty appetites, Roald Dahl had to create other women of a more three dimensional nature. One of these is Tanaka's beautiful assistant, Aki, whose daring saves 007 many times. Spinning through the Tokyo traffic in her zippy Toyota 2000 sports car, she was Dahl's tribute to the Japanese woman of the Sixties who was gradually breaking away from traditional restraints.

Had Ken Adam been asked to build a new hotel on the Pinewood lot, his problems would have been no less complex than the ones he faced in constructing Blofeld's secret rocket base. For *You Only Live Twice,* Adam had to create not only the interior of a huge hidden rocket base but a set that included a functional heliport, a closing steel curtain that covered the entire cone of the volcano, a monorail that transported personnel and equipment throughout the complex, numerous working elevators and cranes and a labyrinth of stairways and catwalks that ringed the fortress.

With a budget of one million dollars, Adam built his creation full size on the back lot, the biggest set Adam had constructed. Adam recalled: "One of the problems on the Bond films is that if these big sets were written completely into the original screenplays, we could probably get away with building part of the sets full sized and faking the rest with models and matte paintings. But since we only know at the time of construction that the big finale or the big shoot out takes place in the set, and nothing else, I've got to do it full size. We then work out the action as we go along. I make the designs and then the director and writer come and help plan the actual movements within the set. Since by the time we made *You Only Live Twice* we had a liberal set budget, the main problem was logistics. You can't afford to make any mistakes on a set of this size, especially when you're using an enormous amount of structural steel. You have to consult with structural engineers who calculate your stress factors And you can't keep changing your mind like you often do on an interior set. We had to create accurate models and these had to be followed to a T. And when you work with steel it has to be ordered three months ahead of time."

In January 1967, the *Los Angeles Times* published a few of Adam's more interesting statistics. In constructing the volcano base, his team used two hundred miles of tubular steel, more than seven hundred tons of structural steel, two hundred tons of plasterwork, eight thousand railway ties for the set's working monorail, and more than two hundred and fifty thousand square yards of protective canvas.

Two hundred and fifty men worked on the project and on May 11th, 1966, the first of the steel foundations was completed. The finished set was visible from the main London/Oxford highway, some three miles away. During the period of construction, Adam saw that this kind of set was a designer's dream, but suffered from insomnia, wondering whether his design would work in practical terms, since, unlike a normal building, this gigantic set had no precedents.

In addition to the Volcano creation, Adam and his assistant Harry Pottle were responsible for other key sets, including Blofeld's underground apartment, complete with indoor piranha infested pond; the supersonic headquarters of Tiger Tanaka's Japanese Secret Service with the drop chute which rudely greets any western visitors and the offices of Mr. Osato, a millionaire industrialist whose operations form a convenient front for Blofeld.

While Adam realised his concepts full size, special effects wizard John Stears was creating his in miniature. Stears had just returned from Hollywood where he had received an Oscar for his special effects on *Thunderball.* Like stuntman Bob Simmons, editor Peter Hunt and composer John Barry, Stears was another member of the Bond team who received little publicity during the early years, but who was nevertheless responsible for a great deal of the creative longevity of the series.

During his time in the British army, Stears had developed an interest in pyrotechnics and ballistics. He cultivated some film contacts and in 1952 was asked to work on the miniatures for the film about the British flier Douglas Bader, *Reach for the Sky.* Stears later specialised in matte paintings and was involved in the first Bond film, *Dr. No,* creating the miniature bauxite mine and in *From Russia with Love,* blowing up the SPECTRE helicopter and speed boats. In *Goldfinger* he flew the miniature Goldfinger and presidential jets and in *Thunderball* he was responsible for the destruction of the hydrofoil Disco Volante. Whenever a scene featured aerial action or explosions Stears was called in to offer his expertise. On *You Only Live Twice* with its outer space

Three views of Ken Wallace's incredible autogiro "Little Nellie," which became a flying version of the Aston Martin. *(Wide World)*

German actress Karin Dor and Connery on the set of YOU ONLY LIVE TWICE. *(UPI)*

sequences and helicopter chases he was kept particularly busy.

Wing Commander Ken Wallis joined the special effects team on the film, contributing his invention, a miniature auto-giro, which Harry Saltzman had spotted in an aviation magazine. The portable helicopter, "Little Nellie", was soon equipped with the proper 007 defence mechanisms, including heat seeking air to air missiles, aerial mines, machine guns and flame throwers. Wallis himself flew "Little Nellie" for the cameras.

Meanwhile, in Japan, the Toyota Automobile Corporation offered to create a special version of its new GT sports car, complete with a convertible top, the first of its kind ever seen in Japan. Into this dream car, Stears added a functional closed circuit television which allows Bond and Aki to communicate with Tiger Tanaka's Tokyo head-quarters.

Before they left for Japan, Lewis Gilbert and the first unit completed a number of interiors at Pinewood including the "murder" of 007 in Hong Kong. To trick Blofeld into lowering his guard on British Secret Service activities in Japan, screenwriter Dahl had Bond's death faked in a Hong Kong hotel room when two machine gun wielding Japanese break in and pump lead into Bond's relaxing form. Under the eye of SPECTRE agents, Bond is given a proper Naval burial at sea aboard a destroyer in Hong Kong, and his body is sent to the bottom of the harbour where a team of frogmen recover it and bring it to a waiting submarine. Bond is alive, thanks to a special aqualung and he reports to "M" aboard the submarine. To avoid further detection, he is placed in one of the submarine's torpedo tubes and fired towards the Hong Kong shore.

The elaborate ruse was filmed in three stages. The "death" of Bond in the hotel room was completed on the first day of shooting at Pinewood (July 4th 1966), and involved Connery, Chinese actress Tsai Chin, six Chinese extras, Patrick Jordan and Anthony Ainley who portray British police officers, and stuntman Bob Simmons who, as Connery, gets thrown into the hideaway bed.

Five months later, Peter Hunt's second unit crew filmed the "burial at sea" sequence aboard the British Destroyer HMS *Tenby,* anchored in Gibraltar Harbour. The rescue of Bond's body from the bottom of Hong Kong harbour was actually filmed in the Bahamas where cameraman Lamar Boren was once again hired to handle the underwater photography. The actual interior of the British submarine was located in the East Tunnel of Pinewood and was completed in mid-October 1966.

After seventeen days of interiors, Gilbert and sixty two others boarded a chartered jet and headed for Tokyo. On July 27th 1966, Sean Connery arrived and was mobbed by 007 fans. Already hugely popular in Japan, Bond's reputation grew when it was announced that the latest film in the series would be filmed partially in their own back yard. Connery appeared rumpled and bleary eyed for the press conference, without his toupé and dressed in baggy knockabout trousers, shower sandals and a blue shirt open at the neck to reveal his hairy chest. The disappointment of the reporters was not appeased by Connery's admission that he did not find Japanese women sexy. His comment resulted in a hostile press during the six weeks of filming in Japan.

Only second unit director Peter Hunt and his helicopter unit staging over Kyushu seemed to be protected from the press hordes. This was fortunate for Hunt's crew had the dangerous assignment of working with Wing Commander Wallis and his autogiro, a flying machine that made the Wright Brothers aeroplane look technologically sophisticated.

As the first unit skipped round Japan, filming in an Ama village, where Bond meets Kissy

Suzuki, and then at the Kobe docks where 007 is trapped by SPECTRE gunmen, Hunt began to prepare the helicopter chase across volcano country.

The original script had called for three car chases which would have been difficult to devise in a way that would have retained the audience's interest. It seemed impossible to come up with something new until the idea of a helicopter chase across the mountains was mooted.

Photographing the second unit's helicopter sequences was Johnny Jordan, a cinematographer who specialised in aerial photography. He was filming from inside one of the speedy French Alouette helicopters where a special Panavision camera was rigged to the helicopter's metal skid. Four Japanese stunt pilots flew the four SPECTRE helicopters while Wing Commander Wallis, the only person who could fly the autogiro with any degree of expertise, doubled for Connery.

Stuntgirl Jenny Le Free, doubling Karin Dor, falls into Blofeld's piranha-infested pool. Dor looks on, surrounded by press photographers. *(UPI)*

On the afternoon of September 22nd 1966, Jordan was filming above the little village of Ebino when the four enemy helicopters began their dive on Bond. Hunt was on the ground, observing the action from a jeep. The main problem was that the helicopters were always getting too spread out since the Japanese pilots were nervous, and wary of flying in close formation. It was difficult for the camera to keep them in frame.

This same afternoon, Jordan's Alouette was keeping pace with two black Hillers when one of the action helicopters struck an updraught, hurtling it towards the helpless camera ship. Before the pilot could react, Jordan's ship was struck by the Hiller's rotor blades which sliced through the Alouette's skids and Johnny Jordan's extended foot. Hunt remembers with amazement that Jordan, a cameraman through and through, had photographed his own foot when he got hit, saying that it might be useful for the surgeons. Japanese doctors were able to stop the loss of blood and preserve the leg until Jordan returned to England, where, three months later, it was amputated.

The loss of Jordan completely demoralised the second unit crew and Peter Hunt requested that they abandon the helicopter stunts and return to London at once.

When Jordan was hit, little of the helicopter shooting had been finished. Only a couple of the establishing shots of the helicopters moving across the volcanoes had been completed. The rest of the fight was later filmed, before Christmas, over Spain above Torremolinos on the Costa del Sol. Hunt changed his entire crew, using French stunt pilots this time, including Chomat, reputed to be the best helicopter pilot in Europe. Tony Brown replaced Jordan as unit photographer.

Back in London on the completed Volcano set at Pinewood, stunt coordinator Bob Simmons whipped his group of fighting Ninjas into shape. Within a few days, this special team of English muscle and co-ordination was asked to wind its way through the girder work one hundred and twenty feet above the set, grab hold of individual stunt ropes and then slide into a full-fledged battle below them, with machine guns blazing.

Virtually every stuntman in England had been called to Pinewood for the battle sequences. Later, a crowd of 120 men were called for the master shots. Simmons had whittled his group down to forty Tarzans who would work the ropes. It was a tricky stunt. Several of the men had to ride down with one hand, firing a sub-machine gun with the other. Their progress on the rope was controlled by a mountaineering device, a piece of rubber hose that was squeezed to break their fall. Once a stuntman hit the ground he had to move off quickly, for a comrade was coming right behind him. The forty regulars were also required to do trampoline stunts which would be intercut with Stear's explosions.

One of Simmons's specialists was George Leech, one of England's finest stuntmen, and an associate of Simmons since the early fifties when the pair rode war horses in a series of American-financed costume dramas like *Quentin Durward* and *Ivanhoe*.

Simmons had worked with Broccoli's company, Warwick Films before the Bonds on films, like *Paratrooper* and *Zarak*. When *Dr. No* went into production, he was assigned to the unit as Sean Connery's double. Leech joined him on *Dr. No* doubling Joseph Wiseman in the climactic fight in the reactor room. Replaced by Peter Perkins on *From Russia with Love,* the pair re-teamed on *Goldfinger.* It was Leech who drove the Aston Martin into the wall at Auric Enterprises (actually the Pinewood Lot), and it was Simmons who doubled for actor Michael Mellinger, who as Kisch is thrown off the top of Fort Knox by Oddjob.

You Only Live Twice was one of Leech's most difficult assignments. For the battle sequences, a number of new techniques were used to give the action a spectacular feel. Approximately twelve of the best men were used on the trampoline. "It was an interesting form of trampolining", Leech comments, "It wasn't your expertise in tumbles and perfect sommersaults that mattered. You just had to look as if you were being blown up. No pointed toes or classic positions. You went off screaming with your arms and legs flailing every which way. You landed into a made-up

Bond and Kissy (Mie Hama) ignore the approach of a SPECTRE killer copter. *(UPI)*

bed about twenty feet away. The special effects team timed their explosions to your jump".

Work on the Volcano set commenced during the first week in November 1966. Lewis Gilbert and Peter Hunt had combined their units for the master shots, using three separate camera crews. The finished set was magnificent with its gleaming polished metal and yards of form fitting concrete. Everything worked like a child's gigantic playset. Its proud creator Ken Adam walked on to the set at least twenty times a day, admiring the level of craftsmanship and looking for any undue stress.

On the first day of shooting, the Brantley helicopter was flown expertly through the volcano cone and down on to the special landing pad built on raised concrete above the rocket.

On November 11th Czech actor Jan Werich was taken ill and, after a hasty conference, it was decided to find another actor to play Blofeld. With time running out, the producers signed Donald Pleasence, a popular British actor who had recently starred in 20th Century Fox's *Fantastic Voyage*. Pleasence proved to be a disappointing choice, as John Brosnan points out in his book on James Bond: "Blofeld, as with all of Fleming's villains is a larger than life character and should therefore be portrayed by an actor with these same qualities. Gert Frobe, for instance, who played Goldfinger is a perfect example. After all, Blofeld as described by Fleming was a big man who weighed twenty stone when he first appeared in *Thunderball*". Brosnan recounts that in the make up room at Pinewood,

attempts were made to make Pleasence look more unusual with a hump, and then a limp, a beard and a lame hand. Eventually they settled for a scar. But the last minute casting never really worked.

During the last week of November, Peter Hunt reassembled the helicopter crew and left for Finmere in Scotland to shoot the crash landing of Helga's Aero Commander light plane. From Finmere he flew to Gibraltar for Bond's sea burial and then to the skies above Torremolinos for the final battle with the SPECTRE helicopters. All the camera work in Ken Adam's rocket base was finished by the last week in December 1966. In January, John Stears began working on the film's elaborate special effects which featured orbiting American and Russian space vehicles.

You Only Live Twice was still being filmed as late as March 1967 and when shooting was officially completed the statistics ran off the blackboard. Before he left to pursue other projects, Lewis Gilbert's final cut of the film was 133 minutes long. It needed severe editing and it soon appeared that Thelma Connell was not getting very far with it. Hunt returned from Torremolinos in mid December and Broccoli and Saltzman implored him to resume editing charge of the picture. Hunt's first impression of *You Only Live Twice* was not favourable. As in *Thunderball*, the continuity lapsed, the film was too long as in his view the best films in the Bond series were under two hours. Hunt reluctantly accepted the task and reduced it on his own.

Even the billboard designers were getting Bond fever. Here two pedestrians admire the upside-down handywork. *(UPI)*

The new team: Diana Rigg, director Peter Hunt,
George Lazenby, and Cubby Broccoli on location
in Switzerland in 1968. *(Life Picture Service)*

7

THE MODEL BOND

George Lazenby, an Australian model with no acting experience, became James Bond number two in 1968 when he signed to play 007 in the sixth Bond film *On Her Majesty's Secret Service*.

Neither John Barry's fine score nor the last minute editing prowess of Peter Hunt could help *You Only Live Twice* which was beaten to the box-office in 1967 by Charlie Feldman's long overdue Bond entry *Casino Royale*. Feldman had finally obtained the proper financing and distribution deal from Columbia Pictures and the result was a huge film, top heavy with international stars and a multi-faceted publicity campaign to match. The lumbering satire on the whole world of James Bond (Feldman had originally planned the film as a serious thriller but when he failed to get Sean Connery to play Bond he abandoned the idea of competing with the Broccoli and Saltzman products) featured the work of no less than five directors and five screenwriters.

The result was less than successful. The long-winded, patchwork romp of a story which

ON HER MAJESTY'S SECRET SERVICE (1969) PC. Eon Productions – A United Artists Release 140 mins Col. **PROD.** Albert R. Broccoli and Harry Saltzman **DIR.** Peter Hunt **SCR.** Richard Maibaum from the novel by Ian Fleming **PH.** Michael Reed **ED.** John Glen **PROD DES.** Syd Cain **MUSIC.** John Barry **SP EFFECTS.** John Stears **STUNT ARRANGER.** George Leech
CAST. George Lazenby (James Bond), Diana Rigg (Tracy), Telly Savalas (Ernst Stavro Blofeld), Ilse Steppat (Irma Bunt), Gabriele Ferzetti (Marc Ange Draco), Yuri Borienko (Gruenther), Bernard Horsfall (Campbell), George Baker (Sir Hilary Bray), Bernard Lee ("M"), Lois Maxwell (Miss Moneypenny), Desmond Llewelyn ("Q"), Angela Scoular (Ruby), Catherina von Schell (Nancy), Dani Sheridan (American Girl), Julie Ege (Scandinavian Girl), Joanna Lumley (English Girl), Mona Chong (Chinese Girl), Anoushka Hempel (Australian Girl), Ingri Black (German Girl), Jenny Hanley (Italian Girl), Zara (Indian Girl), Sylvana Henriques (Jamaican Girl), Helena Ronee (Israeli Girl), Geoffrey Cheshire (Tousaint), Irvin Allen (Che Che), Terry Mountain (Raphael) James Bree (Master Gumpold), Virginia North (Olympe), Brian Worth (Manuel), Norman McGlen (Janitor), Dudley Jones (Hall Porter), John Crewdson (Draco Copter pilot), Josef Vasa (Piz Gloria Attendant), Les Crawford (Felsen), George Cooper (Braun), Reg Harding (Blofeld's Driver), Richard Graydon (Draco's Driver), Bill Morgan (Klett), Bessie Love (American Guest), Steve Plytas (Greek Tycoon), Robert Rietty (Chef du Jeu), Elliott Sullivan (American).

At the baccarat table, Tracy (Diana Rigg) loses francs but wins James. *(Life Picture Service)*

dragged on for months, prompting a number of last minute offers on the part of Broccoli or Saltzman, it finally became apparent that a search would have to begin for a new James Bond.

Whilst Connery went off to film *Shalako,* in Spain, for half his normal salary, rumours that Eon Productions would soon collapse without his services were quickly quashed by publicists who suggested that the Bond myth was more potent than any individual who came to embody the hero.

George Lazenby, the second actor to play James Bond for Cubby Broccoli and Harry Saltzman, was 25 years old when he entered the modelling profession. An Australian, he had come to England in 1964, after a couple of successful years selling cars in his own country. Tipped off by fashion photographer Chard Jenkins that he could make more money as a model than as a salesman, Lazenby soon progressed from thirty pounds a week selling Mercedes sportscars to five hundred a week modelling orlon fabrics and appearing in advertisements for British Petroleum. On the prompting of his agent, who knew about the search for a new Bond, Lazenby suggested himself for the role to Harry Saltzman, who was impressed by the Australian's looks and physique.

By April, Broccoli and Saltzman had narrowed the field down to five actors. Besides Lazenby, they were considering John Richardson, who had recently starred alongside Raquel Welch in *One Million Years B.C.,* and three young English actors, Anthony Rogers, Robert Campbell and Hans de Vries.

Elaborate action tests began in April 1968 when the full crew was assembled. Both producers were already aware that United Artists wanted to see some fighting footage of the Bond applicants. The archetypal Bond fight is spectacular and, although over in seconds, it is generally choreographed like a ballet, with shots of the stuntmen and stars intermixed, and edited tightly. His performance in the test fight won Lazenby the role of Bond. To choreograph the key battle, Peter Hunt hired George Leech, this time as chief of stunts, and the pair picked a sequence from the script where Bond is surprised by a

featured several James Bonds, including Peter Sellers, David Niven and Woody Allen, failed to match the quality appeal of the United Artists James Bond films.

Though funny in parts, with interesting cameo roles by many major stars, including William Holden, John Huston and Deborah Kerr, *Casino Royale* did little to hurt the serious interest in Bond around the world. It did, however, hurt the box-office success of *You Only Live Twice.*

The box office was not the most important of Eon Production's worries that summer of 1967. Sean Connery's threats to leave the series became fact in June when the actor adamantly refused to do the next film – the often cancelled *On Her Majesty's Secret Service.* Although negotiations

Lazenby and Rigg. *(Wide World)*

would be assassin in a hotel bedroom on the Portuguese coast. For the test, Leech asked the former wrestler, Uri Borienko to double the villain, a Union Corse gunman.

Uri Borienko had little experience in film fighting, and Lazenby had even less. Leech instructed both of them in the basic mechanics. Lazenby was good, physically, Leech remembers,

Returning from the American premiere of ON HER MAJESTY'S SECRET SERVICE, George Lazenby arrives at Heathrow Airport in London. Broccoli and Saltzman both objected to the new beard, but to no avail. *(Wide World)*

so he could learn how to punch easily enough, but his main problem was learning not to flinch when a punch came his way.

Both producers considered that Lazenby was the perfect replacement. United Artists in New York agreed and plans were immediately finalised to sign up George Lazenby for shooting in the autumn.

On Her Majesty's Secret Service, the best of Ian Fleming's later novels, had been postponed as a film project several times, since its original publication in 1963. Originally, it was intended to follow *Goldfinger* but when Kevin McClory came on the scene in 1964 with his *Thunderball* project, *Secret Service* was promptly shelved. When *Thunderball* was finished, it was felt that *Secret Service* was too similar ("a *Thunderball* on skis") since it took place primarily in the snows of Switzerland.

Yet *Secret Service* was much more than this. It was an emotional story that revealed more of the world of James Bond. It starts with Bond ready to resign from the Secret Service rather than keep up his frustrating search for the elusive Blofeld. However, with the help of a Union Corse Capo named Marc-Ange Draco, Bond eventually finds the head of SPECTRE in the Alps, where he is plotting germ warfare against the United Kingdom. It is Draco's daughter though, the ravishing Tracy, who makes this book much more than the average Fleming adventure.

Bond intends to marry Tracy once Blofeld is destroyed. Unlike Bond's one dimensional girl friends, Tracy is a fully developed character whose murder by Blofeld in the book's closing pages leaves the reader distressed.

Once again scriptwriter Richard Maibaum was signed to adapt the story to the screen. Originally, it was planned to open the film in an English hospital where Bond is undergoing plastic surgery to change his face – a strategy designed to outwit his many enemies and to introduce George Lazenby. It was an idea that everyone hated immediately and Maibaum was happy to throw it out. The plastic experimentation idea, however, was to resurface at the beginning of the next Bond film, *Diamonds Are Forever*, in which Blofeld creates duplicates of himself to confuse the British.

Maibaum finally decided that Lazenby would be introduced in a normal way, in the new film's teaser, in which, on the beach in Portugal, he rescues Tracy (Diana Rigg) from the ocean. Concluding the teaser, he added a little humour to ease the transition. After Lazenby disposes of the thugs on the beach, only to find Tracy running off in her car, Lazenby picks up her lost shoe and turns to the camera saying in perfect seriousness, "This never happened to the other guy".

Following the teaser, Maibaum continued the reference to the other James Bond in 007's office where Lazenby resigns and begins to clean out his

desk. With John Barry's music in the background, Lazenby begins to look over his mementoes which include Honey's knife belt from *Dr. No* and the strangler watch from *From Russia with Love*. Scenes such as this, combined with the titles which showed sequences from all the previous Bond films reinforced the idea that this new Bond was still a member of the same team – a man who answered to a crusty old retired Admiral named "M" and still engaged in sexy banter with a secretary named Moneypenny.

Although Eon Productions had reversed the continuity of Fleming's novels by filming *You Only Live Twice* before *Secret Service*, the change had little effect on the new film. James Bond is still on the trail of Blofeld, who, having escaped

The wedding of Bond and Tracy in Portugal. It was to be a short-lived marriage for 007. *(Wide World)*

the destruction of his Japanese rocket base, is now holed up in Switzerland, in a mountain fortress dubbed Piz Gloria.

Here in the Alps, Blofeld's new plan is to wage biological warfare against the agricultural and livestock producers of the world.

His agents are ten beautiful girls who sincerely believe that Blofeld is a famous allergist. Brainwashed, and equipped with a deadly atomiser in their makeup kit, the girls are cured of their allergies and plans are made to send them back to their respective countries where they will receive radio communications from Blofeld who will then order them to spread their cargo of disease throughout the world. The scheme is about to be put into operation when Bond arrives once more to spoil his plans.

Harry Saltzman had organised a half-hearted reconnaissance to Switzerland in 1964 when *Secret Service* was an active project. However, a serious location search did not begin until the winter of 1967-1968. The first stop was France, where Saltzman and production designer Syd Cain, who had returned to Eon Productions after a gap of a few years, entered a segment of France's infamous Maginot Line, the string of fortifications that had been constructed as a barrier prior to World War II, but had been totally ineffective against Hitler's invading armies. Saltzman was interested in seeing whether Blofeld could actually make his base inside an old Fort on the Western Front, but Syd Cain decided that everything could be built in the Studio. Cain and Saltzman left for Strasbourg and then made a quick flight to St. Moritz where they were joined by Peter Hunt and production manager David Middlemas.

This time, Broccoli and Saltzman were hoping that Fleming had based his conception of Blofeld's fortress on something real. They were looking for a mountain retreat accessible only by cable car and situated above a small village. Although they found a railway ascending Mount Pilatus, they could find no mountain hideaway at the top. There was also a big Swiss army base nearby and Hunt doubted whether the crew would be given permission to ski on a military reservation. In the end, they learned that a new revolving restaurant was being built above Murren on top of the Schilthorn Mountain, and was approaching

completion. Hunt was thrilled to find exactly that for which they had been looking.

The construction of the restaurant had begun in 1961 with the help of helicopters which transported the building materials to the top of the Swiss peak. By Christmas 1967, the structure was completed, as was the cable car run to Murren below. Everything was brand new and plans were being made to furnish the restaurant's interior when the James Bond crew arrived.

Negotiations began the following spring to secure the location for filming. The agreement committed Eon Productions to furnishing the interior of the restaurant as well as building a helicopter landing port next to the main building that could be used for rescue missions. In return, the film makers were given permission to film throughout the five story mountain top complex.

Syd Cain was in charge of the operation to transform the bleak restaurant into Blofeld's exotic retreat. It was not an expensive task, and cost only sixty thousand pounds, compared to

Still in top form, George Lazenby was the guest of honour at the fabled James Bond Weekend in Los Angeles (summer 1981). He is seen here with Martine Beswicke.

While Sean Connery had seemingly retired from Bond, his younger brother joined the ranks, portraying a secret agent in the Italian film *Operation Kid Brother,* here with ex-Bond girl Daniela Bianchi. *(UPI)*

the nearly three hundred thousand that Ken Adam had needed for Blofeld's former habitat. Most of the money went into construction of the heliport, which was accomplished by the Swiss Government working to Cain's designs.

Not only were there excellent ski runs near Murren but it proved to be a good location for the bobsled run, which was built on the site of an older run that had been closed since 1937.

Sid Cain began supervising the construction activity on Piz Gloria in the spring of 1968. Back in London, Richard Maibaum was completing his

script. Since the actual locations closely matched Fleming's descriptions, the final draft was very close to the novel, with a few important changes. One of these was the sprawling party sequence to celebrate Draco's birthday during which Bond resumes his friendship with Tracy. Maibaum gave Draco, the sympathetic Mafioso, an interest in livestock, making him someone who raises bulls as a pastime. This background lends weight to Draco's decision to support Bond's attack on Blofeld. The sumptuous Da Vinho estate in Portugal which sported a private bullring, provided the background to the birthday sequence.

Maibaum also created the tense vignette in which Bond arrives in Berne to photograph documents in Blofeld's lawyer's office that reveal the SPECTRE chief's plans to adopt a noble title. In the sequence, Bond cracks Master Gumbold's

safe with a portable computer slipped to him through the lawyer's window by a Swiss agent, manning a heavy industrial crane across the street. The computerised safe cracking device, Bond's only gadget in the entire film, also has a built-in copying machine that automatically copies Blofeld's secrets as Bond relaxes in a chair reading the latest copy of *Playboy*. Maibaum's script then follows the general line of the book in which Bond impersonates a British genealogist to gain entrance to Piz Gloria, where he learns of Blofeld's evil plans, and then escapes into Murren with the vital information.

He is soon helped by Tracy who arrives unexpectedly in her Red Cougar (once more, compliments of the Ford Motor Company) and spirits Bond away from his enemies. Casting Tracy, the most important of all Bond's women was difficult. For the first time, it was felt that the company should sign up an established actress, someone who could work well with the inexperienced Lazenby and intensify the love scenes in this, the most romantic of all the Bond films.

Since Fleming had described Tracy as a blonde in the book, Hunt's first choice for the role was Brigitte Bardot. Bardot, however, had, ironically, just signed to star opposite Sean Connery in *Shalako*. Hunt's second choice was the exquisite French actress Catherine Deneuve who had just finished working with Terence Young on *Mayerling,* but she was not interested in the idea. Giving up his quest for a blonde, Hunt then approached Diana Rigg who was currently featured on British television in the series, *The Avengers*, as the acrobatic British agent Emma Peel; she had replaced the leather-suited Honor Blackman's Mrs. Gale. Diana Rigg agreed to play Tracy.

Joining her on the film as Blofeld, was her recent co-star in *The Assassination Bureau,* American actor Telly Savalas. For Blofeld's assistant, Irma Bunt, Harry Saltzman suggested Greek actress Irene Papas but Hunt felt she was too sympathetic for the role and eventually cast the popular German actress Ilse Steppat. Saltzman then suggested the Italian actor Gabriele Ferzetti for Draco. Although he spoke good English, his

Telly Savalas was the second actor to play SPECTRE chieftain Ernst Stavro Blofeld, who this time is hiding in the Alps as a world famous allergist.

voice was dubbed for the final film as Saltzman was worried about audiences misunderstanding his Italian accent.

Many of the film's action sequences were filmed on location that autumn, in Murren, with a unique team of Olympic skiers and camera specialists. Because of insurance regulations, none of the main actors, including George Lazenby, were allowed on skis. All their scenes had to be shot in the studio with a process screen or with the use of a special sled upon which the actors pretended they were skiing at forty-five miles per hour.

Leading the team of experts was the ski champion Willy Bogner Jr., practically a contortionist on skis, who was subsequently praised for his unorthodox camera techniques. Equipped with a modified Arriflex (with an adapted Hasselblad viewfinder) Bogner hand held his camera while skiing backwards, catching the swift moving Olympic skiers as they flew down the slopes above Murren. At times, he would even shoot backwards, looking through his legs. His skis were modified with curved tips at both ends to allow him proper mobility.

Joining Bogner on *Secret Service* was Johnny Jordan, the aerial cameraman who had been so seriously injured in *You Only Live Twice,* but had returned to action with an artificial limb and still filmed daredevil action from the skies. Jordan designed his own camera rig which hung down from the belly of a helicopter, like a parachute harness. By using such a platform, Jordan drifted above the treetops with complete freedom of movement. He was responsible for some of the film's most beautiful aerial sequences, including the shots of Draco's phony Red Cross helicopters headed across Switzerland for their attack on Piz Gloria and the aerial view of the hair-raising bobsled chase in which Bond has one last chance to eliminate Blofeld.

The rest of Hunt's crew included second unit director/editor John Glen who was responsible for half the location sequences; Alex Barbey, a skiing cameraman who had come over from Basle; Ken Higgins who was mainly shooting with day-for-night filters; and Michael Reed who was the director of photography on the film and who was working directly with Hunt on the interior sequences at Piz Gloria and Murren.

It was originally planned to shoot the entire

Nestled 9712 feet above sea level, rotating restaurant Piz Gloria was a perfect SPECTRE installation.

location in one go and then return to the studio for interiors. However, by the middle of November, Hunt not only found the weather clouding up his ski chases, but the snow level in Murren was getting dangerously low. Work on the Christmas festival in Grindelwald, and the rally car chase was postponed and plans were made to return to the studios until February 1969. Suddenly, Hunt found himself sixteen days behind schedule.

Fortunately the fifty four days in the snow had netted them some good chase footage, the completion of the Piz Gloria interiors and a hair-raising stunt on the cable car run. In the film, Blofeld sees through Bond's disguise and locks the agent in the cable car wheel-house, a clocklike maze of cables and gears with a tiny opening above. Bond tears out the pockets of his trousers to make a pair of gloves, winds his way through

The cable car that almost cost Bond his life makes the run from picturesque Murren to the Schilthorn peak. Non-secret agents pay a small fee.

the gear system, catches hold of the departing cable and is whisked out of the mechanical prison. Once he is in the open air, Bond holds on to the cables and then jumps on an arriving cable car that takes him back into the Piz Gloria reception area where he steals some skis and heads for Grindelwald.

The interior of the wheel house was filmed at Pinewood on a set designed by Syd Cain, while stuntman Chris Webb did the dangerous location stunt work where he clung expertly to the icy cables. George Leech, who co-ordinated the sequence was intended to be Lazenby's double in the sequence but when he started doing the cable climb, he fell off and twisted his arm. It was a dangerous stunt in freezing cold weather 10,000 feet up, with cables that were greasy and caked with ice and a hundred foot drop below.

Since Leech was injured, he employed two stuntmen to double Lazenby, Chris Webb and Dicky Greydon. To protect them, Leech fastened a metallic rigging device inside their sleeves. Should they lose their grip, the metal hook would prevent them from falling. As a second safety precaution, a drop bed was placed below the cable to catch the stuntmen if their primary device failed them. Peter Hunt wanted Leech not to use the metallic aide, but as the days wore on and it became colder and Leech felt it was impossible to do the stunt without it.

Ironically, it nearly killed Dicky Greydon. It was so cold that he could not get a grip on the moving wire and began to slide down the mountain on the cable. Fortunately, Leech had stationed somebody at the first pylon who stuck his foot out in time and prevented him from sliding any further. He could have slid down the rope all the way to Murren.

Also, getting used to the oxygen levels on the 10,000 foot Schilthorn peak was not easy for Hunt's stunt crew. Breathing normally was one thing, but when the men began to throw punches and skid around on the icy patios, it became difficult to catch their breath.

Walking in the snow on the edge of the Piz Gloria was another problem. Men with ski poles were always checking the snow level, making sure the unit did not stray over a crevice that could break open and send them careering down the mountain.

To play James Bond, Eon Productions offered George Lazenby virtually the same salary they had offered Sean Connery before *Dr. No,* a sum of twenty-two thousand pounds. In addition, he was given the use of a chauffeured limousine and a furnished London apartment. As the world press began to concentrate on him, Lazenby became something of a prima donna.

One thing that particularly irritated him was Peter Hunt's aloofness. As director in the snows as well as on the stage, Hunt found little time to coach Lazenby in the Bond character. Lazenby found to his consternation that he was alone most of the time on the set, trying to memorise the dialogue and get his movements down while his director was off elsewhere. The scenes on the first leg of the Swiss location were certainly not over demanding on his acting since most of the footage shot that winter was second unit material, but Lazenby began to sense that he would not be treated with kid gloves.

As a model, he was used to constant direction. Learning the acting ropes on his own was difficult for him to accept. Hunt later claimed that this was part of his strategy in getting a performance from a non-professional, especially in the film's more emotional moments when Bond begins to fall in love with Tracy.

The strained relationship between actor and director soon spread to other parts of the production, creating a long running controversy that was picked up and fuelled expertly by the English press. One of their favourite items was the so-called "flap" between Lazenby and Diana Rigg. There was the "garlic incident" which supposedly took place in the Pinewood commissary on a Wednesday afternoon prior to the first love scene. As Lazenby tells it, midway through their lunch, Rigg called over to him jokingly: "Hey George, I'm having garlic with my pâté, I hope you are too." Lazenby smiled and went back to his meal. The headlines next day read: "DIANA RIGG EATS GARLIC BEFORE KISS WITH GEORGE LAZENBY". Contrary to the newspaper accounts, Lazenby claims that he and Diana Rigg did not hate each other. He did, however, acknowledge that he was the cause of the eventual collapse of his relationship with Hunt and the producers.

By the beginning of 1969, plans were being

made to send a second unit crew back to Switzerland to finish the location sequences. On January 3rd John Glen arrived in Murren to resume the ski chases. While his fleet of streamlined Alouette helicopters ferried equipment and manpower to the ski slopes, a second crew of construction workers began work on the stock car rally in Lauterbrunnen, one of the film's funniest sequences.

In the novel, Bond and Tracy elude a SPECTRE Mercedes when 007 switches around a Swiss road warning sign and the enemy car goes plunging over a cliff. In the film, Maibaum continued the festive mood present in Grindelwald by creating a Monte-Carlo Rally that is rudely interrupted when Tracy's Cougar and the big, lumbering SPECTRE Mercedes come smashing into the race course. While the astonished crowd watches, the cars continue their game of cat and mouse, to the confusion of the rally drivers, whose smaller cars are being smashed like toys.

The rally took place on an icy track in Lauterbrunnen only two miles from Murren. John Glen assigned racing specialist, Anthony Squires, to choreograph the race, which featured a number of spectacular crashes, one involving the SPECTRE Mercedes which overturns and explodes. Shooting began at Lauterbrunnen on February 2nd and continued until heavy snow began to fall at ten o'clock in the evening. On the 7th George Lazenby and Diana Rigg braved a snow blizzard at London airport and left for Lauterbrunnen to do their close-ups, with Glen's cameras mounted on the hood of Tracy's Cougar. Peter Hunt directed the close-ups of his principals in the stock car sequence. When this was finished, he left for the village of Grindelwald where a haggard and besieged Bond finally bumps into Tracy on a skating rink.

Hunt was now twenty nine days behind schedule. He recalls that the skating rink was melting while shooting took place. "Some nights we had to wait to see if the temperature would drop below zero. We would wait till midnight or one o'clock in the morning and then ask 'Is it freezing yet?' and we would be informed 'No way'. So, in the end, I just had to mark off certain areas and make sure the skaters didn't wander." Adding visual interest to the skating sequences were Rudi and Gerda Johner, a skating duo who were given the centre spotlight on the festive evening.

Since Diana Rigg was unable to skate with any degree of proficiency, the key sequence in the film where Tracy skates up to the bedraggled Bond was done with her skating double. Hunt kept his camera panned on the double's legs as she skates up to Bond and then cut to a head shot of Diana Rigg in close-up.

When they signed Peter Hunt to direct, Broccoli and Saltzman had injected a different style into their sixth film. Whereas on *You Only Live Twice* Lewis Gilbert and Roald Dahl had been more concerned with the fantasy elements of Bond's world, by creating huge workable sets and unbelievable stunts, Hunt pressed for a return to the basics of Fleming's writing. This is apparent in several sequences that were transferred directly from the novel to the screen. One of these was a visit to "M"'s house. Hunt had always wanted to show the Admiral's home, complete with sixteenth century cannon guarding the driveway, an ocean front view and a servant named Hammond. On *Secret Service*, he was given his chance and Richard Maibaum wrote a sequence where Bond comes to tell his chief that Blofeld has been found in Switzerland.

Hunt went searching near the studio in Buckinghamshire for a suitable house for "M" and found Thames Lawn a river-front mansion that was remarkably similar to the house described in the novel. On April 9th he completed the exterior sequence where Bond drives up to the house in the Aston Martin.

In May, Hunt took his crew to Portugal for several key sequences in the film, including the teaser opening during which we first see the new Bond. Whilst a number of critics and many of his own crew members later lambasted Lazenby, stunt co-ordinator, George Leech, was impressed with the actor's physical ability. Leech himself was kept busy on the Guincho Beach that May, preparing the fight sequence where Bond takes on two of Draco's henchmen. Leech wondered how to create a spectacular fight on a plain beach without any props. He lined up a few fishing boats near the water line and these had some oars and nets lying around, which could be used. In the eternal search for a fight gimmick, he decided to take the fight into the water just before sundown, when it would photograph well. Meanwhile, Peter Hunt was filming Draco's birthday party on the magnificent acreage of the De Vinho Estate at Zambuljal.

On Her Majesty's Secret Service was officially completed on June 23rd 1969, fifty eight days over schedule. Most of the delay had been caused by the weather in Switzerland. However, Hunt's main problem had been a very long and involved script. Once shooting stopped, John Glen left his job as second unit director and entered the editing rooms of Pinewood. Prior to the first fine cut, *Secret Service* was only ten minutes short of three hours, more than an hour longer than any of the previous Bond films. Glen cut the film down to two hours and twenty minutes, a fact that Hunt kept secret from Broccoli and Saltzman who had informed United Artists that the final print would be less than two hours.

Composer John Barry, returned in *Secret Service* to create what is probably the best score in the series. It also featured Barry's favourite song, "We Have All the Time in the World", which was sung by Louis Armstrong. Armstrong had been in a New York hospital for nearly a year when Barry and writer Hal David decided that he was the best person to sing their main song. They needed an elderly man who could sing the line, "We've got all the time in the world" with real emotion. The line itself was taken from the last paragraph of Fleming's novel.

"Louis Armstrong was the sweetest man alive," recalled Barry solemnly, "but having been laid up for over a year, he had no energy left. He couldn't even play his trumpet. And still he summoned the energy to do our song. At the end of the recording session in New York City, he came up to me and said, 'Thank you for this job.'" He was such a marvellous man. He died soon after that. The song didn't do a thing when the film came out. It was a very heavy song so we couldn't use it as the title track. It was buried inside the film and that probably hurt its chances for success. Interestingly, two years later it suddenly became number one in Italy.

"The song itself was written for a very emotional moment. I had pictured Sean Connery in the role of Bond when Hal and I first wrote the lyrics. If it had been Sean who married Diana Rigg and then lost her to Blofeld, then the song would have been beautiful and highly appropriate. Having Sean Connery and Diana Rigg together in the last scene would have really created a bombshell of a moment. With all due respect for his inexperience, in that scene, George Lazenby couldn't have created a boiled egg . . ."

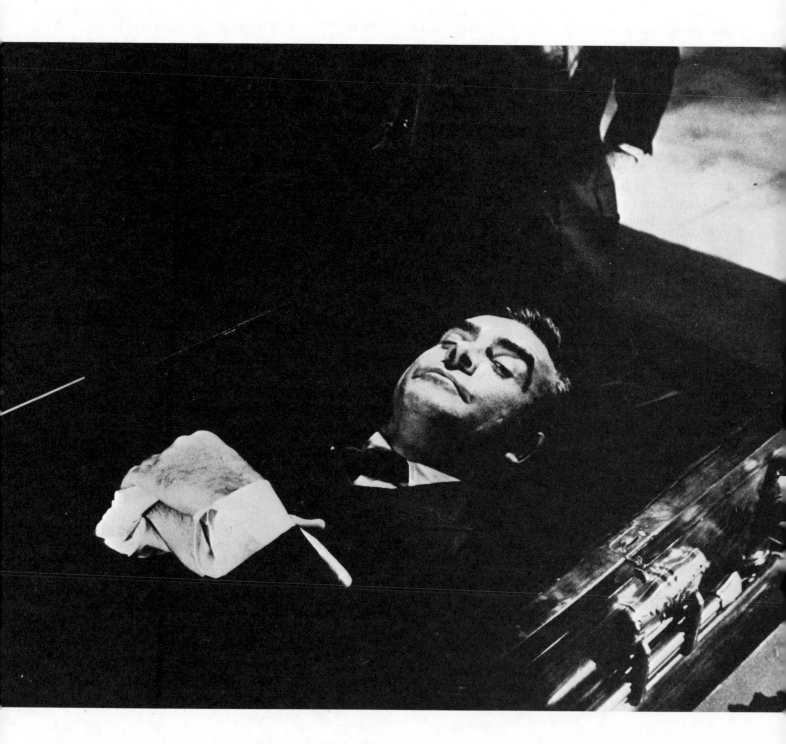

"Who says I'm dead?" Sean Connery returns to Bond in DIAMONDS ARE FOREVER. *(UPI)*

8
DIAMONDS ARE FOREVER... BUT CONNERY IS NOT

The box office performance of *Secret Service* proved that a new James Bond, as well as a return to the seriousness of the early films, was not a winning combination. *Secret Service* was no failure: it made twenty five million dollars in 1970 and 1971, but despite its monetary success, it did little to enliven the James Bond series, which many felt was doomed without the services of Sean Connery. George Lazenby's sincere performance was universally panned by the American and English critics while the film itself was dismissed with a polite nod to Peter Hunt's vigorous direction and the usual slam-bang stuntwork.

In the spring of 1970, a new Bond film was already in the planning stages – *Diamonds Are Forever*. Peter Hunt was gone, anxious to make it as a film director outside the Eon fold. In his place was Guy Hamilton, the director of *Goldfinger*, who had spent some of the intervening years working for Harry Saltzman on the pro-

ducer's pet project *The Battle of Britain*. Teamed once more with Hamilton was production designer Ken Adam who was again commissioned to dazzle audiences with his outsized sets. With these two veterans in control, the plan this time was to return to the glitter and fantasy which had been played down in *Secret Service*.

As James Bond entered the Seventies, it became increasingly evident that Ian Fleming's. novels were becoming more and more dated What was fresh and exciting in 1956 now seemed trite and mundane. This was especially true in *Diamonds Are Forever*, a relatively straightforward suspense story in which Bond infiltrates a diamond smuggling pipeline and does battle with a group of American gangsters from England to Las Vegas to South Africa. Like all Fleming's novels, the book is humourless.

While diamonds were a good subject for the new Bond film, smuggling, by itself, was thought

---

DIAMONDS ARE FOREVER (1971)
PC. Eon Productions – A United Artists Release 119 mins Col. **PROD.** Albert R. Broccoli and Harry Saltzman **DIR.** Guy Hamilton **SCR.** Richard Maibaum and Tom Mankiewicz based on the novel by Ian Fleming **PH.** Ted Moore **ED.** Bert Bates and John W. Holmes **PROD DES.** Ken Adam **MUSIC** John Barry **SP EFFECTS.** Leslie Hillman and Whitey McMahon **STUNT ARRANGERS.** Bob Simmons and Paul Baxley

CAST. Sean Connery (James Bond), Jill St. John (Tiffany Case), Charles Gray (Ernst Stavro Blofeld), Lana Wood (Plenty O'Toole), Jimmy Dean (Willard Whyte), Bruce Cabot (Burt Saxby), Putter Smith (Mr. Kidd), Bruce Glover (Mr. Wint), Norman Burton (Felix Leiter), Joseph Furst (Dr. Metz), David Bauer (Nathan Slumber), Bernard Lee ("M"), Desmond Llewelyn ("Q"), Leonard Barr (Shady Tree), Lois Maxwell (Miss Moneypenny).

John Gavin, here with Mary Tyler Moore, was signed to play Bond in DIAMONDS ARE FOREVER but was replaced at the last minute by Sean Connery. *(Universal Pictures)*

to be too tame a project in which to involve SPECTRE. If Ernst Stavro Blofeld was to have his organisation involved in diamonds, it would be for more sinister purposes. The writers came up with the idea of SPECTRE kidnapping a Howard Hughes-type recluse whose worldwide industrial interests include dealings with the US space programme, one of whose satellites becomes a pawn in SPECTRE's new plan for world domination. Rather than use the smuggled diamonds for jewelry purposes on the black market, Blofeld plans to take his cache of jewels and build a huge crystal fan. When attached to a normal communications satellite, this will harness the power of the sun and fuel a huge laser, the force of which can destroy targets on the Earth's surface.

The glitter in *Diamonds Are Forever* was reflected in the settings themselves, especially that

of Las Vegas, Nevada, a land of obviously beautiful girls, unsavoury gangster types and nonstop gambling. Although the scriptwriter Richard Maibaum completed a first draft of the story, it was Tom Mankiewicz, the son of Joseph Mankiewicz who finished the final shooting script for the seventh James Bond film. Like Maibaum, Mankiewicz has a ready wit that earned him assignments on the next four films in the series. Earlier, between 1964 and 1966, he had worked on a number of projects including a Nancy Sinatra television special which won seven Emmy awards. In 1967 he wrote his first film, a surfing movie entitled *The Sweet Ride*, which starred a young Jacqueline Bisset, and simultaneously completed a disastrous musical version of *Georgy Girl*, which was staged on Broadway, and closed after three nights.

When Mankiewicz heard that he was wanted for the Bond film, he was delighted. Broccoli and Saltzman were keen to have a young American writer since the film took place largely in the United States and David Picker of United Artists who had seen *Georgy Girl* and, despite its failure, liked it, recommended him for the job.

The big question now was who would play James Bond. George Lazenby was definitely out. Despite his sincere performance in *Secret Service* his sour relations with the producers alone precluded a second offer. A number of actors were considered including some Americans. Burt Reynolds's name was mentioned a number of times (he was still short of superstardom with *Deliverance* in production) but it was forty two year old John Gavin who seemed like the inside favourite. Gavin had once played the young Julius Caesar in Stanley Kubrick's *Spartacus* and had recently starred in two short-lived American television series: *Destry*, a western, and *Convoy*, a dramatic study of naval activities in the North Atlantic during World War II.

Gavin had tested well, was athletic enough to handle the numerous stunts and was not a well known personality, a factor that prohibited the producers from choosing a number of other American performers. But even while preparations were made to give Gavin a multi-picture contract, United Artists president David Picker was still wondering whether Sean Connery could be lured back. After *Secret Service* it was obvious to Picker that Connery and not Bond was the key selling point in the films. United Artists had once offered the actor a million dollars to return to the role. Picker realised that they would have to sweeten the pill considerably to attract Connery's attention.

Since the release of *You Only Live Twice*, Connery had become involved in the political affairs of his native Scotland and had joined the Scottish National Party. In 1971, he used his influence to win for Glasgow the European premiere of *The Anderson Tapes*, the proceeds of which were given to Connery's own Scottish International Educacational Trust. Education was very close to Connery's heart and he believed that by setting up a trust for needy Scots he could help provide some of the opportunities which were missing when he was growing up in Edinburgh.

In February, Picker flew to London with a huge and unprecedented offer. Not only would he give Connery a base salary of one and a quarter million dollars and a percentage of the profits on *Diamonds Are Forever*, he would also agree to back, with United Artists' funding, two films of Connery's choice. Connery could star in the films, or he could direct.

Connery told Picker that if he accepted the offer, he wanted a provision included in the one picture contract declaring that should the film go over its eighteen week shooting schedule, he would get an extra ten thousand dollars a week. It had always been the length of the Bond production schedules that had particularly irritated Connery who did not like to spend so much of his time on a single project. David Picker's offer was too tempting for the actor to refuse and *Diamonds Are Forever* was finished within its eighteen week schedule, sparing United Artists the extra cash outlay to their star.

Only a few months after the release of *On Her Majesty's Secret Service* Richard Maibaum was called back to work up a story on the new Bond. The producers kept harking back to *Goldfinger*, the pride of their fleet. With this in mind, Maibaum composed a new story which featured Goldfinger's twin brother as a power-mad Swedish shipping magnate who houses a laser cannon in the hull of one of his fleet's super tankers. Plans were even made to find Gert Frobe and have him play the twin.

Having succeeded with a laser which nearly killed Bond in *Goldfinger*, Maibaum thought it was a good idea to bring the weapon back as an expanded technological threat against the world, and it became even more appropriate when Maibaum discovered that the first laser was

Connery with Jill St. John, who shone as pretty jewel smuggler Tiffany Case. *(UPI)*

actually projected through a diamond. In order to build such a powerful laser it was easy enough to have Goldfinger use a diamond smuggling pipeline to gather the correct number of gems.

From this fantastic beginning, Maibaum's script went off in all directions. Harry Saltzman immediately suggested locations in Thailand and India where the crew could shoot inexpensively and, using the Far East as a setting, Maibaum's script began to feature treks through the jungle and tiger hunts in India. Broccoli complained that the Bond film was turning into a latter day Tarzan epic.

One night Broccoli had a dream that turned the script around. Broccoli had always maintained a friendship with the billionaire industrialist, Howard Hughes, and, in his dream, Broccoli visited the ageing Hughes at his luxurious suite in Las Vegas. It was mid afternoon and Broccoli found himself peeking through a window in Hughes's suite where he saw a familiar figure sitting behind a huge oak desk. The man turned around and Broccoli started. It was not Hughes at all, but an imposter. Broccoli recounted the dream to Maibaum who immediately took it up for use in the script.

He outlined a SPECTRE operation, based around Las Vegas. The supertanker was eliminated and replaced by a secret installation outside the city where Blofeld is preparing his laser firing satellite for shipment to the US Air Force which is one of the Hughes-like character's government contacts. In the early script, Howard Hughes became Willard Whyte, whose base of operations is a huge Las Vegas hotel named the Whyte House.

Another interesting aspect of Maibaum's script was the ending which featured a high speed motor boat chase on nearby Lake Mead. Maibaum had discovered that each hotel in Las Vegas maintained its own yacht on the Lake for recreation and publicity purposes. Caesar's Palace owned a Roman galley while the Riviera owned its own pirate frigate, and the other hotels possessed various types of strange lake dwelling craft. In the film's conclusion, Bond tracks an escaping Blofeld to the Lake and watches as the SPECTRE chieftain takes off in a high-powered boat.

Bond jumps on a power boat himself, but

Connery takes a breather during the filming at Los Angeles International Airport. *(Danny Biederman)*

before he gives chase, he speaks through a loud speaker, summoning the captains of all the colourful yachts to do their duty for Las Vegas and blockade Blofeld's escape route. With that, the whole flotilla gives chase, eventually cornering Blofeld above the awesome Hoover Dam.

In the autumn of 1970, after eight months of constant work, Maibaum turned in his final draft and went off to pursue new projects. It was Danny Reisner, a United Artists vice president who suggested that Broccoli bring in another screenwriter to tighten up the Maibaum script.

In rewriting a number of Maibaum's scenes, Mankiewicz created new elements as well. He was responsible for the interesting subplot in which Blofeld is conducting cloning experiments in order to produce duplicates of himself, a necessary safeguard against a revenge-seeking James Bond who is close at his heels. *Diamonds Are Forever* begins where *On Her Majesty's Secret Service* left off with Bond searching for Blofeld who had murdered Bond's wife in the last scene of *Secret Service*.

While Maibaum's script featured a teaser in which Bond flies a hang glider towards a cliff house where he meets a girl who will give him information on Blofeld's whereabouts (a sequence that was used in the next film *Live and Let Die*), Mankiewicz took Bond to several locations where Bond roughs up three different enemy agents to gain the proper information. In the final sequence, Bond meets a beautiful girl on the beach, dressed in a very revealing bikini. He walks up to her, introduces himself, and then rips off her top, twists it around her neck and, before she chokes to death, obtains the location of Blofeld.

Bond finds the SPECTRE stronghold in South America where Blofeld is concluding his cloning experiments in huge vats of steaming mud. Bond drowns one near perfect Blofeld duplicate and then, after disposing of Blofeld's guards, knocks what he thinks is the real Blofeld on to an operating table which he sends rolling into a vat of boiling mud. Is Blofeld finally dead? We can but wonder as the camera focuses on a white cat looking on sorrowfully, its diamond bracelet coming into focus for the first time as the credits begin to roll and we hear the welcome voice of Shirley Bassey.

Mankiewicz also changed Maibaum's ending.

Connery and Norman Burton, who became the fourth actor to portray American CIA agent Felix Leiter. *(Danny Biederman)*

The entire motorboat chase on Lake Mead was replaced by a helicopter attack on Blofeld's last line of defence: an oil rig off the Pacific coast whose computers control the guidance system of the laser satellite. Bond substitutes a fake computer tape that destroys the satellite and before

On the streets of Las Vegas with Jill St John and Sean Connery. (*Las Vegas News Bureau*)

Blofeld is able to escape in his mini-sub, Bond wrests the crane controls away from a guard and smashes Blofeld's sub into the control room, an end to Blofeld which, to some viewers, seemed a bit too quick. In fact, Mankiewicz's original script did not end on the oil rig.

In his first version of the ending, Blofeld was escaping under water in his bathosub when Bond sees it idling in twelve feet of water. Bond dives off the oil rig, holding on to the long string of a huge weather balloon which he ties to the sub's conning tower. Thus, when the sub moves under the water, Bond rides along the surface holding on to the weather balloon.

Blofeld arrives at a beach somewhere in Mexico, thinking he is safe, only to turn around and see Bond hanging from this big balloon. Blofeld was to have said something like: "Mary Poppins I presume", and to have shot down the weather balloon. Bond would fall in the water and both

would start running for the shore. They were to have ended up in a giant salt mine. As this was long and involved after the lengthy battle for the oil rig, the mine was eliminated.

In *Diamonds Are Forever*, Bond's principal female interest is Tiffany Case, an independent young felon whom Fleming described as "a good woman who simply grew up on the wrong side of the tracks." Tiffany at first defies Bond's charm but when the going gets rough she succumbs and joins him on a king size circular waterbed filled with tropical fish.

The key to casting Tiffany was her "cockiness". Ideally, Guy Hamilton wanted someone like Jane Fonda or Faye Dunaway to play her but both producers were against going after name actresses for the role. With Connery back, they intended to return to the well-tried formula of casting unknowns in the principal female roles. Broccoli did mention Raquel Welch as a possibility but Hamilton was against it and the idea was dropped.

In Los Angeles, attorney Sidney Korshak, who

was helping the producers set up location deals in Las Vegas, asked whether a small role could be arranged for his close friend, actress Jill St. John. Broccoli suggested her for the role of Plenty O'Toole, a character newly created for the film, a glamorous society girl who meets the heavy-betting Bond at a Las Vegas crap table. Hamilton, however, began to think that Jill St. John might make the ideal Tiffany and at his instigation, Broccoli signed her up for this role. She proved to be a versatile enough actress to cope with the varied moods and emotions that the part demanded.

In the new script, billionaire Willard Whyte (excellently played by singer Jimmy Dean) owns a beautiful desert house which is protected by two female karate experts nicknamed Bambi and Thumper. The acrobatic stunt girls, Trina Parks and Donna Garrett were signed to play these deadly bodyguards who give Bond a rough time until he corners them in the swimming pool and they tell him where the missing Mr. Whyte is imprisoned. Charles Grey, one of Harry Saltzman's favourites, who had played the small part of Dikko Henderson on *You Only Live Twice*, was cast as Blofeld.

Blofeld's homosexual assassins, Mr. Wint and Mr. Kidd, were in the original book but both were very tough thugs in Maibaum's script as well as in Fleming's novel. Hamilton and Mankiewicz later decided to make them "gay and fun". The film was originally planned to end in Tiffany's cabin where she was tied to the bed with a bottle of hot fondue about to fall on her and Bond was to throw Kidd through a porthole. At the last minute, Saltzman and Broccoli decided that the action was too enclosed in this setting and that the characters were to be brought out on deck instead.

Although they approved Mankiewicz's final rewrite, both producers were confused by some of the sophisticated dialogue scenes. In one sequence on the oil rig, Bond tells Blofeld that he has won, to which Blofeld replies: "As La Rochefoucauld once observed, Mr. Bond, humility is the worst form of conceit." When Broccoli read the line, Mankiewicz recalls that he said: "What is this thing here with the Roquefort cheese? Get it out of here, it doesn't belong." Despite his complaints, Hamilton shot the se-

quence with the line intact. Broccoli complained when he saw the rushes, but Hamilton insisted that the line had to stay as he had only shot the sequence with one angle. Another argument blew up over Mankiewicz's favourite pun in *Diamonds Are Forever* where CIA agent Felix Leiter says to Bond: "I know the diamonds are in the body but where?" To which Bond replies "Alimentary Dr. Leiter". Again, despite Broccoli's protests the line remained.

Diamonds Are Forever was the first Bond film to utilise American interiors and the facilities of a Hollywood studio. When David Picker disclosed to Broccoli how much Sean Connery was going to cost United Artists, Broccoli suggested that they try for an Eady subsidy for the film, rather than shoot entirely in America. The subsidy was granted. All the Las Vegas locations were completed in the Nevada city except for the parking lot car chase which was filmed on the Universal Studios lot in North Hollywood. Guy Hamilton

Connery and director Guy Hamilton discuss a scene. Hamilton directed four Bond films, including one of the best, GOLDFINGER. *(Danny Biederman)*

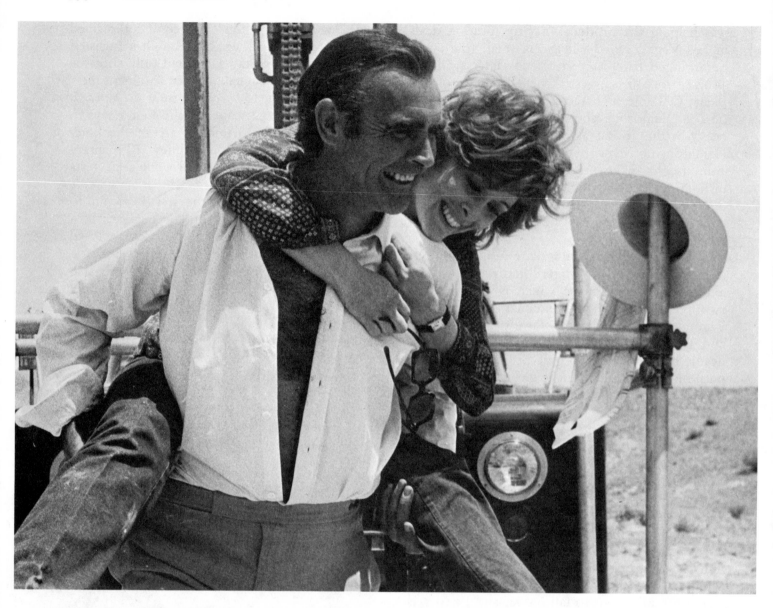

Clowning in the Nevada desert are Sean Connery and Jill St. John. According to Tom Mankiewicz, "there was now an old pro's grace to Connery's Bond." *(UPI)*

also did some shooting outside Palm Springs, California, in a luxurious split level desert home which became the winter residence of Willard Whyte; on the outskirts of Las Vegas, the John Manville Gypsum plant became the Whyte Missile Laboratories; the outside of Las Vegas Visitors Bureau Building on Highway 10 became the headquarters of the Slumber Mortuary business; and off the coast of Southern California a temporary oil rig was equipped with a battery of anti aircraft guns.

James Bond's Las Vegas hotel suite was originally planned as a Las Vegas interior and after a thorough search of the city, a suitably garish suite was found at Caesar's Palace. Ken Adam, however, thought that he could design one better and it was instead built at Pinewood.

Having lost their momentum with the ineffectual *On Her Majesty's Secret Service*, Broccoli and Saltzman were delighted to find themselves once more in the limelight on *Diamonds Are Forever*. Reporters flocked to Nevada to see Connery back in action as Bond. He now looked heavier by at least twenty pounds. His face was fuller, his eyebrows bushier and his hairpiece was not close fitting. To many of his fans, he looked terrible but to Mankiewicz: "It was the

While looking for the missing Willard Whyte, Bond is attacked by his lucious bodyguards, Bambi (Donna Garrett) and Thumper (Trina Parks). *(UPI)*

only time in any of his films that he looked mature and there was an old pro's grace about him."

The winter reconnaissance to Las Vegas allowed Tom Mankiewicz to write much of the city into the final script. The city's newest hotel, the International, became the snazzy Whyte House. The Circus Circus Hotel and Casino, built under a huge concrete tent and featuring high wire experts parading above the slot machines and gaming tables was also used to good advantage as a rendezvous for Tiffany and Bond. Fremont Street, perhaps the brightest boulevard in the world, was ideal for a high speed chase. Fords had once more come to the rescue with a brand new 1971 Mustang which Bond handles expertly in the Casino Center traffic as he is pursued by the entire Las Vegas Police Department. For three straight nights, Las Vegas's most famous boulevard was cordoned off so that

Hamilton's team of American stunt drivers could practice their unique game of cat and mouse. In the film, Bond leads the police on a wild chase through Fremont traffic, turns off the main drag and heads for a parking lot where he succeeds, through acrobatics, in demolishing a half dozen of his pursuers.

After the completion of this sequence, Hamilton returned to the Riviera Hotel and filmed James Bond's obligatory foray into a typical Las Vegas Casino where he quickly wins fifty thousand dollars and Miss Plenty O'Toole. In the distance, Bond hears the concluding remarks of Shady Tree, a nightclub comedian who is actually a member of the smuggling operation. Wise-cracking comedian Leonard Barr played Tree, a withered old man who saves Bond from a roasting at Slumber Inc. but is later killed by Wint and Kidd. The original script called for a name cele-

Bond gives Thumper a taste of her own medicine. *(UPI)*

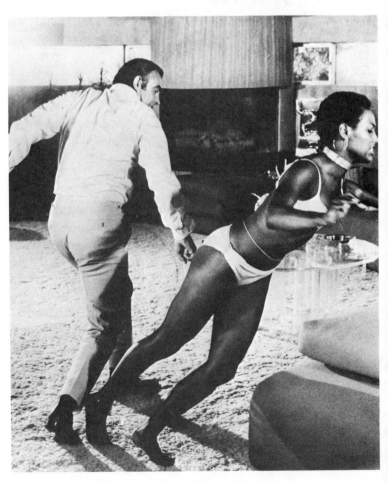

On board the oil rig, Tiffany Case takes matters into her own hands with the help of a SPECTRE submachine gun. *(UPI)*

brity to appear in the casino sequence and complain to the casino boss Burt Saxby (Bruce Cabot) about his contract. The producers signed Sammy Davis Jr. to make the cameo appearance but the short sequence later ended up on the cutting room floor.

Diamonds Are Forever featured two different stunt crews, one in the United States which was responsible for the car stunts, and another English team led by veteran Bob Simmons and George Leach. Simmons's first assignment was to choreograph a fight sequence between Bond and Peter Franks (Joe Robinson) a diamond smuggler, whose place Bond takes in the first part of the pipeline. The fight was to take place in the old iron and glass lift, only four foot square, of Tiffany Case's Amsterdam apartment building.

The art department made a wood mockup of the elevator before the actual set was built and Leech and Simmons worked out a beginning and an ending as well as certain movements when somebody's elbow would strike a button causing the lift to reverse directions. At first, they did not believe that it was possible to stage a fight in a four foot square box and make it interesting. For three weeks they worked out a couple of moves, went away and had a cup of tea and then came back and worked out some more. Leech remembers, "We would say things like 'What would happen if I hit you with my elbow, then you could wrap your hand around my ear and then pull me into that corner where I could get my knee up . . .'" These ideas would have to be tried out because they did not know if they would work.

In the sequence, Joe Robinson, a judo and wrestling teacher, played Franks, but a double had to be used because Robinson's contract prohibited him from doing any stunts. As a result, the film had to feature a judo expert doubling a judo expert!

After Bond destroys Blofeld on the oil rig, he and Tiffany are sent back to England on the Queen Elizabeth II for a relaxing vacation. At dinner time, they sit down to a glorious meal served by Mr. Wint and Mr. Kidd who, disguised as waiters, attack the pair with flaming shish kebab. In the eery fight, Bond dumps brandy on Wint and the flames from the shish kebab spread to the rest of his body, turning him into a human torch. Aflame from head to toe, he runs to the railing and jumps into the Atlantic. This interior was filmed on a sound stage at Pinewood while the dive into the water was filmed later as an exterior.

George Leech doubled Putter Smith. As Wint, meets his fiery death, Leech was nearly consumed as well. The sequence was done with the help of a special effects makeup man who designed a mask for Leech, made of fire-proof rubber and perfectly moulded to the stuntman's features which, on the outside, featured the image of bespectacled Putter Smith. The mask had two copper gauze pieces which were placed over the eyes, through which Leech could see, and a copper gauze plate over the mouth so that he could breathe. Protecting the rest of his body was an asbestos car racing suit. If something had gone wrong in the take,

Leech could not have got out of the suit but would have had to wait for someone to put him out with a fire extinguisher. When it came to the actual stunt, Leech had to stagger a little in front of the camera and then go to the edge of the boat set and jump over the edge on to a pad, where a fireman stood by with an extinguisher. The fireman was instructed to extinguish the fire as soon as Leech hit the pad, but when the time came, he did nothing, waiting for the director to say "cut". By this time, Leech's hands were burning because some of the fiery jell had leaked through his fireproof gloves which had cracked under the extreme heat. In stunt work, the best laid plans are never foolproof.

9

BEWARE CROCODILES CROSSING

"Diamonds are Forever" was Sean Connery's swan song as James Bond. Starting with the next film, *Live and Let Die*, Roger Moore ushered in a whole new era of Bond films when he began his duties as the world's most desirable secret agent.

It had been over a decade since Cubby Broccoli and Harry Saltzman first considered Roger Moore as a possible James Bond. Moore had spent the years in a series of American and British television programmes, establishing himself as a light comedian. His forte was playing the dashing hero who spent a great deal of time with the ladies, drank champagne before he went off to deal with the opposition and used his brains to befuddle

There's good reason to smile, for Roger Moore is indeed the newest James Bond. (Wide World)

even the most cunning of enemy agents. In short, Roger Moore used his wits rather than his fists to survive in television adventures, such as the popular *Saint* series in which he played Simon Templar.

After a couple of film roles, Moore gained some weight, let his hair grow and joined Tony Curtis in another British romp for television, *The Persuaders*, which carried him through the summer of 1971. It was probably because Moore was not a household name in America, that encouraged Harry Saltzman to approach him for the Bond role in the spring of 1972. Moore was certainly closer than Connery to Ian Fleming's original conception of a well tailored agent who was fastidious about the clothes he wore, the food he consumed and the women he bedded.

In contrast to the tough, belligerent Connery,

LIVE AND LET DIE (1973) PC. Eon Productions – A United Artists Release 121 mins Col. **PROD.** Albert R. Broccoli and Harry Saltzman **DIR.** Guy Hamilton **SCR.** Tom Mankiewicz based on the novel by Ian Fleming **PH.** Bob Kindred **ED.** Burt Bates, Raymond Poulton and John Shirley **PROD DES.** Syd Cain **MUSIC.** George Martin **SP EFFECTS.** Derek Meddings **STUNT CO-ORDS.** Eddie Smith, Ross Kananga, Joey Chitwood, Jerry Comeaux, Bill Bennett and Bob Simmons **CAST.** Roger Moore (James Bond), Yaphet Kotto (Mr. Big/Kananga),

Jane Seymour (Solitaire), Julius H. Harris (Tee Hee) Geoffrey Holder (Samedi), Earl Jolly Brown (Whisper), David Hedison (Felix Leiter), Bernard Lee ("M"), Lois Maxwell (Miss Moneypenny), Desmond Llewelyn ("Q"), Clifton James (Sheriff Pepper), Gloria Hendry (Rosie Carver), Tommy Lang (Adam), Roy Stewart (Quarrel Jr.) Lon Satton (Strutter), Arnold Williams (Cab Driver), Ruth Kempf (Mrs. Bell), Joey Chitwood (Charlie), Madeline Smith (Miss Caruso), Michael Ebbin (Dambala), Kubi Chaza (Salesgirl).

Moore and colorful Harry Saltzman on location in New Orleans. Saltzman would soon sell his share of the Bond empire. *(UPI)*

Moore was the typical "nice guy" with much more of the flavour of the Etonian dropout that Fleming envisaged than his predecessor. His personality inevitably influenced the Bond films in which he starred and he brought to the role a sophisticated sense of comedy which was not a feature of Connery's style. Even in the gadget rigged days of the middle sixties when Bond was lost in the technological shuffle for bigger stunts and more complex gadgetry, there was still an obsession with tough fight sequences, occasional moments of bloodshed not for the squeamish, and the Connery machismo.

From this point, the emphasis began to be towards comedy, an emphasis that benefited Moore, but which radically altered the whole Bond mystique. Eon Productions had done well with *Diamonds Are Forever* which grossed over thirty five million dollars worldwide. American audiences especially, enjoyed the return of Sean

Connery and identified with the Las Vegas locations. In their next project, the producers made plans to return to the United States for location work in the bayou country of Louisiana, as well as street scenes in New Orleans and New York City.

Live and Let Die, Fleming's second novel, was one of the author's best, but because it dealt with a powerful crime syndicate run by a black man, the story had been left untouched until the early seventies when Tom Mankiewicz was asked to do a script.

In the novel, Bond's opponent is a ruthless Moscow-backed hoodlum named Mr. Big, who uses the voodoo superstitions of his Haitian background to discipline his followers and put fear in the hearts of his enemies. Based in Harlem, his criminal activities extend to the Caribbean where smuggled buried treasure is being used to fuel Russian espionage operations in the United States. Fleming's most interesting characters were a beautiful fortune teller from Haiti named Solitaire, two unsavoury thugs named Whisper and Tee Hee and the legendary Baron Samedi, the most feared of all voodoo spirits who is the king of the legion of the dead and the guardian of all cemeteries and whom many fear has been brought to life in the person of Mr. Big.

When *Diamonds Are Forever* was begun in 1970, a United Artists executive quipped that "for its annual one hundred thousand dollar fee, the Fleming estate was giving us a few nice characters, ten per cent of a usable plot and a great Fleming title." The same pattern re-emerged in *Live and Let Die* as indeed it did in all the later Bonds. The screen writers were now creating entirely new stories, that bore little resemblance to anything of Fleming.

In the *Live and Let Die* script, the buried treasure of Morgan the Pirate was replaced by a heroin smuggling racket which is operated by a sinister island diplomat named Dr. Kananga, who masquerades in Harlem as the infamous Mr. Big. It is on Kananga's island of San Monique in the Caribbean that the poppy shrubs are being harvested wholesale for shipment to the United States, where the drugs are to be distributed through a chain of Filet of Soul restaurants. San Monique does not appear on any nautical chart. Fleming's reference to the Russians was also gone. Kananga has no political affiliation. He is simply a crook.

Early on, Mankiewicz decided that Solitaire was the key character in the story, especially with her affinity for the occult. He also decided to capitalise on the wave of black exploitation movies such as *Shaft* and to introduce Fleming's beautiful white fortune teller as a black girl. At the last minute, however, United Artists, nervous enough at the prospect of launching a new Bond and uncertain of Moore's star potential, vetoed the idea. To Mankiewicz's chagrin, the British actress Jane Seymour was cast in the role. She had been "discovered" by the producers in the BBC television series *The Onedin Line* and had some difficulty in conforming to the one dimensional sex object role marked out for her in Mankiewicz's script as a young fortune teller who uses Tarot cards to predict the future for her boss, the drug smuggler, Dr. Kananga.

An arresting Tarot deck was created by a young Scotsman, Fergus Hall, whose surreal figures later influenced the film's unusual advertising campaign which featured Roger Moore in front of cards symbolising Death, Fortune, Devil, and Lovers.

In the Mankiewicz script, each character had his or her own alter ego in the Tarot pack. Solitaire was symbolised by the High Priestess, a card whose figure deliberately bore a strong resemblance to Jane Seymour. James Bond was featured as the personification of many cards including the male half of the Lovers, a card that shows two lovers wrapped in a passionate embrace. In the film, Bond has a phony pack of Tarot cards created, consisting solely of cards depicting the Lovers. With this deck he tricks Solitaire into believing that they are destined to make love.

The Tarot cards help Bond in other ways. Solitaire alerts Bond to the treachery of the CIA operative, Rosie Carver, when she sends 007 a card depicting the Queen of Cups in an upside down position. This card means that Bond is involved with a deceitful woman. When Solitaire is recaptured and sent to San Monique for execution, it is three Tarot cards, the High Priestess, Death and the Moon that lead Bond back to the island, to her rescue. Every time Solitaire sees Bond, the card known as the Lovers appears, hinting at the inevitability of their entanglement.

It was through this sense of "destiny" that Mankiewicz was able to get round the customary taboo on Bond going to bed with a virgin, and to make it seem acceptable.

If Broccoli and Saltzman were tired of playing musical chairs with Bond, they continued to play

Lovely Jane Seymour who portrayed Solitaire, mistress of the Tarot Card.

A Glastron motorboat similar to one command-eered by 007 in LIVE AND LET DIE. (The Glastron Boat Company)

them with their art directors. Ken Adam was gone and Syd Cain was back, the veteran of *On Her Majesty's Secret Service* and *From Russia with Love*. In March 1972, Cain accompanied director Guy Hamilton to Jamaica, searching for locations to match those described in Mankiewicz's first draft screenplay. In the first draft, Mankiewicz had Dr. Kananga drop Bond into a huge sugar granulator, a processing machine common in Jamaica. However, when Cain and Hamilton arrived in Jamaica, they immediately found the granulator too unwieldy and dangerous even for Bond. Mankiewicz joined the team and the three men moved into the jungle, searching for alternative ideas.

Outside Montego Bay, on a jungle road, they passed a sign saying "Beware Crocodiles Crossing". Further on, they passed another saying, "Trespassers will be eaten". They had come upon a crocodile farm, a discovery which influenced the final script. In this, Bond is captured in New Orleans by Dr. Kananga and is sent out to the crocodile farm for execution. Tee Hee escorts Bond to a huge stagnant pond filled with reptiles, and leaves him stranded on a concrete island.

To determine how Bond would escape this death trap, Mankiewicz consulted the crocodile farmer, himself named Kananga, who said that he would try to jump over the backs of the crocodiles. This was a stunt that could only be done if the crocodiles were immobilised. The farmer tied the feet of half a dozen reptiles to weights on the bottom of the pond so they could not move, while their jaws and tails were left free. When the crocodiles were tethered in place, creating a reptilian bridge of snapping teeth and swishing tails, he prepared to jump their backs, a stunt he had never before attempted.

The entire pond was later cleared of excess

crocodiles so that Hamilton could bring in his small team of film makers, including a contingent of London craftsmen who fashioned the retractable bridge which strands Bond on the island. For the stunt, the farmer had to wear a pair of trousers and shoes, to resemble the outfit worn by Moore, who would be watching his own escape from a safe distance.

The first four times Kananga tried the stunt, he slipped and fell into the pond. On the third attempt, one of the crocodiles actually nipped his shoe. He realised that the street shoes were preventing him from getting across the slippery surface. Even with specially prepared soles designed to give him traction, he continued to slip and land in the water. Each time, he had to return to the wardrobe shack, change into a fresh pair of slacks and row out to the little concrete island. Each time he failed, the stunt became more difficult because the crocodiles were learning to expect him. Only on the fifth try did he manage to keep his footing and race across their backs to the shore.

One of Mankiewicz's most important jobs on the first script was to move away from Fleming's snobbishness and to portray the black antagonists believably, without being patronising. What finally emerges in *Live and Let Die* is a typically Bondian terror organisation as powerful as Smersh or SPECTRE, but much more interesting. While one SPECTRE agent seems to look like another, Mr. Big's group of criminals are all individuals. Actor Yaphet Kotto played the dual role of Mr. Big, the brash Harlem bigshot with a tough no nonsense attitude towards interlopers and Dr. Kananga, the soft spoken island diplomat, who can hold his own in a United Nations assembly and still talk the ear off any CIA snoopers who question his activities on San Monique.

Julius Harris, equipped with an articulating metal claw, is a terrifying Tee Hee, a laughing villain who terrorises Bond especially on the train ride home from New Orleans. Whisper played by portly Earl Jolly Brown is more of a subtle influence in the film, flitting in and out of scenes like a soft spoken spirit and providing comic relief at key moments, especially in the grotto sequence. The six foot six-inch dancer Geoffrey Holder steals the show as the mortal manifest-

ation of Baron Samedi. An extension of Kananga's power in voodoo country, Holder plays the role on two imaginative levels. At times, he is simply one of Mr. Big's associates, an extremely conspicuous presence, but a mortal one. At others, Holder becomes Baron Samedi, the king of the dead who officiates over a sacrificial rite on San Monique in which Solitaire is nearly murdered by snake-bearing fanatics.

Holder, with his huge powerful laugh and dancer's movements is the film's most enduring image and it is fitting that he is the last character we see, riding the cow catcher of Bond's homeward bound train, laughing as usual, and warning us that the supernatural cannot be lightly dismissed.

Yaphet Kotto, who portrayed the sinister diplomat turned drug smuggler, Dr. Kananga. *(Courtesy of NBC)*

Screenwriter Tom Mankiewicz, the master of Bond's onscreen wit. *(Richard Schenkman)*

Holder's appearance in the film's last scene was an afterthought. It was felt that having killed off practically all the black villains, it was important to end the film without a clear victory for Bond. Little does 007 know who is sitting on the front of his train. With Samedi riding the end titles, the producers were throwing a sop to the potential black audience. Such careful attention to the black antagonists appealed to those critics who were ready to pounce on this Bond film for exploiting the new wave of black films.

Filming Roger Moore's first Bond began in the Louisiana bayou country in October 1972. Director Guy Hamilton had assembled an armada of high speed motor boats and a tough group of seasoned stunt men including ace driver Joey Chitwood and his "Greatest Show on Wheels" troupe of auto daredevils, a contingent

of black stunt boat specialists from Hollywood, and Hamilton's own cadre of Pinewood professionals.

Derek Crachnell, Hamilton's right hand man in the bayou country, and the art director Peter Lemont had been in Louisiana for over a month choreographing a dazzling motor boat chase in which Bond eludes Dr. Kananga's henchman on the narrow bayou waterways. In the Mankiewicz script, the water chase becomes comical when members of the Louisiana State Police, led by the pot bellied sheriff J. W. Pepper, attempt to round up the speeding fugitives.

Hamilton initially wondered whether any of Mankiewicz's ideas for this sequence could be brought to the screen without killing off his hand-picked stunt crew. In the script, motor boats fly across highways, skid across lawns, land in swimming pools, slam into tree trunks, smash into deserted landing craft and skim through narrow channels at 70 miles per hour. The com-

CIA man David Hedison reteamed with Roger Moore in the 1980 film, "ffolkes." *(Universal Pictures)*

plexity of jumping high speed motor boats across a road was solved when the crew hauled in a huge water ski ramp which would give the boats the proper elevation. One of these special platforms was placed in position on October 16th 1972 as Jerry Comeaux prepared to jump a road which crossed the Crawdad Bridge outside Phoenix, Louisiana.

Comeaux was working with one of the jet pumps, a type of motor boat that uses a jet stream of water for propulsion. The engine sucked in the water and pumped it out in a fast jet that propelled the boat forward and provided rudder control. Without the jet stream the boat had no steering, a fact that Roger Moore had already learned painfully. The previous Wednesday he had been practising some tight turns on a nearby bayou when his motor cut out, leaving him with zero steering at forty five miles an hour. Losing control, the boat smashed into a dock, an unfortunate accident that sent the new James Bond to the local doctor with a jammed leg, a fractured front tooth and general bruising. That afternoon, Comeaux overturned his own boat while negotiating the jump across Crawdad bridge, but was able to walk away, with only minor concussion.

In one funny scene, Bond is being chased down a bayou by two pursuers when the trio come upon a wedding ceremony on a peninsula of land wedged between two bisecting waterways. In the script, Kananga's agent, Adam, makes the turn into an adjacent waterway by detouring along the grass, but the other villain ends up smashing through the wedding cake and the refreshment tent.

Murray Cleveland started the day doubling the wayward enemy boat handler and at 11.00 a.m. he revved up his CV-19 power boat and glided down the bayou opposite the Treadway Estate, a

The author Steven Jay Rubin playing secret agent with actress Jane Seymour.

stunts the following week when Joey Chitwood's stunt drivers tore up the Lakefront Airport outside New Orleans where Bond commandeers a training plane and, accompanied by an astonished old woman (Ruth Kempf, a non-professional), is chased round the airport by carloads of gun-toting enemy agents. Chitwood seemed to have a seemingly inexhaustible amount of ways to demolish the company's cars. He crashed into airplanes, over airplanes, around airplanes. He even crashed an airplane through some partially closed hangar doors, sheering off its wings.

In the Fleming novel *Live and Let Die*, James Bond arrives in Jamaica to destroy Mr. Big's yacht, the Secatur, and thus to smash the illegal pipeline in Spanish doubloons which is fuelling Smersh operations in America. 007 teams with

Roger Moore picks up a Swiss machine gun during a trip to the Alps to promote LIVE AND LET DIE. Here he is flanked by beauty contest hopefuls. (Wide World)

former Indian Reservation where the wedding ceremony was in progress. Cleveland, moving at ramming speed, never tasted the icing on the targeted wedding cake as his boat swerved out of control, slamming into a nearby oak tree. The driver was unhurt but his boat was lost for the day.

As Crachnell's assistants hauled the wrecked boat away, it was Jerry Comeaux's turn. When the area was clear of debris, he took his own CV-19 at a perfect 65 miles per hour and also lost control, slamming into another oak tree. Eddie Smith was next, and he too was handling one of the powerful CV-19's. He dropped his speed five miles an hour, down to sixty, maintained steering control and was able to head straight through to the wedding cake.

Boat stunts became car stunts and airplane

Hang glider expert Bill Bennett instructs Roger Moore on location in Jamaica on LIVE AND LET DIE. *(UPI)*

Strangeways and Quarrel (his two Jamaican contacts destined for further adventure in *Dr. No*), crosses a moonlit channel underwater, afixes a limpet mine to the hull of the enemy yacht, gets captured in the process and is almost flayed alive on the Jamaican reefs when at the very last moment, the Secatur is destroyed in a terrific explosion, setting Bond and Solitaire free.

All these plot elements were jettisoned in the new *Live and Let Die*. In Mankiewicz's script, Bond returns to Jamaica to blow up Kananga's poppy groves and to rescue Solitaire who is about to be executed by the voodoo fanatics. In a trick graveyard where the sacrificial rites are being held, Bond destroys a Baron Samedi statue that is raised from the ground mechanically by Dr. Kananga's underground technicians. He then defeats the real Baron Samedi in sword combat, and flees, with Solitaire, into Kananga's underground fortress. There he is once again captured by Kananga and Whisper. But using his bag of tricks which this time includes a special watch which cuts through his bonds and catches a compressed air bullet in its magnetic grip, Bond is able to overpower Kananga who is killed when Bond shoves the gas bullet into his mouth. This

Bond airborne for LIVE AND LET DIE. *(UPI)*

causes Kananga to super inflate, rise to the roof and explode. As Bond quips: "Kananga always did have an over-inflated opinion of himself."

On November 25th, Geoffrey Holder donned his white top hat and tails and began parading around as Baron Samedi, this time in a nightclub show staged at the unit's Jamaica hotel, the Sans Souci (once Miss Taro's mountain home in *Dr. No*). A crowd of 95 tourists was rounded up by the assistant directors and transported over to the Sans Souci where Holder choreographed a mock voodoo ceremony, with Jamaican fire eaters and a strange contortionist named Don Topping who, as the crab man, uses his double jointed body to mystify audiences.

Holder illustrated his versatility the next day by exchanging his top hat and tails for a frock of rags in a sequence where he greets Bond and Solitaire in a jungle graveyard. Holder looms ominously over a tombstone, playing a ghostly flute, and wishing the two escapees a good day. In a film that features one mindless chase sequence after another, the graveyard interlude stands out. Mankiewicz illustrated that he had not forgotten a maxim employed by the previous Bond writers, that Bond could be involved in humorous action as long as the audience was led to believe their secret agent was truly in peril. With Samedi lurking about, warning Kananga of Bond's arrival, the stage was set for a carefully planned chase sequence through the Jamaican countryside. His appearance, bedecked in rags, served to further mystify the audience as to Samedi's true identity. Was he simply another of Kananga's hoods, or was he really a spectre of the supernatural?

On November 29th, Hamilton's crew left Ocho Rios for Montego Bay where the actor Roy Stewart had arrived to play Quarrel Junior, Bond's Jamaican assistant, while down the road from the Montego Bay exteriors a large group of stunt men was preparing for the long awaited double decker bus chase.

Maurice Patchett, the London bus driver, who had been waiting for a chance to display some fancy driving skills arrived in Montego Bay on November 30th driving a Leyland R.T. double-decker fresh off London's No. 19 bus route. Sprayed a greyish green by Syd Cain's roving art department the bus was christened a member of San Monique Transport. Looking at it, it was impossible to notice that a team of metal workers had actually sawn off the top half of the bus body, placed it on metal rollers and attached it to the lower body so that when Patchett hit the low level trestle bridge, the upper half would easily smash off, leaving Patchett and Seymour free to drive off in the single decker.

Before this wild stunt was attempted, Patchett

During a voodoo ceremony, Solitaire (Jane Seymour) is nearly done in by a snake. *(UPI)*

earned his salary by skidding the bus through a water patch, a manoeuvre which surprises three chasing motorcyclists who are catapulted into the nearby brush. He also swerved the bus from side to side along the Montego Bay/Lucea Highway, forcing two enemy patrol cars off the road. In these sequences, Roger Moore was available for

Bond effects the inevitable rescue. *(UPI)*

close-ups and certain driving sequences, but for insurance reasons, Patchett did all the stunt work, spinning, swerving and at last approaching the trestle bridge. He had already worked out the stunt with a mathematician who verified that a thirty mile an hour speed would sheer off the specially prepared top section.

While Patchett gave the bus a final check, the assistant director Richard Jenkins and twenty

Jamaican policemen attempted to control a crowd of two hundred locals who had heard about the stunt and were already lining up along the country road.

Finally, on the morning of December 7th 1972, Patchett climbed into his Leyland, adjusted the mirrors, waited for Jane Seymour to station her-self in the undercarriage and then gunned his engine. Hamilton gave his signal and Patchett began heading for the bridge. He started to pick up speed and was still watching his odometer when there was a terrible crash and the stunt was suddenly over.

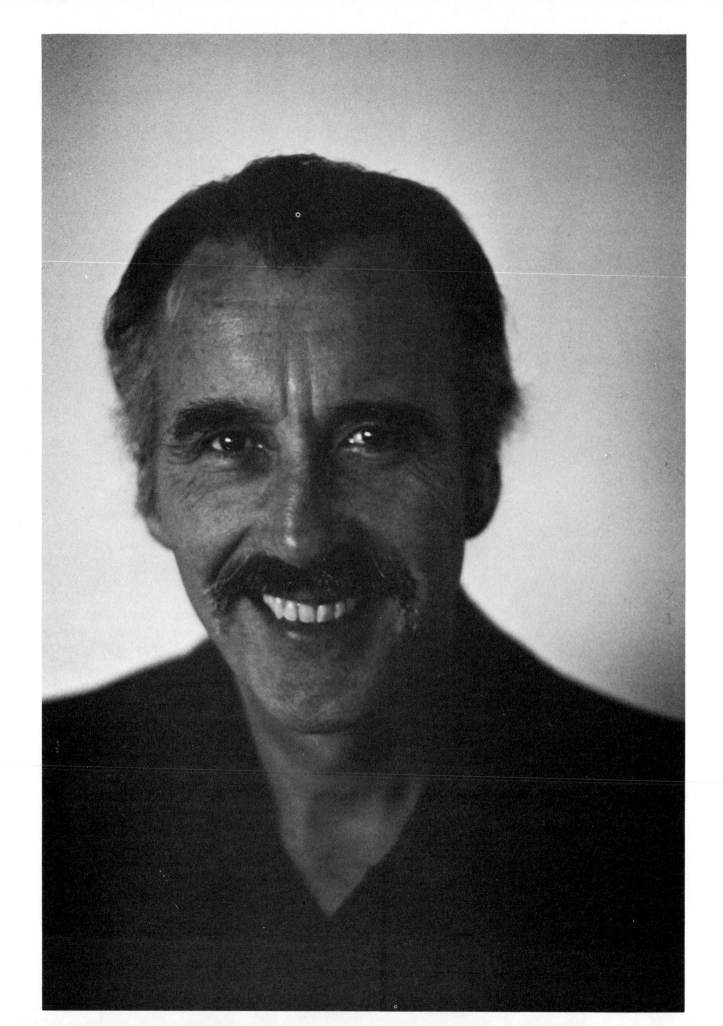

10

DRACULA MEETS BOND ON AN ISLAND IN THE SUN

Live and Let Die was Harry Saltzman's swan song as a full time James Bond film producer. Since that first meeting in Broccoli's office in the early 1960's, their partnership had been a stormy one. Saltzman was the more volatile, Broccoli the more phlegmatic, a man who would establish his position in an argument and calmly wait until he got his way. Scriptwriter Richard Maibaum considered Saltzman to be an imaginative contributor to the early films in the series, but disruptive in later years.

The Man with the Golden Gun was Ian Fleming's last James Bond novel. Serialised in *Playboy*, and a best seller within weeks of its publication, it was, nevertheless, a weak entry in the Bond

Christopher Lee abandoned his Dracula image as suave Francisco Scaramanga, the "villainous" MAN WITH THE GOLDEN GUN.

series and repeated many incidents in the previous twelve adventures.

In this book, James Bond is brainwashed by the Russian Secret Service and sent to assassinate "M" in London. The plan fails and "M" sends Bond to a psychiatric clinic where he recuperates under the care of battle-hardened chief psychiatrist Sir James Maloney. When fit for duty, Bond is sent on still another suicidal mission. This time, his target is freelance assassin, Francisco "Pistols" Scaramanga, "the man with the golden gun", a vicious KGB assassin, responsible for the deaths of several British Secret Service agents. The mission takes Bond back to one of Fleming's old haunts, Jamaica, where he eventually tracks Scaramanga through remote jungles, and silences the golden gunman forever.

Since *Live and Let Die* was filmed in Jamaica,

THE MAN WITH THE GOLDEN GUN (1974) PC. Eon Productions – A United Artists Release 125 mins Col. **PROD.** Harry Saltzman and Albert R. Broccoli **DIR.** Guy Hamilton **SCR.** Tom Mankiewicz and Richard Maibaum based on the novel by Ian Fleming **PH.** Ted Moore and Oswald Morris **ED.** John Shirley and Raymond Poulton **PROD DES.** Peter Murton **MUSIC.** John Barry **SP EFFECTS.** John Stears **STUNT CO-ORD.** W. J. Milligan Jr. **CAST.** Roger Moore (James Bond),

Christopher Lee (Scaramanga), Britt Ekland (Mary Goodnight), Maude Adams (Andrea), Hervé Villechaize (Nick Nack), Bernard Lee ("M"), Desmond Llewelyn ("Q"), Lois Maxwell (Miss Moneypenny), Richard Loo (Hi Fat), Marc Laurence (Rodney), Clifton James (J. W. Pepper), Soon-Tak-Oh (Hip), Marnie Maitland (Lazar), James Cossons (Colharpe), Chan-You-Lam (Chula), Carmen Sautoy (Salda), Michael Osborne (Navy Lieutenant), Michael Fleming (Commanding Officer).

Fleming's vision of Dr. No, perhaps? Actually it is a scene from Christopher Lee's film *The Brides of Fu Manchu*. Lee, who starred as Scaramanga in THE MAN WITH THE GOLDEN GUN, was Fleming's original choice for Dr. No. Note: Burt Kwouk next to Lee. *(Seven Arts)*

it was planned to dispense with many of Fleming's original settings for *The Man with the Golden Gun* in the film version. As usual, the producers decided to take the Fleming title, a few of the author's interesting characters and create an entirely new story.

Even before *Live and Let Die* opened in Ameri-

Britt Ekland joins the ranks of Bond women as 007's daffy secretary Mary Goodnight. *(UPI)*

can cinemas, scriptwriter Tom Mankiewicz was racking his brain for a new Bond plot. His only staple ingredient was Scaramanga, the world's most expensive assassin who murders for a million bucks a shot. Mankiewicz ended up writing a story about a duel between the best assassin in the world and James Bond. "M" receives a gold bullet in the mail with 007's number engraved on its surface. This is a signal from Scaramanga that Bond is the assassin's next target. "M" eventually suggests that Bond sort this issue out himself and Bond decides to trace the bullet back to the assassin. Near the end of the script, it is discovered that Scaramanga never sent the golden bullet to Bond. It was his girlfriend who sent it, hoping Bond would kill Scaramanga and free her from sexual slavery. She knows of Bond because Scaramanga has always spoken highly of him. Tired of being used, she begins to leave clues for Bond along the way – a trail of information that eventually leads 007 to his quarry.

Mankiewicz recalls that the film was originally to be a reworking of the Jack Palance versus Alan Ladd gun battle in *Shane* – the greatest heavy against the greatest hero in the world. He had nearly finished his first draft along these lines when conflicts began to develop with director Guy Hamilton and by the late summer of 1973, Mankiewicz was asking for his release.

Despite a very tenuous relationship with Harry Saltzman, Richard Maibaum agreed to come back and work on Mankiewicz's script. Although he retained the idea of Scaramanga's girlfriend sending Bond the golden bullet in a bid for quick rescue, Maibaum shelved the idea of a one to one gun battle and instead introduced the energy crisis as a relevant 1974 background to the story. The key to the story became the Solex – a solar energy unit owned by a Chinese industrialist named Hi Fat, who employs Scaramanga to guard the costly apparatus from enemy agents.

A desperate search began for new and interesting locations. Mankiewicz had hinted at the Far East when he mentioned Hi Fat's Macao gambling ship. With that in mind, a major reconnaissance team left London in the autumn of 1973, headed east. Suitable sites were discovered piecemeal. In Hong Kong harbour, the team found the rusty wreckage of the Queen Elizabeth which had caught fire under mysterious circumstances and had then half sunk on the edge of the harbour. It became a memorable background shot, and later, at Pinewood, its interior became the Far Eastern headquarters of "M".

The three week reconnaissance reaped a harvest of locations in Hong Kong, in Macao, in Bangkok (the capital of Thailand) and along the Thai klongs, a series of narrow canals that crisscrossed the latter city and which were traversed by knife-like motor canoes. But the real find came in October when Broccoli, Hamilton and production designer Peter Murton travelled southwest out of Bangkok to Phuket, a tiny hamlet on the west end of the Malay Peninsula. It was near Phuket that the team found a chain of tiny islands so extraordinary in appearance that Murton

Clifton James returns as wacky sheriff J. W. Pepper. (MGM)

thought that they had crossed the time barrier and were back in the prehistoric age. Covered with jungle foliage, shaped like overturned boulders and appearing from the air like a series of giant stepping stones, each island was a photographer's delight. One of these strange pieces of Asian geography was to become the island of Scaramanga. In the Thai geography book it was called Khow-Ping-Kan, and it featured a lovely sandy beach fronting a grotto that would later accommodate James Bond's seaplane, as well as the beach duel between Bond and Scaramanga. In the background, there were smaller, unusually shaped islands that lent the scene a sense of exotic mystique far removed from anything the crew, let alone the film audience, had ever imagined.

With shooting scheduled for April 1974, the reconnaissance team returned to London for logistical planning, a knotty problem on Khow-

An early publicity photo of Roger Moore. In 1961, Broccoli and Saltzman felt Moore was too much of a "pretty boy" to play the original 007.

Maud Adams as the treacherous Miss Ice.
(American International)

Ping-Kan, where the unit would have to be entirely self supporting.

Tom Mankiewicz had originally envisaged Jack Palance as the perfect actor to portray Francisco Scaramanga, the "man with the golden gun". Guy Hamilton, however, was particularly keen on tall, gaunt Christopher Lee who was ready to branch out of his long series of horror film roles in which he was typecast as Britain's answer to Bela Lugosi. Interestingly, he was a distant cousin of Ian Fleming and had been a frequent golfing partner of the author. Fleming had actually told Lee that he imagined him when he created the Dr. No character in 1957 and had voiced the hope that some day he would play one of the Bond villains.

Departing from Fleming's description of the thuggish assassin, Hamilton saw Scaramanga as a smartly dressed hit man, who, like James Bond, appreciated the finer things in life, who loved to kill for a million dollars a shot, and yet was not the typical down at heel killer.

To complement that image, Christopher Lee was fitted out with a unique weapon, a gun that could be taken apart and appear as normal trinkets – a cigarette case, a ball point pen, a cuff link, a lighter and a bullet hidden in a belt buckle. As such, the golden parts were totally inconspicuous and allowed Scaramanga freedom of movement through X-ray machines and physical searches, a factor that enabled the assassin to kill with surprising ease.

Guy Hamilton encouraged Lee to develop a light approach to the character, and the wardrobe department at Pinewood provided him with the most streamlined wardrobe of any Bond villain.

Lee was surrounded by a very unusual group of supporting players. Stealing the show was three foot nine inch Hervé Villechaize, an extraordinary actor who was given the role of Nick Nack, Scaramanga's manservant – a kind of miniature Odd job. A Frenchman with a squeaky voice, Villechaize had a series of tiny mannerisms that perfectly fitted the fantasy tradition of the Bond films. Certainly the smallest of Bond's adversaries, Nick Nack was no less formidable for this. On Scaramanga's island, he controls the mysteries of the fun house – an ultra-sophisticated maze in which Scaramanga matches wits and shots with the world's best hired guns.

Playing Scaramanga's winsome but treacherous girlfriend was cover girl Maude Adams, tall, slender and exotic looking. Swedish bombshell Britt Ekland played Mary Goodnight, Bond's Far Eastern girl Friday. To Richard Maibaum, the casting of Britt Ekland was a mystery. Maibaum's lines were written with a very intelligent girl in mind who could offer Bond some assistance. Britt Ekland however played the character as a "female buffoon" in Maibaum's view.

One of the reasons that Mankiewicz dropped out of his third Bond effort was his inability to meet the need for a new set of stunt ideas. Helping Maibaum this time, various crew members came up with contributions. On *Live and Let Die*, Derek Cracknell had become friendly with the stunt driver, Joey Chitwood, and when the film was finished, he was invited to meet a friend of Chitwood's named Jay Milligan who had a stunt idea to sell. Milligan, a well known car stunt specialist had spent months working out the "spiral jump", the ultimate car stunt in which a car is sent up a ramp, turned entirely round in the air and lands on another ramp right side up.

He drew up a plan and went to the Cornell University computer which worked out the mathematical aspects of the stunt. It would involve a set speed, a specially designed car,

Cover girl Maude Adams as the icy Miss Andrea.

take off and landing ramps designed to give the car the proper lift and turn so that it could land on all fours.

When *The Man with the Golden Gun* entered the pre-production phase, Milligan was hired by the producers to do the stunt in Bangkok. Eon Productions purchased a two year option which prohibited Milligan and any other stunt driver from performing it in public. It was to be kept as secret as possible. The producers were especially nervous of quickie television productions stealing their material and beating the Bond films to an audience.

In Bangkok Peter Murton had supervised the construction of specially designed take off and landing ramps over a Thai klong. The ramps were skilfully disguised as a fallen bridge and in the story, Bond, attempting to overtake Scaramanga's

car has to cross the canal in a hurry. With no bridge in sight, resourceful 007 spies the fallen bridge, backs up his car and rams it forward over the fallen timbers doing the turnaround and landing perfectly across the water.

For a stunt that lasted a matter of fifteen seconds in the film, the producers did not stint on building the fake bridge or on the approach road. The cars themselves were provided *en masse* by American Motors Corporation who were well aware that an appearance in a Bond film would promote their new line. Though an AMC Hornet could not compete with Aston Martin in the styling, it met Milligan's specifications perfectly. The stunt driver and a team of engineers redesigned its chassis, placing the steering column in the centre of the car, cutting down the body in certain places and widening it in others as well as adjusting certain weight factors that could affect the eventual jump.

By June 1974, the Hornet was ready to jump the klong. The stunt was performed by Bumps Willard, one of Milligan's drivers. Cranes and ambulances were standing by should Willard end up in the water and Hamilton had set up a number of cameras to catch the stunt from separate angles. The Hornet threw up a little dust, revved up its engine and then hit the launch ramp. "Before you knew it," Christopher Lee remembers, "it had flown across the canal, turned perfectly around and landed right on four tires. He made it look easy." In the final film, Hamilton presented the jump in slow motion.

On paper, there was no reason to think that *The Man with the Golden Gun* would not work as well as the eight James Bond films that had preceded it. It had a healthy budget (between 7.5 and 8 million dollars) good locations, some unusual characters and the typical 007 breakneck pace. Unfortunately, this time, the whole was not equal to the impressive parts.

The fact remains that there is no real threat in *The Man with the Golden Gun*. Without strongly defined danger, the new Bond film lost its edge. It became a series of set pieces: Set piece 1 – Fun house; Set piece 2 – Karate battle; Set piece 3 – Car jump; Set piece 4 – Fight with Nick Nack. It really looked, as Peter Murton pointed out, as if the film was put together piecemeal around its locations.

One aspect of *The Man with the Golden Gun* that intrigued James Bond fans was what was left out of the picture. A key sequence takes place on the beach of Scaramanga's island where Nick Nack oversees a classic gun duel between Bond and Scaramanga. It is the Walther versus the Golden Gun and each duellist prepares to walk twenty paces turn and fire. However, when Bond turns around, Scaramanga is gone. Fans complained that bits of footage featured in the film's trailer were not in the actual film.

In the duel, footage was cut which would otherwise have slowed the overall pace of the picture. In the final film, when Bond turns round

to find Scaramanga missing, Scaramanga is next seen coming round the corner of the fun house. According to Christopher Lee, the way the film was originally shot is evident from the expression on his face suggesting that he was not going to play by the rules of the duel. As Bond walks away from him he dives out of the frame and disappears. Bond realises Scaramanga is hiding in the rocks and the two have a long conversation shouting at one another, with Bond also hiding behind rocks. Bond tries to flush Scaramanga out by flinging a thermos of petrol into the air and exploding it above Scaramanga's head. This incident was shot and actually appears in the trailer. Scaramanga dodges the thermos and he and Bond end up in the fun house.

Principal photography on *The Man with the Golden Gun* began in Hong Kong harbour on November 6th 1973 when Hamilton and a skeleton camera crew filmed "Magic Hour" on the Queen Elizabeth. The key to shooting the decapitated Queen, lying in state, was to shoot at a special time just before dawn, when there was enough light to register on film naturally and yet enough darkness to simulate nightfall or dusk. This was known as "Magic Hour". In the sequence, a motor launch takes Bond across the harbour to the Queen Elizabeth which Bond discovers is "M" 's Far Eastern headquarters. For this early sequence, actor Mike Lovatt was doubling Roger Moore who was not due in Hong Kong until the following April. The sequence works well and is one of the film's most vivid moments. Later in the processing lab, at Pinewood, a painting of the illuminated Hong Kong skyline was matted into the scene.

Five months later, in mid April 1974, a major Eon crew assembled in Phuket and journeyed out to Khow-Ping-Kan. The first scene shows the landing of Bond's seaplane in Scaramanga's grotto. An accident nearly destroyed the plane as well as its pilot, Colonel Claire, who was doubling for Moore. John Stears went to work and destroyed the plane properly with explosives. In the film, Scaramanga demonstrates his solar cannon by blasting the seaplane apart.

Once the amphibian stunts were completed, Hamilton began working with his principals. Meanwhile, second unit director Derek Cracknell was filming the exterior of a Red Chinese listening post which guards the approaches to Scaramanga's island. After that sequence was completed, the unit moved to Hong Kong and then returned to London for Peter Murton's interiors.

Peter Murton became the third man to be employed as production designer on a James Bond film. He had worked with Ken Adam on *Dr. Strangelove* in 1963 and Adam asked Murton to join him on *Goldfinger*. From 1965 to 1968, Murton was art director on such films as *Thunderball*, *The Ipcress File*, *Funeral in Berlin* and in 1968, he was given his first job as chief production designer on *The Lion in Winter*.

One of the major criticisms of *The Man with the Golden Gun* was that the script failed to make good use of Murton's interiors. The most ambitious of all the sets, the solar energy room, was barely used in the film and was attended by only one actor. The solar energy room featured huge generators and a background utilising blinding colours and computer consoles that controlled the huge fan-like refractor which caught the sun and fueled the entire apparatus.

More time was spent in Murton's fun house which though repeated in a tiresome way in the film's finale was fascinating in the film's teaser in which Scaramanga takes on the Mafia hit man. On Murton's drawing board, the fun house combined the features of many amusement park attractions, including a maze, a house of mirrors and a shooting gallery.

Murton's other sets included Scaramanga's bedroom on the Chinese junk (his sea-borne base), Bond's hotel suite where he beds first Mary Goodnight and then Andrea, and the slanting headquarters of the British Secret Service which are hidden aboard the sinking Queen Elizabeth. Murton's interiors were well up to the standards expected on a Bond film. Responsibility for the failure of *The Man with the Golden Gun* lay elsewhere.

11
ESTHER WILLIAMS SWIMS AGAIN

The Spy Who Loved Me featured the most daring stunt of the entire James Bond series. The idea had come to Cubby Broccoli via a Canadian Club whisky advertisement in which ace ski-jumper Rick Sylvester was pictured flying off Greenland's Asgard. Making enquiries, Broccoli learned that the Arctic stunt had been faked and that it had really been done off the El Capitan peak in Yosemite Valley, California. Sylvester had at-

Ski jumper Rick Sylvester. For $30,000, he ski jumped off Baffin Island's 3000-foot Asgard peak and parachuted to safety in THE SPY WHO LOVED ME.

tempted to jump the Asgard but weather conditions had made it impossible.

Broccoli contacted Sylvester and made him a James Bond sized offer to do the stunt for *The Spy Who Loved Me*. The script called for Bond to be chased out of his Berngarten ski lodge by four Russian ski troops carrying machine guns. Bond eludes most of them but ends up skiing down a one way precipice that leads to a 3000 foot drop. Without flinching, he goes over the cliff and falls and falls and falls, losing skis and poles until his parachute opens to reveal the British Union Jack. Bond glides gently into the cool Arctic snow.

The stunt was so outrageous that Broccoli could hardly believe it was possible. The spiral

THE SPY WHO LOVED ME (1977)
PC. Eon Productions – A United Artists Release 125 mins Col. **PROD.** Albert R. Broccoli **DIR.** Lewis Gilbert **SCR.** Christopher Wood and Richard Maibaum from a novel by Ian Fleming **PH.** Claude Renoir **ED.** John Glen **PROD DES.** Ken Adam **MUSIC.** Marvin Hamlisch **SP EFFECTS SUPERV.** Derek Meddings **UNDERWATER PH.** Lamar Boren
CAST. Roger Moore (James Bond), Barbara Bach (Major Anya Amasova), Curt Jurgens (Karl Stromberg), Richard Kiel (Jaws), Caroline Munro (Naomi) Walter Gotell (General Gogol), Geoffrey Keen (Minister of Defence), Bernard Lee ("M"), Shane Rimmer (Captain Carter), Bryan Marshall (Commander Talbot), Michael Billington (Sergei), Olga Bisera (Felicca), Desmond Llewelyn ("Q"), Edward de Souza (Sheik Hossein),Vernon Dobcheff (Max Kalba), Valerie Leon (Hotel Receptionist), Lois Maxwell (Miss Moneypenny), Sidney Tafler (Liparus Captain) Nadim Sawalha (Fekkesh), Sue Vanner (The Cabin Girl), Eva Reuber-Staier (Rubelvitch), Robert Brown (Admiral Hargreaves), Marilyn Galsworthy (Stromberg's Assistant), Milton Reid (Sandor), Cyril Shaps (Bechmann), Milo Sperber (Markovitz), Albert Moses (Barman), Rafiq Anwar (Cairo Club Waiter).

jump in *The Man with the Golden Gun* had been worked out by computer. Here it was a matter of chance. Scriptwriter Christopher Wood had even taken the stunt further by having the parachuting Bond land on a lake behind a speedy motorboat, where he fires a grappling iron which hooks to the boat and becomes an instant water skiier.

Second unit director/editor John Glen was scheduled to lead a team to the ski site to shoot the stunt before principal photography began in August 1976. Sylvester found the Asgard ideal.

New Yorker Barbara Bach plays Russian superspy Anya Amasova, the title character in THE SPY WHO LOVED ME. *(UPI)*

The Asgard is a 3000 foot narrow ledged peak in the Auquittuq National Park on Canada's Baffin Island fifteen hundred miles north of Montreal. Its summit is a football field's length, covered with a carpet of snow and accessible only by helicopter.

The first requirement was a vertical cliff, meaning a true ninety degrees; the second was skiable terrain. The cliff had to be high. The higher the better since it would be not only more spectacular but safer. It would give time to get rid of the skis and deploy the parachute, not to mention more time to react if something went wrong. A suitable landing area and the right wind conditions were obvious essentials.

Sylvester was flanked by his friend Bob Richardson, an expert climber who was to handle safety on the Asgard, working with camera rigs and keeping a watchful eye on the less experienced climbers, and Jim Buckley, a parachute expert who was in charge of repacking Sylvester's parachute if the need arose and of keeping track of wind conditions. Monsieur Claude, the proprietor of a Montreal film production company served as local liaison. Other personnel included a doctor, René Dupont, the film's production coordinator in Canada, Alan Hume, the principal cameraman, two other cameramen, one assistant cameraman, two helicopter pilots and one helicopter mechanic.

In early July 1976, Glen's crew arrived at the little village of Pangnirtung and settled in a comfortable ex-Hudson Bay hunting lodge to wait for suitable weather. The Asgard was fifty miles away. While waiting, Glen shot some test footage as well as the actual approach shot which showed Sylvester skiing to the take off point. Long hours were spent determining the camera positions and responsibilities. After ten days had elapsed, impatient calls from London began to come in. Nothing could be done, however, without the right conditions. Even when conditions were eventually deemed to be satisfactory for filming the stunt there was considerable pressure on the crew to complete the attempt swiftly since it seemed that the clouds might shortly regroup to obscure the Asgard.

Nearby, the Jet Ranger camera helicopter hovered out of range of the cliff face so that the draught of the propeller would not interfere with Sylvester's parachute. Alan Hume manned the helicopter camera which was to take the master shot of the sequence. The other two cameras were of secondary importance.

Exactly three minutes before a huge cloud blotted out the sun and enshrouded the Asgard in shade, Sylvester received the go ahead from Glen, dropped into the egg position and started his ski run. He bumped across a mini-ice bulge, remained steady and then shot over the cliff, practically over the head of one of the cliff placed cameramen.

On top of the Asgard, Glen was too busy cueing his cameramen to actually see Sylvester's stunt. He was already learning that, despite the tests and the painstaking precautions, Hume, in the helicopter, had lost Sylvester soon after he dropped over the wall. It was up to the ledge cameramen to save the day.

To the relief of all concerned it was later confirmed that the film was "adequate". Although the helicopter had lost Sylvester, one of the ledge cameramen had caught the entire stunt intact. The parachute had opened, not quite perfectly, to reveal the Union Jack and looked beautiful.

Like *From Russia with Love*, Ian Fleming's tenth novel, *The Spy Who Loved Me* was an experiment that was only partially successful. This time, Fleming chose to tell the story through the eyes of a woman, a young English girl named Vivian Michel who journeys to America in search of adventure. Vivian rents a little motor scooter and tours the Eastern seaboard of the United States until she ends up in a deserted motel in upstate New York. Here, in a *Psycho*-like setting, the girl is tormented by two American thugs who are intent on burning down the motel for insurance money.

It is only near the end of the book, when Vivien is about to be raped and killed that James Bond, like the US Cavalry, arrives to clean up this backwoods situation. To Vivian, Bond's English accent is a whisper from God. In true form he despatches the loathsome villains, restores Vivian's faith in the male, takes her to bed and then leaves before the story gets too mushy.

Broccoli was alone now. In desperate need of capital, Harry Saltzman had sold off his interests in the Bond films to United Artists for a reputed thirty million dollars. United Artists were now partners in this rejuvenated Bond series and

Moore and Bach at the London premiere of THE SPY WHO LOVED ME. *(Wide World)*

Broccoli was the sole producer. No sooner was *The Man with the Golden Gun* in general release than Broccoli began the process of developing an entirely new story to fit the Fleming title.

The writing of *The Spy Who Loved Me* was something of a nightmare. No less than twelve script writers had a crack at it and there were at least fifteen different drafts of the script on Broccoli's desk at any one moment. It became a question of who could be the most innovative and yet stay within the bounds of credibility.

On this new project, the writers were asked to work from scratch, bearing in mind a guideline from Broccoli who thought that "The Spy" in question should be a Russian agent who falls in

Code-named Esther Williams in an early draft screenplay, Bond's Lotus submarine car was the highlight of the film. *(Don Griffin, Perry Submarines)*

love with Bond. Broccoli's stepson, Michael Wilson, now a practising lawyer who, along with executive William Cartlidge divided the production load once shared by Saltzman, was intensely involved with the negotiations with script writers.

Wilson remembers the many legal problems they faced in getting the project cleared with the Fleming estate. Through a prior agreement, they had the right to create new Bond stories beyond those written by Fleming. This allowed them to negotiate for the use of *The Spy Who Loved Me* title which they were allowed to use only if they created an entirely new story line.

A New York comic book writer and author, Cary Bates, submitted a script on the recommendation of Roald Dahl. This was an adaptation of Fleming's *Moonraker* novel which was also being considered as a possible title for the series. Bates had taken the character of Hugo Drax and given him a SPECTRE association with a huge underground base at Loch Ness in Scotland. The story concerned a SPECTRE plot to hijack a nuclear submarine and Bond's attempt to foil the plot with the help of Russian Agent Tatiana Romanova (the girl in *From Russia with Love*). It was an interesting script but Broccoli was hesitant to proceed with it. Instead, he hired the novelist Ronald Hardy to start afresh. Ironically, Hardy also developed a story about nuclear submarines, this time featuring a sophisticated electronic tracking device that allows the villain to pinpoint and capture enemy submarines. If the script itself did not impress Broccoli, the tracking device idea encouraged him to explore this field further with another scriptwriter, Anthony Barwick.

Barwick took the tracking device and gave it to a villain named Zodiac whose henchmen

Model nuclear submarines stand in crates on the docks of Perry Submarines in Florida prior to assembly of electrical motors. *(Don Griffin, Perry Submarines)*

include the sinister triplets, Tic, Tac and Toe. If the Western powers fail to surrender their art treasures, Zodiac intends to destroy fleets of nuclear submarines with his long range torpedoes.

Barwick left the project and was followed in order by Derek Marlowe; Sterling Silliphant, John Landis and Anthony Burgess (the author of *A Clockwork Orange*). Burgess developed the most outrageous of all the scripts, an undisguised parody of the world of James Bond. Michael Wilson felt that in writing their Bond scripts, the writers tended to fall into the same trap, thinking mainly in terms of set pieces, to the detriment of a strong story line. When Richard Maibaum was eventually brought in to work on the script, Guy Hamilton was once again signed up to direct his fifth Bond film.

Early in 1976, Maibaum decided to retain the SPECTRE influence but to get rid of the typical Blofeld-type old guard. He introduced a young cadre of international terrorists, members of the Red Brigade, the Bader Meinhof gang, the Black September Organisation and the Japanese Red Army, who had come together to form the new SPECTRE.

Uninterested in blackmail or extortion, they intend to destroy the world, by capturing a nuclear submarine and wiping out the world's oil fields. In the script's opening scenes, the youngsters burst into SPECTRE headquarters and assassinate the old guard. Then they put their plan into operation.

Maibaum was completing his script with some location scouting in Budapest when Guy Hamilton suddenly left the project. Broccoli subsequently signed up Lewis Gilbert who had directed *You Only Live Twice* a decade earlier. Gilbert brought with him his own choice of scriptwriter, Christopher Wood, who began reworking the Maibaum draft.

Broccoli had liked Maibaum's script but he felt that the young SPECTRE group of terrorists was much too political. Wood eliminated the terrorist group and instead brought back a Blofeld-type character. His name is Stavros, a shipping magnate who owns a huge supertanker. The supertanker is equipped with a special bow that allows it to open up and swallow nuclear submarines. The tanker idea was Maibaum's, dating back to 1970 and the *Diamonds Are Forever* script when Blofeld commandeered a huge tanker as a firing platform for his laser cannon.

In the final Wood draft, SPECTRE uses the special tracking system to capture a Russian and a British submarine. Bond and a Russian agent named Major Anya Amasova (Maibaum's creation) are sent to Cairo to find a SPECTRE traitor who is putting the tracking system on the open market. Each agent thinks the other is behind the hijacking. They play a game of spy versus spy in Cairo until it is revealed that a third party has been playing them off against each other (in typical SPECTRE style). Bond and Anya then join forces and trace the tracking system to Stavros's base off the coast of Sardinia.

Stavros's chief henchman finally became the Jaws character, replacing earlier tentative ideas of look-alike bodyguards in both the Bates and the Barwick treatments. Jaws, a giant of a killer with cobalt steel teeth, became a one man indestructible army and survived to return in the next Bond film *Moonraker*. He is the only Bond film henchman ever to do so. In casting the part, Broccoli at first considered Will Sampson, the huge Indian in *One Flew over the Cuckoo's Nest,* but then decided on the seven foot two inch Richard Kiel to play the part.

Practically overnight, Kiel became a cult figure and established a name for himself in an industry that had almost always relegated him to the part of the bit villain in numerous television dramas. Broccoli had seen him as Patrick McGoohan's assistant in *The Silver Streak* where he was an awesome sight on a train, with his shoulders often wedged near the ceiling. The effectiveness of his train-borne presence probably influenced the writers to include him in the train sequence in *The Spy Who Loved Me,* when, on a trip from Cairo to Sardinia, Bond and Anya are attacked in their compartment by the huge

Curt Jurgens as evil shipping magnate Karl Stromberg. *(20th Century Fox)*

assassin whose dinner plate sized hands give Roger Moore outsized trouble.

With SPECTRE, Stavros, and Jaws established as the film's villains, the writers began to work on Bond and his equipment. In *The Spy Who Loved Me,*

Roger Moore finally grew into the James Bond part. The gadgets and set pieces were there, but this time it was a three dimensional Moore who brought 007 to life. In the Maibaum/Wood script, Moore has two key dramatic moments that were entirely lacking in his previous efforts. Both of them occur with the American actress Barbara Bach, who, as Anya, makes a very fine Russian agent.

The most impressive moment is in their hotel suite in Sardinia after a hair raising chase sequence in which Bond eludes a combined assault by enemy motor cyclists, cars and helicopters, by taking his specially equipped Lotus Esprit into the Mediterranean where it becomes an instant submarine. Bond lights a cigar with a special cigarette lighter which Anya admires. When she asks him where he got it he tells her it came from

English actress Caroline Munroe turned many heads in THE SPY WHO LOVED ME as Stromberg's seductive helicopter pilot Naomi.

Berngarten in Austria where he had been skiing. This startles Anya whose lover, a Russian agent, was recently killed in Berngarten while on a mission (a mission to kill James Bond.)

She shows him a picture of her lover and Bond replies that he does know the face. However, when Anya states that he was killed while on a mission, Bond confesses that he probably killed him during a high speed ski chase. Anya turns cold and informs Bond that when the mission is over, she will kill him. She then walks away. *The Spy Who Loved Me* is not a serious film in the Bond series and much of it is, as usual, tied into slapstick and pun saturated dialogue. However, this short emotional scene (perhaps no more than five minutes) serves to elevate the film above the usual buffoonery. In Roger Moore's case, it was his best scene for years, warmly nostalgic of the early Connery Bonds when things were handled differently. The look on Moore's face during the sequence, his mannerisms, the whole feel of the moment seems to be from an earlier age.

The budget of *The Spy Who Loved Me*, almost fourteen million dollars, indicated that United Artists was ready to invest in the most expensive and impressive effects ever used in the series, despite having received rather disappointing box office returns on the previous Roger Moore Bonds. *The Spy Who Loved Me* was to be another globe trotter, with expensive location work in the Bahamas, Switzerland, Sardinia, Egypt, Scotland, and Baffin Island. The special effects budget was trebled and plans were drafted to create the ultimate Bond gimmick, a submarine car.

The submarine car had gone through several transformations in the various screenplay drafts. It had appeared as early as the Cary Bates script when its code name was "Esther Williams". In later drafts it became "Wet Nellie", a kind reference to the "Little Nellie" auto-giro which had been such a hit in *You Only Live Twice*. The submarine car was actually the product of two creative geniuses, production designer Ken Adam and special effects coordinator Derek Meddings, who had replaced John Stears five years earlier as Broccoli's effects wizard.

Meddings, who deserved an Oscar for his special effects work on *The Spy Who Loved Me*, but had the misfortune of competing with *Star Wars* and *Close Encounters of the Third Kind* in the

On location in Sardinia with Moore and Bach.
(Wide World)

same year, recalls that when it was decided to turn the sports car into a submarine, Ken Adam suggested they use the shell of the new Lotus Esprit. Neither knew anything about the aquadynamics of underwater driving but they went ahead with the Lotus considering it to be the most beautiful car in England. They were given the car in shell form from the Lotus factory. With half a dozen of these, they built separate operating effects into each one.

To give the car an underwater streamlined effect, wheels had to be created that could disappear inside the body and wheel arches that could come down to fill the space. Louvres were built over the windscreen to create the impression of strengthening the glass against underwater pressure.

Only one car was equipped to work under-

water. It had an engine and could be driven underwater like an aeroplane. When it turned, it banked, and it could dive and climb. Two men were assigned to drive it. The special modifications such as the surface to air missile launcher, the underwater rockets and the mine laying panel were all constructed and perfected in the Pinewood special effects shop.

When the Pinewood effects unit had finished with their modifications, Meddings transported the shell of the Lotus to Perry Submarines, in Miami, a unique underwater engineering firm building submarines and underwater scooters for the US Navy. They were the final authority on "Wet Nellie's" workability. The plan was to have two skin divers driving the vehicle wearing breathing apparatus. They did not want a dry submersible. "When you build something that has an air compartment, you have problems with ballast. You're faced with the problem of continually pumping ballast in and out of the car. And

Celebrating his 49th birthday at the base of the Pyramids, Roger Moore takes a turn with a local belly wiggler. *(Wide World)*

that was something we wanted to avoid," said Ken Adam.

Perry Submarines looked at the designs and said they could motorise the car. They also gave Adam the idea of having the car drivers use a rebreather unit that did not leave a telltale trail of bubbles. However, regular aqualungs were used in the end, not only because they were safer but also because Adam and Meddings realised that without any bubbles coming from the car a degree of conviction would be sacrificed. With the bubbles trailing the car from the aqualungs there was a much more persuasive picture of a car moving underwater. The last thing Adam wanted was the impression that a model car was being used in the studio tank.

The underwater sequences with the motorised Lotus Esprit were filmed in the clear waters of the Bahamas by veteran underwater photographer Lamar Boren returning to the Bond films after a long absence. Michael Wilson was in charge of the Bahamas location and his unit included Derek Meddings whose special effects team was also handling all the miniatures, including the sixty three foot super tanker – hardly a miniature!

In the final Maibaum/Wood screenplay, the super tanker Liparus opens her special bow doors and swallows three nuclear submarines. While all the ocean work was handled in the Bahamas by Meddings's men the interior of the tanker, where the captured submarines are docked was duplicated on the largest soundstage ever constructed at Pinewood.

The script called for Ken Adam to build a full-sized interior of the Liparus with three captured submarines in her belly. The "Jonah" set would also include another working monorail, miles of steel girder work, a dock area, a huge brig, an arsenal, and an impregnable control room with computer banks controlling the submarines' nuclear warheads.

It was originally intended that Ken Adam would design his set within a traditional sound stage. If not at Pinewood, he would make use of another installation, perhaps an old airship hangar like that at Cardigan.

Adam found his airship hangar but the expense of converting it into a sound stage with a huge water tank to accommodate the nuclear sub-

Production designer Ken Adam who holds the secrets to 007's fantasy world. *(Charles Sherman)*

marines was equal to that of constructing an entirely new stage at Pinewood. Add to this the cost of transporting crews back and forth between the studio and the hangar and the total was prohibitive. Adam reasoned that the only way to do it right was to follow the example of *You Only Live Twice* and build it on the lot.

So Eon Productions entered the real estate business, investing a million dollars in a brand new sound stage, to be constructed near the old Fort Knox exterior that had been torn down soon after its construction. The decision to build a whole stage was based on Adam's experience with the volcano set on *You Only Live Twice* when the elements continually hampered filming. This time, four walls and a roof protected the tanker complex.

The stage was built to accommodate three nuclear submarines five eighths actual size. A real nuclear submarine is about 425 feet long. That size of vessel would require a set in excess of 600 feet. Adam could not build to that scale because the scale of the men to the ships would have looked awkward.

He first constructed a model of the set which was viewed with awe by the director and the screen writers. The script called for a huge battle to take place within the tanker when Bond releases the captive submarines, who then attempt to take over the tanker before the enemy submarines can fire their nuclear missiles on Moscow and New York. The battle would rage over the entire dock area, on the cat walks, up staircases

A scale model of Stromberg's Atlantis fortress. (Note: Camera and light meter at left indicate size of model.) *(Don Griffin, Perry Submarines)*

and along the corridors where the prisoners break out of their brig and gather weapons in the tanker's arsenal. When the special effects team was finished, the interiors of the Liparus would be set ablaze with dozens of fires and explosions.

In one of the early scripts, the super tanker is controlled from the bridge area, located above the deck of the tanker. In that script, Bond and his men battle to the surface and then attack the bridge along the deck of the ship. When Adam formulated the design for his interior set, it was decided to move the control room inside the tanker (where it strongly resembled Blofeld's communications centre in Adam's volcano set for *You Only Live Twice*).

Adam gives much of the credit for the accuracy and swiftness with which the set was constructed to the Pinewood construction crews who were, by now, used to the type of way-out set design featured in a Bond film. Upon completion the 007 stage measured 374 feet in length, 160 feet in width and 53 feet high. It included an exterior tank

into which Adam placed his nuclear submarine mockups. The set was officially christened Number 007 on December 5th 1976 in a ceremony attended by the British Prime Minister, Harold Wilson.

Rivalling the spectacle of Adam's tanker interior was his exquisite design for Atlantis, Stavros's spider shaped marine laboratory, and the nerve centre of his plans for world destruction. Like the original Atlantis, Adam's structure sits on the bottom of the ocean but has the ability to rise to the surface on huge metal stilts. It becomes the centre of a proposed underwater city to which Stavros will retire once the world is destroyed.

The Atlantis idea was not in the original scripts. Broccoli, Lewis Gilbert and Ken Adam had gone to Okinawa because they had heard about a Japanese structure which could rise out of the water. When they arrived, it turned out to be a

white elephant since Adam found it impossible to use. He decided to design something entirely new and, for the interiors, he determined to get away from his customary straight line concepts. Instead he planned to use circles and ellipses, a style partly influenced by location scouting in Sardinia where much of the architecture along the Costa Smeralda utilises that style. The fish tanks in Atlantis were elliptical, the escape corridors featured elliptical exit ways and Stavros's big shark pond was circular in shape.

Only a short time before shooting started in Sardinia, Broccoli received word that Kevin McClory was filing an injunction against *The Spy Who Loved Me* to hold up production immediately. In what was to become another long and complicated legal battle, McClory claimed that the final Broccoli script was unusually similar to McClory's own Bond project which he had co-written with thriller author Len Deighton and Sean Connery. The McClory script had been written in 1975, ten years after McClory had

A Lotus Esprit arrives from London for underwater conversion. *(Don Griffin, Perry Submarines)*

The Shark Hunter II, a rocket-firing, two-man
submarine. *(Don Griffin, Perry Submarines)*

signed an agreement with Broccoli and Saltzman
that, after *Thunderball*, he would wait a full decade
before producing another Bond film. Whether or
not McClory had the rights to do another project
beyond a remake of his original *Thunderball*, he
was still interested in Broccoli's *The Spy Who
Loved Me* script. The McClory script, variously
referred to as *James Bond of the Secret Service* and
Warhead, also featured a spider-like underwater
headquarters, a shark pond, and concerned itself
with a SPECTRE plot to destroy the world.

Perhaps fearing the possibility of a legal battle
with McClory, who, according to the favourable
decision in the 1963 case with Ian Fleming, had
sole film rights to the SPECTRE organisation,
Broccoli had already told Christopher Wood to
remove all traces of SPECTRE from the final
shooting script of *The Spy Who Loved Me*.

Stavros became Karl Stromberg, a multi-

millionaire shipping magnate who alone plans to
destroy the world. Any reference to his SPECTRE
contacts was eliminated and even his supertanker
security troops wear red, rather than black
SPECTRE uniforms. Such a transformation in
the final script convinced McClory that Broccoli
was definitely poaching on his rights. But there
was little chance that McClory could stop Broccoli
and *The Spy Who Loved Me* at this time. Rather than
pay Broccoli's legal fees in a long and abortive
case, McClory chose instead to withdraw his writ
of injunction and to begin planning his own
production, *Warhead*. The possibility that Sean
Connery would indeed return to play the part of
Bond was a constant thorn in the side of Broccoli
and United Artists. Although satisfied with the
public acceptance of Roger Moore, they were
naturally concerned about the return of Connery
in a rival camp.

Egypt and the Nile play an important part in the
early scenes of *The Spy Who Loved Me*. In Cairo,
Bond searches for the traitor who sent British

Intelligence a tracing of the unique tracking system, and meets his Russian counterpart, Agent Triple X, Anya Amasova.

In the shooting script, Bond finds his old school friend Sheik Hossein in the middle of the desert and learns that the tracking system is being marketed by an Egyptian nightclub owner named Max Kalba. To meet Kalba, Bond is told to contact a man named Fekkesh.

Bond goes to Fekkesh's apartment in Cairo, dallies with his luscious secretary Felicia, and is nearly killed by Sandor, an assassin of Stromberg's. Bond kills Sandor but before the huge muscleman dies, he tells Bond that Fekkesh can be found at the pyramids.

Bond goes to the Pyramids at Gizah only to find that Fekkesh has been murdered by Jaws. Near one of the tombs, Bond meets Anya and her two agent subordinates who are dealt with handily by Bond in a vicious fight. "Hope you enjoyed the show", smiles Bond as he walks away. Anya merely stares. She is impressed. Bond and Anya later resume their acquaintance at Kalba's club and are about to bid for the tracking system when Kalba is called away to a bogus phone call and killed by Jaws. They follow Jaws in a telephone repair truck, a journey that leads them to a ruined city in the desert where they recover the plans for the tracking system and head back to Cairo.

Certain details present in the scripts were eliminated in the final film. Fekkesh is first identified as a curator at the Cairo Museum of Antiques, and Bond goes to the museum instead of the Pyramids for his first rendezvous. In the museum, he encounters the two Russian agents and a big fight occurs in the mummy room. Glass cases are smashed, mummies disintegrate and inane one-liners prevail. (In one sequence after one of the Russians hurls a bust of King Tutenkhamen at Bond, Bond ripostes "Tut Tut").

Bond is overpowered and knocked out to awaken in another part of Cairo, to a powerful electric shock. He looks down the length of his body and sees that electrodes have been applied to his vital areas. The Russians, unaware that a third party is involved, demand to know the location of their missing submarine. Bond remains silent and is about to be given another jolt when Anya arrives. She walks in, takes a look at the situation and screams at her Russian subordinates. She reaches down to detach the electrodes saying, "I can handle this". Bond smiles, quickly knocks out the two guards and jumps out of the window.

In the early treatments, the meeting with Kalba at the nightclub featured a tense high stakes game of backgammon in which Bond comes from behind to win fifty thousand pounds from Kalba who dies before he can pay off. Bond and Anya still go after Jaws, but this time they follow in a sportscar. The desert sequence was much more elaborate with the two agents fighting off marauding bands of Tuareg bandits with Anya's pearl necklace providing them with mini hand grenades.

Beneath the perplexing eye of the Sphinx, Richard Kiel discusses a scene with Cubby Broccoli and Moore. *(Rachard El Koussy, Gamma Liaison)*

The advertisement which inspired THE SPY WHO LOVED ME's teaser sequence. *(Rick Sylvester)*

In the shooting script, the pair team up when their superiors "M" and General Gogol (head of the KGB) inform them that a third party is responsible for the missing submarines. Both are ordered to collect their equipment from "Q" branch. In an earlier version of the script, Anya has her own equipment officer, a bearded Russian named "P" (a codename that prompted the most obvious of one liners).

The role of Anya Amasova was the most important female role in a Bond film since that of Tracy in *On Her Majesty's Secret Service*. Lewis Gilbert was pleased with the casting of American actress Barbara Bach and felt that the relationship between Bond and Anya was something new for the Bond films. He felt that with the advent of the women's liberation movement it was no longer possible to portray a woman simply as window dressing, even in a Bond film.

Sultry Barbara Bach shined as tough KGB agent, Anya Amasova. *(American International)*

Preparing for the Wetbike sequence are Roger Moore, production designer Ken Adam, and Roger's wife, Luisa. *(Emilio Lari, Gamma Liaison)*

Anya is independent, a major in the KGB and Russia's top agent. She is capable of stealing a march on Bond and does so. In *The Spy Who Loved Me*, Bond does not always win and this makes him more human. A certain vulnerability allows Bond's other accomplishments to appear all the more impressive. Barbara Bach was deliberately chosen for her serenity and maturity. It was felt that a very young girl would be quite inappropriate.

Although the big 007 stage was not scheduled for completion until Christmas, it was decided to begin shooting in the studio with the smaller sets. The summer heat of the Egyptian location and tourist problems in Sardinia meant that location shooting had to be postponed.

Broccoli had picked Egypt for the Bond location because he felt that the Middle East was still as mysterious as ever and had never yet been used to advantage in the Bond series. Lewis

Bond's newest toy: the Wetbike, a water motorcycle. *(Emilio Lari, Gamma Liaison)*

Construction of full-sized fragment of the Atlantis fortress, which will be lowered into the ocean off Nassau. Weight: approximately 13 tons. *(Don Griffin, Perry Submarines)*

Lamar Boren's underwater camera. *(Don Griffin, Perry Submarines)*

(Left) photographer Don Griffin, pilot of the Lotus submersible, and Keith Anderson, who commands the Shark Hunter II. *(Don Griffin, Perry Submarines)*

A rear view of the Lotus submersible, AKA Esther Williams, AKA Wet Nellie. *(Don Griffin, Perry Submarines)*

Photographer Lamar Boren (right) explains a new scene to his underwater actors manning the Shark Hunter II. *(Don Griffin, Perry Submarines)*

The Shark Hunter II preparing to go into action. *(Don Griffin, Perry Submarines)*

Gilbert, working with French cinematographer Claude Renoir (grandson of the famous impressionist painter and nephew of the film director) achieved some genuinely atmospheric moments in the desert near Cairo, especially in the ruins of a great Egyptian temple where Bond and Anya stalk Jaws. When their return journey takes them into the desert proper, Renoir's photography and Marvin Hamlisch's pleasing musical score combine for a brief moment to give the film a nostalgic mood – a reminder of simpler times when camels ruled the sands. This atmosphere was well timed in a film which tended to be over glossy and superficial. While the early Bond films always mixed fantasy with the reality of Sean Connery, the Roger Moore Bond films frequently depended on clever stunts and obvious one liners to carry sequences. Seldom is the audience given more than a glimpse of the scenery or a hint of musical mood.

Frogmen preparing an attack on the Lotus. *(Don Griffin, Perry Submarines)*

And then there was one. *(Don Griffin, Perry Submarines)*

A rocket fired by the Shark Hunter barely misses the Lotus. *(Don Griffin, Perry Submarines)*

Atmospheric quality (not simply an ability to "think big") is also at the heart of production designer Ken Adam's achievement in *The Spy Who Loved Me*. His particular ability to combine a feeling for drama with a spontaneous sense of fun is apparent in the continuity sketches for the film. Unlike other projects, "in a Bond film, we create the design of the film as we go along," Adam explains. "We start out with a basic story line, and as location ideas and stunts come our way, we develop the finished film." If the later Bond films can be recognised as the offshoot of those early classics, *Dr. No, Goldfinger* or *Thunderball*, Adam's production design may well be a key factor. The tradition is one he began and it has been developed in the films ever since. In the absence of a strong script, a heavy responsibility is thrown on the designer to keep the audience mesmerised. Ken Adam's ingenuity in this respect is a dazzling feature of *The Spy Who Loved Me*.

NASA's Space Shuttle, instrument of Hugo Drax's
MOONRAKER operation. *(NASA)*

12

THE HARRY HOUDINI SYNDROME

The international box office success of *The Spy Who Loved Me* was followed almost immediately by plans to create *Moonraker*, which, at a final budget of thirty million dollars cost nearly as much as the first eight films combined. This was a huge outlay, but, on the basis of the receipts from *The Spy Who Loved Me*, hardly a risk to Broccoli and United Artists. *The Spy Who Loved Me* had been something of a test for Broccoli. Its success proved that he and his new production team of executive producer Michael Wilson, associate producer William Cartlidge, director Lewis Gilbert and writer Christopher Wood could survive the departure of Harry Saltzman.

With *Star Wars* and *Close Encounters of the Third Kind* pointing the way, it was obvious that now was the time for James Bond to move into outer space, although it took the producers a few months to get the title straight. At the end of *The Spy Who Loved Me* it had been announced that James Bond would return in *For Your Eyes Only*, the title Fleming had given to his 1961 collection of short stories. Only a few months later, however, Broccoli announced that the new James Bond film would be entitled *Moonraker*. This was Fleming's last available novel and a property once owned by the Rank Organisation and the American actor John Payne.

To help finance the film, Broccoli allied himself to a French production company. The eleventh film was to be the first Franco-British co-production in the Bond series. *Moonraker* interiors

---

MOONRAKER (1979) PC. Eon Productions (London) Les Productions Artistes Associés (Paris) 126 mins Col. **PROD.** Albert R. Broccoli – **EXEC PROD.** Michael G. Wilson **DIR.** Lewis Gilbert **SCR.** Christopher Wood based on the novel by Ian Fleming **PH.** Jean Tournier **ED.** John Glen **PROD DES.** Ken Adam **MUSIC.** John Barry **VISUAL EFFECTS SUP.** Dereck Meddings **STUNT ARRANGER.** Bob Simmons
CAST. Roger Moore (James Bond), Lois Chiles (Holly Goodhead), Michael Lonsdale (Hugo Drax), Richard Kiel (Jaws), Corinne Clery (Corinne Dufour), Toshiro Suga (Chang), Bernard Lee ("M"), Desmond Llewelyn ("Q"), Lois Maxwell (Moneypenny), Geoffrey Keen (Frederick Gray), Blanche Ravalec (Dolly), Irka Bochenko (Blonde Beauty), Emily Bolton (Manuela), Michael Marshall (Colonel Scott), Leila Shenina (Hostess on Private Jet), Anne Lonnberg (Museum Guide), Jean Pierre Castaloi (Pilot on Private Jet), Walter Gotel (General Gogol), Douglas Lambert (Mission Control Director), Arthur Howard (Cavendish), Alfie Bass (Consumptive Italian), Brian Keith (Shuttle Pilot), George Birt (Captain of 707), Kim Fortune (FRA Officer), Lizzie Warville (Russian Girl), Funambulists (Johnny Traber's Troupe).

were filmed on soundstages in both France and England. Derek Meddings, once again handling the special effects, used the 007 stage at Pinewood as his base of operations.

Broccoli's first step was to bring in the Bond veteran Tom Mankiewicz to work up an original story with Lewis Gilbert. Mankiewicz was happy to work on the story but he told Broccoli that he wanted no credit for his work. He was now blazing new paths as a writer/producer and no longer wanted his link with Bond to be publicised. Once a new story line had been developed, responsibility for the shooting script was left to Christopher Wood.

In the autumn of 1977, Broccoli and Mankiewicz agreed that Bond should be sent into space via America's new space shuttle, a manned rocket plane that could orbit the earth and yet re-enter the atmosphere like a conventional piloted aircraft.

Work on the film began in earnest with a trip to the National Aeronautics and Space Administration's testing complex in Northern California, where Mankiewicz quickly incorporated NASA's centrifugal force test chamber into the plot of the new film. He took only one look at the G-force trainer to picture Bond strapped in there with someone interfering with the controls.

For Mankiewicz, the problem of attaching a completely new story line to an existing Fleming title was a familiar one. Initially, ideas like that of the centrifuge stimulated him but his method was to put such set pieces to the back of his mind and to pursue his story line until he found appropriate places to insert them. His working method was similar to that of Roald Dahl on *You Only Live Twice*.

Since 1970 and the completion of *On Her Majesty's Secret Service* it was obvious that Broccoli and Eon Productions had bled the Fleming estate of all the best books in the James Bond series. Consequently, they were forced to simply adopt titles, creating, with the estate's permission, reasonably updated stories. Since Broccoli was intent on topping his previous efforts to please his increasingly demanding audiences, attempts were made to find more outlandish stunts, locations, and plot elements. The process had developed into the Harry Houdini syndrome: "Please the audience at all costs".

Yet, so much had been achieved in this area in the earlier films, that real innovation seemed impossible. The scriptwriters therefore applied themselves to bringing a new angle to old ideas. Bond enthusiasts must have observed the similarity between *Moonraker's* gondola chase through Venice and the Dong chase through Bankok's canals in *The Man with the Golden Gun*. The motor boat chase in Brazil in *Moonraker* was clearly based on the motor boat chase in *Live and Let Die*. A cable car fight, a wrestling match with a huge snake, a space age battle in outer space, and a fight in a glass factory were hardly new ideas but with thirty million dollars to spend, Broccoli was able to disguise *Moonraker's* borrowed quantities.

Certain ideas for *Moonraker* came from the previous efforts of a number of scriptwriters,

Borne piggyback on a Boeing 747, the Space Shuttle is later hijacked by Drax's men. *(NASA)*

Spaceborne, and code named MOONRAKER, the
Space Shuttle heads for Drax's radar-proof space
station. *(NASA)*

particularly Richard Maibaum. His motorboat
chase on Lake Mead, cut from *Diamonds Are
Forever,* was brought back for *Moonraker.* The
tactic of rallying a fleet of hotel yachts to cut off
Blofeld's escape and send the SPECTRE chief
over the Hoover Dam was reworked by
Christopher Wood so that Bond is being chased
across a Brazilian river valley by Jaws until the
moment they are about to go over the falls,
whereupon Bond flies off in a converted hang-
glider, leaving Jaws to plummet to his doom, a
variation of the escape routine used by Bond in
The Spy Who Loved Me teaser, when he escapes his
ski-pursuers by parachuting over a cliff. Bond's
armoured Glastron motor boat in *Moonraker* was
yet another version of the *Goldfinger* Aston Martin.
Maibaum's fight in the mummy room of the Cairo
Museum, an interesting set piece dropped from
The Spy Who Loved Me, is reworked in *Moonraker*
when Bond fights with Drax's Chinese manservant, Chang, in the Venice Glass Museum.
However, even with the expertise of the veteran
stuntman Bob Simmons, the sequence is predict-

able and lacks the suspense of similar fights in
You Only Live Twice and *Goldfinger.*

Even the plot of *Moonraker* resembled *The Spy
Who Loved Me.* Hugo Drax, a billionaire industrialist and inventor of the Moonraker fleet of six
shuttle craft plans to send them into outer space
where their human cargo will populate a huge space
station from which lethal orchid bearing cylinders
will depopulate the Earth. Once mankind is
poisoned, Drax's super-race will recolonise the
planet.

When one of America's shuttle craft is hijacked
by Drax's henchmen while being ferried to
England on a Royal Air Force jumbo jet, James
Bond is called in to investigate. Having lethal
orchids depopulate the Earth was a plot device
reminiscent of the plant and animal killing viruses
borne by Blofeld's allergy victims in *On Her
Majesty's Secret Service.* Nevertheless, the con-

Jaws (Richard Kiel) returns to torment Bond in Rio, while Holly Goodhead prepares to strike. Note: Artificial background of Rio skyline had yet to be added to this studio scene. *(Gamma Liaison)*

nections made with Mayan legend and super-stition, which told of the disappearance of an entire race, placed the idea in a novel light and enabled the director Lewis Gilbert to compile some exquisite footage of the Brazilian jungles. This, combined with some exotic exterior work in Rio de Janeiro, recalled the old romanticism associated with 007, although Bond was hardly the first to benefit from the mystique of the Brazilian jungle. One of the best of the Bond

spoofs, Jean-Paul Belmondo's *That Man from Rio* had taken rather better advantage of the South American location in 1964.

Even the tradition of including a few topical references (established as early as *Dr. No*, with the shot of the stolen Wellington portrait) fell a little flat in *Moonraker*. Christopher Wood's use of a computerised entry panel in Drax's Venetian laboratory which has a five note musical tone similar to the five note prefix uttered interminably by the alien mother ship in *Close Encounters of the Third Kind*, seems too contrived. The addition of the musical theme from *The Magnificent Seven* to a scene showing Bond dressed as a Brazilian gaucho, galloping up to Secret Service headquarters in

South America is another mistaken attempt at wit, reminiscent of the *Lawrence of Arabia* musical interlude in *The Spy Who Loved Me,* and similarly childish.

A space battle between Drax's space station defence force and a team of NASA spaceshock troops is designed to resemble a scene from *Star Wars* where Empire stormtroopers battle it out with rebels aboard a blockade runner. Here, yet again, the reference lacks any real point. Such devices added nothing to *Moonraker* and served only to emphasise its lack of originality.

The artistic failure of *Moonraker* pinpointed the difficulties that future scriptwriters would face in continuing the adventures of James Bond. Tom Mankiewicz considered that a return to seriousness was not possible.: "The real charm of the books was that they were larger than life, even though Fleming kept them in a kind of believable structure. But once you added the Aston Martin to *Goldfinger,* you couldn't do a serious Bond again."

James Bond today bears little resemblance to the conception of his long dead creator, Ian Fleming. Ironically, although Roger Moore is closer to Fleming's original hero than any other actor who has played him, the dramatic role of Bond in the films steadily diminished as stunts and set pieces took over. The gadgets, the cars, the photography, and John Barry's musical scores all get top billing above Bond in the reviews of recent Bond films.

Broccoli claimed that audiences wanted the Bond films to be more humourous and light hearted and that if there was any change in the character of Bond it was due to audience pressure. Nevertheless, by succumbing to this demand, Broccoli lost sight of the key element in Bond's make-up, the factor that had always made his more outlandish behaviour and abilities believable—his humanity. The literary character of James Bond was an amalgam of many men, but he best reflected his creator, Fleming, a man who smoked too much, drank straight vodka and pushed his body to its physical limits. Throughout his life, Fleming was exposed to health food fanatics, rest and relaxation retreats, pleas from his doctors to slow his pace, and the responsibilities of being a husband and father. Nevertheless, in the end, he gambled everything so that he

"Got you now," intones Richard Kiel to Roger Moore at London's Heathrow Airport. Michael Lonsdale also appears chummy. *(Wide World)*

could maintain the devil-may-care life style he had always wanted.

Fleming's James Bond suffered the same anxieties. Indeed, one of the more important characters throughout the novels and one that is curiously missing from the films is Sir James Maloney, the resident psychiatrist attached to the British Secret Service, one of Bond's best friends, and a comrade who invariably rescues Bond from the brink of retirement and rejection. It is Maloney who convinces "M" that 007 still has one good mission left in him. Nicotine and alcohol poisoning temporarily ignored, Bond is given the chance, gets in shape once more and continues the fight against the evils of a decaying world.

In the early James Bond films, Broccoli and Saltzman, scriptwriter Richard Maibaum, directors Terence Young and Guy Hamilton, editor Peter Hunt, and Sean Connery rallied to bring this characterisation to the screen. The cheap one liners that blanketed the later films, as well as the obsession with mechanical gadgets and gorgeous women, passed over the fact that James Bond was a man with human cravings and weaknesses – never the equivalent of the comic strip Superman. Just as Fleming's wartime experiences combined technological wonders, such as the Enigma decoder, with raw human courage, so James Bond had access to the world's latest weaponry and yet constantly saved his skin with his own two hands.

Ever since 1969 when George Lazenby portrayed Bond as a human agent who shunned gadgets, Broccoli and a growing number of inept scriptwriters began to make the world of Bond all too predictable. Like Superman and the whole range of super heroes that dominate comic books, Bond is always immaculate. His hair is never messy, his suits are never rumpled and it is hard to remember the last time he was actually wounded. The modern Bond invariably takes the easy way out, usually with the aid of some handy gadget. This contrasts with the unpredictable nature of Bond that made Fleming's novels so readable.

In later years, genuine romance also left the series. Bond still ends up with the girl, but the series of events that lead to the climax has become ridiculously contrived and approaches the inanity of a Peter Sellers Pink Panther film.

At one time, Broccoli and Saltzman claimed that their series of spy dramas was "spoof proof ." If true, credit was due to Maibaum's deft writing touch, Connery's one line delivery and Peter Hunt's editing. Today, Maibaum is gone. (Although he co-wrote *The Spy Who Loved Me* his script was changed considerably). Gone too are Connery, Saltzman and Peter Hunt. Broccoli has had a difficult time replacing them. His company now resembles the Union Army before Gettysburg, flushed with manpower and resources but possessing little imagination.

Whereas Terence Young's one time army of rebels created striking adventures on miniscule

Lovely Lois Chiles portrayed CIA agent Holly Goodhead. *(Columbia Pictures)*

budgets, Broccoli's recent productions, despite huge budgets, only seem to imitate the past. With the exception of *On Her Majesty's Secret Service*, Broccoli and Saltzman, and now Broccoli alone have been recycling the same material for ten years, the only change being the name of the villain and the size of the budget.

The fact remains, however, that *Moonraker*, disappointing as it may have been to cultists, has more than succeeded with the cinema-going public. This has to be explained. Not all of Bond's audience are Bond historians and there is a whole generation that may well be unfamiliar with the earlier films. Broccoli's astute insistence on updating the Bond image has meant the continuation of a fantasy that still satisfies the popular imagination. The early Bond films tended to create fashion; the later ones reflect it, absorbing lessons from other films currently successful at the box-office.

Broccoli frequently defends what has become of Bond on the basis of the need to update the hero and this is not unreasonable. Bond's mechanical knowledge has always been sound, even in the early novels where he was capable of making a racing change on his Bentley, or applying a limpet mine to the hull of a yacht. Bond in the eighties must surely possess the latest knowledge about nuclear fission and space chemistry and be able, if necessary, to fly a rocket ship. Bond's women too have moved with the times and are now more active than before. Women like Major Anya Amasova and Holly Goodhead now join battle alongside Bond, fighting off the enemy with equal proficiency.

If Bond's current adventures seem to be the bland artifact of the production line rather than the fruits of individual invention, we must accept that the durability of the myth resides in Bond's streamlined "Superman" image rather than in the tough individualism for which the cultists admire 007. Perhaps the biggest myth of all is to believe that cultists and public identify with the same hero. There is, indeed, every indication that the Bond saga will continue, despite the limitation of new titles.

Richard "Jaws" Kiel once again terrorized Barbara Bach in FORCE TEN FROM NAVARONE. (*American International*)

Adam's marvelous space station set. (*Michael Ginfray, Gamma Liaison*)

Another of Q. branch's marvels: this one waterborne.
(*Glastron Boat Company*)

The Moore family: Roger, Christian, Deborah, and Luisa. (*Wide World*)

007, once again in danger. *(Rick Sylvester)*

13

BASIC EYE EXERCISES

What emerged in the twelfth James Bond movie, *For Your Eyes Only* which was released in America in July of 1981, was a new direction for the series and a long awaited return to the serious fun of the original Bonds. The fact that Roger Moore was consistently beaten up, and endangered, indicated to critics and the public alike that the era of the automaton Bond was ending. For international Bond fans, the summer of 1981 was a summer of joyous celebration. James Bond was back and seemed better than ever.

Soon after the release of *Moonraker* in 1979, producers Cubby Broccoli and his new right arm, stepson Michael Wilson, began formulating plans to bring Bond back down to Earth in a profound way. Abandoning the mindlessness of the Christopher Wood scripts, they immediately brought Richard Maibaum back to write *For Your Eyes Only*.

The plan was to rekindle the adventure and exotic appeal of earlier Bond films like *From Russia with Love* and *On Her Majesty's Secret Service*, Maibaum's best scripts, and apply that class to two of Ian Fleming's best short stories, *For Your Eyes Only* and *Risico*.

In the original *For Your Eyes Only*, written by Fleming in 1960 as part of the abortive TV project, a group of Cuban hitmen led by Gonzalez arrive in Jamaica to buy an English plantation for a renegade ex-Nazi named von Hammerstein. The former Gestapo chief is fleeing the collapse of the Batista regime in Cuba and needs a convenient base of operations.

When the plantation owners, a Mr. Havelock and his wife, refuse to sell their Jamaican property, Gonzalez shoots them down and later threatens their beautiful daughter, Judy. 007 enters the scene when "M," a friend of the Havelocks, sends him to Vermont where the Cubans are hiding out with von Hammerstein. Bond's mission: assassination.

In the dense forest that surrounds the isolated compound, Bond discovers a stalking Judy Havelock, armed with bow and arrow. They join forces and eventually wipe out the nest of criminals.

In *Risico*, another of the aborted TV pilots, 007

FOR YOUR EYES ONLY (1981) PC. PROD.
Albert R. Broccoli **DIR.** John Glen **SCR.**
Richard Maibaum
ORIGINAL TREATMENT.
Richard Maibaum and Michael Wilson
EXEC PROD. Michael Wilson **PROD DES.**
Peter Lamont **DP.** Alan Hume **SP EFFECTS.**
Derek Meddings **FILM ED.** John Grover

STUNTS. Rick Sylvester and Willy Bogner
CAST. Roger Moore (James Bond),
Carole Bouquet (Melina Havelock), Topol
(Columbo), Julian Glover (Kristatos),
Cassandra Harris (Lisl), Lynn-Holly Johnson
(Bibi), Jill Bennett (Jacoba Brink),
Michael Gothard (Locque), John Wyman
(Kriegler).

Special effects experts wire the Esprit with explosives while a 007 dummy looks on. *(Manita, Gamma Liaison)*

is sent to Rome to break up a smuggling ring that is flooding England with heroin. Bond is told to contact a CIA double agent named Kristatos, who will offer to break up the opium trade for a price.

Kristatos agrees to help Bond and soon points the finger at the mysterious Mr. Colombo, an Italian smuggler. Bond journeys to Venice to seduce Colombo's mistress, Lisl Baum, but is captured instead. Aboard Colombo's trawler headquarters, he discovers that Kristatos is the true head of the heroin smuggling operation, taking his orders from the Russians.

Bond joins forces with Colombo and together they disrupt Kirstatos's operations, ambushing an Albanian smuggling vessel and killing Kristatos and his men in a fierce gun battle on the Italian docks.

In the spring of 1980, Maibaum, working directly with Wilson, who shared credit in the story treatment, used the two Fleming short stories as the basis for a more typical Bondian film caper.

At the beginning of the film *For Your Eyes Only,* the St. Georges, a British fishing trawler/ surveillance ship on duty off the Greek mainland, is sunk by an old World War II mine caught in her fishing nets. Lost in the wreck is A.T.A.C. (Automatic Targeting Attack Communicator), a secret device which uses an ultralow frequency coded transmitter to order British Polaris submarines to launch ballistic missiles.

The lost transmitter soon becomes the prize in a typical British–Russian confrontation—the Russians working through their Greek agent, Kristatos—the British, secretly, through an English marine archaeologist named Havelock.

In reading Fleming's short story *For Your Eyes Only,* Maibaum was particularly impressed with the Judy Havelock character, a beautiful, athletic woman who is consumed by revenge for her slain parents. Even Bond's charms are impotent until after the Vermont assassination takes place. The sight of Havelock stalking her enemies with bow and arrow was inspiring enough to provide another subplot to the film story—a tale of revenge.

In the Maibaum script, Judy became Melina, a young Marine archaeologist who returns to the family exploration ship with a Cuban seaplane pi-

lot named Gonzalez. Gonzalez is actually working for Kristatos who through his Russian contacts knows that Havelock is working secretly for the British and is about to launch an underwater search for the sunken St. Georges. While Melina is below deck, Gonzalez dive bombs the ship, raking the deck with machine gun fire, killing Melina's parents instantly.

Armed with a crossbow, Melina begins searching for Gonzalez, a mission that coincides with James Bond's search for the missing A.T.A.C. device. The adventure moves across the face of Greece from the island of Corfu to the mountainous interior and then on to snowbound Cortina d'Ampezza.

Maibaum and Wilson kept the *Risico* plot intact, transferring the Kristatos/Colombo rivalry from Italy to Greece. The two Italian smugglers became ex-Greek partisans with bad blood between them. Colombo became the incarnation of Bond's old friend Kerim Bey, a wonderful fun-loving man who treats Bond like his son (portrayed by Israeli actor Topol).

Kristatos (Julian Glover) comes across as the most believable Bond villain in years, deceiving the audience as the mild mannered sponsor of a young ice skater (Lynn Holly Johnson).

What the new film succeeds in doing is introducing many mysterious characters, an earthy rivalry reminiscent of the Kerim Bey/Krilencu relationship in *From Russia with Love,* a beautiful, motivated woman in Melina Havelock, who is a combination of Tilly Masterson from *Goldfinger* and Domino from *Thunderball,* and for once, some very dangerous activity for Bond.

A Greek monastery atop the Meteora. *(Rick Sylvester)*

A further protest: The Monk's Laundry! *(Rick Sylvester)*

The sign tells all. *(Rick Sylvester)*

As Bond, Roger Moore finally gets his hair messed up, and more. Seldom stopping for as much as a sliver of caviar, he finds himself in one knockabout after another, attacked by sharks and enemy submersibles, his skin flayed along an Aegean reef, his body pummeled by a hockey stick, assailed by spear-carrying fishermen and gun-toting longshoremen, with plenty of daredevil action on the ski slopes and the highways.

Principal photography on *For Your Eyes Only* began in early September 1980, on location in Corfu, Cortina d'Ampezza, and the Bahamas, where veteran filmmaker and photographer Al Giddings was filming the underwater sequences of Bond and Melina recovering the A.T.A.C. from the sunken St. Georges.

Several noteworthy items cropped up in the early pre-production on the film. One concerned Roger Moore's apparent reluctance to do the film unless the pot was considerably sweetened (it was, although a new casting search for Bond was launched). Another story concerned the arrival of a new director, if not an unfamiliar face, John Glen.

Glen was a Bond veteran of many fronts, in-cluding the second units on both *On Her Majesty's Secret Service,* where he coordinated many of the ski sequences, and *The Spy Who Loved Me,* where he was in charge of Rick Sylvester's ski jump off the Asgard in Greenland.

A top-notch editor, Glen was an obvious choice for *For Your Eyes Only.* Lewis Gilbert, Ken Adam and the costly Pinewood interiors they pro-posed were jettisoned this time. Replacing them was a glittering array of exotic locations, earthy settings, and some tough stunt action that will reinspire many an ex-Bond fan and perpetuate the Harry Houdini syndrome. Even the music in the new film is different, the product of Bill Conti's expertise, not John Barry's.

When Bond scales the cliffs below Kristatos's Greek monastery hideout, it is Rick Sylvester who once more dons the stuntman/double's boots. Sylvester, the world's most expensive stuntman, was sent to Greece to perform the haz-ardous climbing chores where Bond breaks into the abandoned monastery complex.

During the climb, Sylvester was asked to lose his footing and fall over 100 feet where Bond hangs from a single rope. The stunt was much deadlier than the Asgard ski jump because Sylves-ter had no idea where he would land, how he would land, and whether the rope would support his fall. Helping him along this time, the special effects department eventually devised a sand bag stabilizing device that would cushion Sylvester's descent.

Tragedy struck the *For Your Eyes Only* crew from two directions in 1981. During the bobrun sequences in Cortina, where a skiborne Bond is chased by spike-wheeled motorcyclists, a bobsled overturned, killing one of the occupants, the first time in many years that a stuntman was injured on a Bond movie. Then, in January, actor Bernard Lee died in London before he could even begin his scenes as Bond's stalwart chief, "M." It was a demoralizing blow to the Bond crew and a personal loss to Broccoli who had used Lee's tal-ents in every Bond film.

Maibaum was forced to rewrite the script in certain parts, introducing Chief of Staff Tanner as Bond's boss in this episode, with "Q" taking over for "M" in other scenes. The forever frustrated Miss Moneypenny, Lois Maxwell, remains the only survivor of all twelve films.

"Welcome aboard the 007 Express!" *(Rick Sylvester)*

The rising star of Roger Moore? No. A funny scene from 1981's CANNONBALL RUN. *(20th Century Fox)*

On the rocks with the 007 crew. *(Rick Sylvester)*

A "Saint" in monk's garb. *(Rick Sylvester)*

Between *Diamonds Are Forever* and *Never Say Never Again*, Sean Connery continued to be one of the world's busiest actors, seen here as King Agamemnon in *Time Bandits* and as Dr Meredith in Fred Zinneman's *Five Days One Summer*. (Avco Embassy-Ladd Company)

14
NEVER SAY OCTOPUSSY AGAIN!

Had Ian Fleming survived to see the summer of 1983 (he would have turned 75 on May 28th), he would have been overjoyed to learn that his venerable hero, James Bond, was more popular than ever. Two 007 spectaculars with a collective price tag of more than $50 million were about to be released within weeks of each other. For the Bond fan, it was an embarrassment of riches.

How could there be two Bond films in one summer? Actually, it wasn't entirely unprecedented. Although they weren't released in the same season, sixteen years ago (1967) two 007 adventures, Columbia Pictures' *Casino Royale* and United Artists' *You Only Live Twice* did hit the box office within a few months of each other. Producer Albert Broccoli later regretted that Charles K. Feldman's spoofy *Casino Royale* had beaten his Connery entry No. 5 to the marketplace. Since *You Only Live Twice* did not repeat the spectacular $52 million gross of the previous *Thunderball*, Broccoli blamed his rival for stealing much of the Bond thunder.

A similar rivalry was introduced when both MGM/United Artists and Warner Brothers announced that their respective Bond entries were targeted for a summer 1983 release. Broccoli's latest entry was *Octopussy*, another entirely new story which utilized the last of Fleming's available titles. Written by Richard Maibaum and Michael Wilson, with additional material supplied by George MacDonald Fraser, it was another multimillion-dollar globe-trotter with Roger Moore returning for the sixth time to play Bond.

In the rival camp, fledgling film producer Jack Schwartzman was offering a monumental updating (read: remake) of the old Kevin McClory/Albert Broccoli/Harry Saltzman *Thunderball* project which had been so successful in 1965. However, the identity of the project was not as important as the fact that Sean Connery was returning to play James Bond. Not surprisingly, the film was entitled *Never Say Never Again,* a sweeping reference to a decade of "Sean is coming back to play Bond" rumours. Those rumours had been swept away by facts when in late September 1982, director Irvin Kershner (*The Empire Strikes Back, The Eyes of Laura Mars*) began cranking his Panavision cameras in Nice, France. Having bought out McClory's rights to the *Thunderball* project, Schwartzman, a shrewd lawyer and ex-studio vice-president (with Lorimar), promptly sold domestic distribution rights to Warner Brothers. Foreign interests were to be handled by the Producer's Sales Organization, an aggressive international distribution company that was rapidly cornering the world film marketplace.

As of spring 1983, both films were hovering in the $25-million range and headed for a summer release against other giants, like 20th Century-Fox's third *Star Wars* film *Return of the Jedi,* Warners' own *Superman III,* Columbia's lavish 3-D space adventure *Spacehunter: Adventures in the Forbidden Zone,* and dozens of other major films. In the media, both Moore and Connery, who were the best of friends, were predicting that both films would be successful. As to the eventual winner at the box office, not even the Las Vegas odds makers could answer that one. It was a classic case of "pick-em."

The roots of *Never Say Never Again* go back nearly twenty-five years to the earliest script conferences

Director Irvin Kershner and Sean Connery previously teamed on the 1966 madcap comedy *A Fine Madness*. (*Warner Brothers*)

between Irish filmmaker Kevin McClory and Ian Fleming. Little did they know that the various film treatments they collaborated on throughout 1959 could form the basis of future 007 adventures, beyond even the *Thunderball* project they were planning.

When Kevin McClory made a deal with Albert R. Broccoli and Harry Saltzman to produce *Thunderball* in 1965, a contract stipulation prevented him from considering a new version of the underwater thriller for ten years. It was one of those points dreamed up by Broccoli's legal brain trust to discourage immediate competition for a series that was

gathering tremendous steam. Broccoli had made a deal with McClory in the first place to avoid a "rival Bond." He wanted to make sure that such competition would continue to be discouraged.

McClory kept to the letter of his contract, collected millions in profits from *Thunderball,* and retired to a more settled life as a plantation owner on Paradise Island in Nassau. The first indication of a new *Thunderball* surfaced right on schedule in 1975. McClory was ready to launch a new James Bond project based on the various treatments of *Thunderball,* the rights of which had reverted back to him. At that time the project was called simply *James Bond of the Secret Service.* Rumor had it that Sean Connery was very interested in the project and had even contributed elements of the script. The title was then changed to *Warhead.*

Much of this material has already been presented in various parts of this book, but it should be noted that despite the concerted efforts of Albert Broccoli to stop the *Warhead* project, as being illegal and of unfair competition to his own series of Roger Moore Bonds, the McClory *Warhead* project was a legitimate film entity. However, McClory didn't have the money, the legal muscle, or the studio support to prevent Albert R. Broccoli from tying him up in various courtroom manoeuverings. While he sat on the sidelines marshalling support for a good project, Broccoli was busy churning out the latest 007 products — *The Spy Who Loved Me, Moonraker,* and *For Your Eyes Only.*

Throughout the late 1970s and into the early 1980s, McClory contacted virtually every studio in Hollywood and London, seeking financial support for a Sean Connery *Thunderball* remake. Wherever he went, an army of corporate attorneys pored over his materials, examining the fine points of agreements, letters of intent, and some of the original McClory/Fleming correspondence. Since he was asking for somewhere in the neighborhood of $20 million, it was natural for such a continual analysis.

Sometime in 1980, the McClory project came across the desk at Lorimar, a television and feature film production company (far better known for its television products "Dallas," "The Waltons," etc., than its motion-picture output *The Fish That Saved Pittsburgh* and *The Big Red One.* One of the top executives working at Lorimar at that time was Jack Schwartzman.

A native New Yorker, Schwartzman was a prize-winning student at the UCLA law school, where he specialized in tax law. Five years after joining his first firm as a tax attorney, he became a partner, and in 1965 he started his own firm, Schwartzman, Greenberg and Grakal, which became one of Hollywood's busiest entertainment law firms.

In 1978, he joined Lorimar as an executive vice-president. During his two-year tenure, he served as an executive producer on their most prestigious film *Being There,* the Hal Ashby film that starred the late Peter Sellers. He was also involved in major production decisions on all Lorimar feature film products. In late 1980, Schwartzman left Lorimar to pursue the career of an independent producer. Nearly two years later, he is about to bring his first project to fruition.

In order to make *Never Say Never Again* a reality, Schwartzman early realized that he could not afford a legal confrontation with Albert Broccoli. It had destroyed McClory's chances, and it could easily destroy his. Convinced that McClory did have the rights to create a new updated *Thunderball,* Schwartzman acquired all of the former's materials in a major transaction. He promptly threw out the *Warhead* script and started from scratch. Legally, Schwartzman had to stay within the remake lines of the *Thunderball* project. While *Warhead* had become an entirely new caper involving a SPECTRE base in the Bermuda Triangle, robot-controlled sharks, an atomic assault on New York, and a spectacular battle on the Statue of Liberty, *Never Say Never Again* was outlined as simply an update of *Thunderball.* Legally, Schwartzman had to retain the same characters, the same situations, and the same basic atom bomb hijacking plot.

Confined to such a regimen, Schwartzman hired Lorenzo Semple, Jr., to write the first Sean Connery Bond film in over a decade. (The last Connery Bond was *Diamonds Are Forever* in 1971.) Bond fans will discover familiar character names, if not familiar faces, in *Never Say Never Again.*

Max Von Sydow becomes the fourth actor to appear on camera as SPECTRE chief Ernst Stavro Blofeld (following in the traditions of Donald Pleasance, Telly Savalas, and Charles Gray), once more plotting to steal two atomic weapons and blackmail the Western world. If all the years of legal manoeuvering had proven anything, they had deter-

Max Von Sydow becomes the fourth actor to portray devilish Ernst Stavro Blofeld in *Never Say Never Again.* (20th Century-Fox)

mined that McClory was the only one who had rights to mention the SPECTRE organization in films. This is borne out in *For Your Eyes Only,* where the Blofeld lookalike in the teaser is unidentified in the credits. Broccoli could dress him up to resemble Telly Savalas, giving him a typical beige tunic, a wheelchair, and the proverbial white cat, but he couldn't mention his name or his origin. A script reference to a "tenth anniversary of their last meeting" — intimating *Diamonds Are Forever* was even excised at the last minute.

Austrian actor Klaus-Maria Brandauer reprises the role of Emilio Largo, SPECTRE's No. 2 man, who ramrods the atomic hijacking. Brandauer had attracted worldwide attention with his starring role in Istvan Szabo's *Mephisto,* which won the 1982

Sultry Barbara Carrera portrays Fatima Blush, a character first created by Fleming in the late 1950s. (*American International*)

Academy Award for Best Foreign Film. Long recognized as a leading actor in Vienna's prestigious Burg-theater, where he has played all the European classics and Shakespeare, he makes his English-speaking debut in *Never Say Never Again*.

Fetching Kim Basinger, who recently starred in the Charlton Heston adventure film *Mother Lode* and who portrayed a hooker in the television miniseries "From Here To Eternity," plays Domino, a part once owned by lovely French actress Claudine Auger. Like Auger, Basinger plays the mistress of Largo, who quickly falls in love with Bond.

One character is definitely missing from this new version of the fabled *Thunderball*. That is SPECTRE assassin Fiona Volpe, who was portrayed by the sultry Lucianna Paluzzi in the original. Harking back to the original *Thunderball* treatment developed by McClory and Fleming back in 1959, screenwriter

Lorenzo Semple, Jr., discovered Fatima Blush, a lovely agent whom Bond meets on a USO plane. In *Never Say Never Again*, Fatima assumes all the deadly characteristics of Fiona, proving to be one of Bond's toughest adversaries. For this part, Schwartzman chose Nicaraguan-born actress Barbara Carrera, the dark-haired beauty of *The Island of Dr. Moreau*, *Masada*, and *I, the Jury*.

Rounding out the cast, black actor Bernie Casey becomes the sixth actor to play CIA agent Felix Leiter (after Jack Lord, Cec Linder, Rik Van Nutter, Norman Burton, and David Hedison), and Edward Fox portrays Bond's superior, "M."

Producer Albert R. "Cubby" Broccoli accepted the prestigious Irving Thalberg Memorial Award from the Academy of Motion Pictures in spring 1982, took it home to his Beverly Hills mansion, placed it on the appropriate pedestal, and went right back to work on his thirteenth 007 adventure, *Octopussy*. More than two decades had passed since

Actor Edward Fox as "M," Bond's Secret Service mentor. (*AFD*)

that first meeting with Ian Fleming in London in 1960. Many people had come and gone in the high rolling world of Eon Productions. Hollywood had changed quite a bit, too. Only a few "big" films were being released each year, and most of those were biting the proverbial box-office dust. It was a credit to Broccoli's incredible track record that he could still mount a $25-million Bond film with hardly a ripple at MGM/UA, the company that had gambled $40-million-plus on something called *Heaven's Gate.*

Two decades and two thousand executive changes later, 007 was still the company's bread and butter — a guaranteed winner. Critics may dismiss what they once treasured and Bond purists may wince at the jokes and situations, but Broccoli still points to the balance sheet and a series that is an international phenomenon after twenty years. When *For Your Eyes Only* was released in the summer of 1981, Broccoli's stepson and heir apparent Michael G. Wilson took delight in pointing out that Bond was beating Spielberg's *Raiders of the Lost Ark* in key marketplaces around the globe. On American television, the Bond films still draw excellent rating points, and sales extend to the videocassette and disc market, where 007 still leads its class. There's just no way to put a lid on James Bond.

However, there are always questions for Mr. Broccoli. Where is the tory? Who is the villain? Ever since the mid-1960s when Fleming's *You Only Live Twice* was considerably updated by the imaginative Roald Dahl, Broccoli and his screenwriters have been changing around the original Fleming plots. Fans of the novels can hardly recognize the film versions of *The Spy Who Loved Me* and *Moonraker.*

As 007 moved in the 1980s, little of Master Ian's agent was left. His name was the same and there was a title and sometimes a villain, but everything else seemed to have floated away. Despite the lack of topical and commercial story lines, the remaining Bond books did supply the screenwriters with hidden ingredients — little touches of mystique that only Fleming could have delivered. Those touches continued to woo audiences around the globe. Although the story was a fresh one, Richard Maibaum's new version of *For Your Eyes Only* retained the intrinsic blood feud between Kristatos and Colombo, so much a part of *Risico.* And lovely

Bernie Casey as Bond's CIA chum, Felix Leiter. (*NBC*)

Carole Bouquet was a perfect incarnation of Miss Havelock, the heroine of the short story. The locations — the Greek Islands and snowbound Cortina, Italy — were still vintage Fleming. Even purists who had scolded Broccoli and Company for the buffoonery of *Moonraker* were grateful for the return in *For Your Eyes Only* to good old-fashioned run-and-gun secret agentry.

Octopussy is based on Ian Fleming's last published works — two short stories entitled "Octopussy" and "The Property of a Lady." The least known of all the Fleming titles, both, nonetheless, proved appealing to screenwriters Richard Maibaum, Michael Wilson, and George MacDonald Fraser, who supplied an early-draft screenplay.

Soon after the release of *For Your Eyes Only* in summer 1981, Maibaum and Wilson began to work up a treatment of *Octopussy,* the title announced at the end of the previous film. Typically, the short story was not much of a Bond adventure. In fact, it was extremely autobiographical, considering Fleming's health situation at the time he wrote it. In *Octopussy,* an ex-British intelligence officer named Major Dexter Smythe is living on the coast of Jamaica, where he occasionally paddles out to a reef to visit a carnivorous octopus, whom he dubs Octopussy. Dying of heart disease and waiting for the Angel of Death to arrive, Smythe spends much of his time spearing the dreaded scorpion fish and feeding them to his forever-hungry pet. The Angel of Death arrives in the personage of 007 who knows that Smythe actually stole a shipment of Nazi gold shortly before the end of World War II, killing a German guide named Oberhauser in the process. Oberhauser, it turns out, was a friendly father figure of 007's, who taught him how to ski at Kitzbühel. In the end, Bond gives his quarry a choice. He can come to England for a scandalous trial or take his own life in Jamaica the so-called honourable way. *Octopussy* ends as Smythe, dying from a scorpion-fish sting, inadvertently falls into the clutches of his reef-hugging octopus.

From initial reactions, it was obvious that the film's Octopussy wasn't going to be a sea creature. It was logical for the writers to conceive of a woman with that name. And in the tradition of Pussy Galore, Plenty O'Toole, Kissy Suzuki, and Holly Goodhead, she was so christened.

Reading on, Maibaum and Wilson discovered the second short story in Fleming's "Octopussy" anthology, "The Property of a Lady." This story revolved around the prized Fabergé eggs, the ornamental Easter gifts custom-built for the Russian royal family by famed jewelry craftsman Carl Fabergé. Smuggling the eggs into Britain, the KGB was using them to reward a Russian agent who had succeeded in infiltrating the highest level of British Intelligence. Little did they know that the identity of the agent was known and that the information she was supplying was carefully prepared by British Intelligence itself. In order to learn the identity of her spymaster contact in London, Bond attends a special Fabergé auction at Sotheby's, where one of the eggs is up for sale. During the course of the afternoon, Bond unmasks the Russian agent, who is discovered in the back of the auction room bidding through prearranged signals. His cover blown, the Russian spymaster is sent packing, destroying another carefully engineered KGB infiltration.

Maud Adams returns to the world of 007 as Octopussy, the leader of a group of female smugglers. (*20th Century-Fox*)

Although its story did not influence the final script, Maibaum and Wilson did make note of the East German locations featured in the third and final story in the "Octopussy" anthology, "Living Daylights," which concerned Bond's plan to foil a KGB assassination attempt.

In the film *Octopussy,* the Fabergé eggs once again figure prominently in the story line. Following the mindless teaser sequence (Bond and his Bede mini-jet), the story opens at an East German circus. A clown breaks away from the festivities and is soon chased through a forest by two knife-throwing twins. In scenes reminiscent of the Renaissance garden sequence in *From Russia with Love,* the clown is eventually stabbed and thrown into an aqueduct. Barely alive, he later stumbles into the British Embassy in East Germany, where he dies, a single Fabergé egg rolling out of his hand.

The clown is actually 009, who was investigating a smuggling ring that uses circuses and fairs for cover. But the plot is far more sinister than a simple smuggling racket. In scenes once again strongly reminiscent of Maibaum's *From Russia with Love,* the plot of a fanatical Russian general is revealed. It is General Orlov's plan to trigger the detonation of an

Frenchman Louis Jourdan portrays the evil maharaja Kamal Khan in *Octopussy*.

atomic device on a U.S. Airforce Base, creating a nuclear accident that will be followed by unilateral Western disarmanent. Their opponent crucially weakened, Orlov can then smash through West Germany with a hundred Russian divisions. General Gogol (our old friend Walter Gotell) denounces the offensive as ridiculous, unaware that Orlov is following through with his "accident."

The instrument of Orlov's plot is the treacherous Kamal Khan (Louis Jourdan), an obnoxious Afghan prince who lives luxuriously in Udaipur, India. Khan's benefactor is supplying him with funds from the smuggled Fabergé eggs. Helping to smuggle the eggs, but unaware that Orlov is involved, is Octopussy (Maud Adams), the awesome leader of a beautiful gang of female smugglers who live on an island in Udaipur.

Back in London, James Bond enters the case to investigate the death of fellow agent 009. Following the thin story material provided by "The Property of a Lady," Bond attends an auction at Sotheby's where a Fabergé egg is being auctioned. There he first sees Khan and his lady friend, Magda (Kristina Wayborn). Aware that Khan must purchase the egg to fulfill some unknown but obviously vital purpose, Bond actually bids against the Afghan prince, rais-

ing the price by hundreds of thousands of pounds. Although Khan eventually outbids him, Bond is able to substitute a fake Fabergé egg for the real one purchased by Khan. Convinced that Khan is somehow mixed up in 009's murder, Bond is soon sent to India.

With its floating palaces, impenetrable jungles, whimsical fakirs, and the continual clash of Eastern and Western cultures, Udaipur became another perfect Bond film location. It wasn't the first time the Bond producers had thought about India. Ex-007 chief Harry Saltzman had mentioned an India tiger hunt as a possible location way back in the days of *Live and Let Die.* In Bond's hotel, Maibaum and Wilson reintroduced the backgammon game, a dramatic confrontation lifted from an early script of *The Spy Who Loved Me.* During the game with Khan, Bond wins 200,000 rupees and a parcel load of trouble delivered by the Afghan's menacing henchman Gobinda, a giant Sikh warrior. A chase ensues through the streets of the crowded Indian city, Bond riding in a three-wheel automobile driven by local operative Sadruddin.

Eluding his captors, Bond is later seduced by Magda, who steals the real Fabergé egg unaware that Bond has hidden a microphone inside. Coldcocked by Gobinda, 007 is taken to Khan's palace, where he eventually overhears a conversation between Khan and Russian General Orlov, where the name Octopussy is first mentioned. Escaping from Khan's palace, Bond meets Octopussy, who is revealed as the smuggler-daughter of British agent Dexter Smythe. Following Fleming's own writings, the screenwriters identify Smythe as an accused murderer who stole a cache of Red Chinese gold seized in North Korea. Given his choice by Bond, Smythe commits suicide rather than submit to a scandalous court-martial. Aware that her father was given an honourable choice, Octopussy bears Bond no grudge. Together they fight off a group of assassins sent by Khan — a successful campaign followed by equally successful moments in Octopussy's bed.

The action then shifts to East Germany, where Bond follows clues that lead him to the circus. Disguised in full clown regalia, he infiltrates the enemy camp, discovers Orlov, and somehow makes it to the American air base in time to disarm the atomic device. The last twenty minutes of the film move at breakneck speed as 007 finds himself atop a train (à la Connery in *The Great Train Robbery*) and then whizzing along the Autobahn in a fast motocar. Although the spectre of actor Roger Moore dressed in clown makeup seems ridiculous at first, it does fit expertly into the plot and is not another farcical moment from the *Moonraker* days.

The scenes at the circus, involving the twin assassins, were the product of George MacDonald Fraser's screenwriting pen. After Maibaum and Broccoli came to an early impasse in the script stage, Fraser (the veteran of the *Flashman* novels) stepped in to produce an early draft screenplay.

Although ridiculous rumours floated around Hollywood in the summer and fall of 1982 that Broccoli had chosen American James Brolin to play 007, Roger Moore was signed to play Bond for the sixth time. At 54, there was now some question as to whether the handsome Roger was getting a little old for the part. He told one reporter that fall, "Actually, I don't think age enters into the playing of a part unless you look senile and then of course it's ridiculous. I don't look senile; I just look as though a wind might blow me over any second. . . . Once you've established a character in a continuing serial, you have to stick with it — it's like giving Hamlet another interpretation in the second act. . . . I've always thought it would be absolutely

wonderful to be a stage actor who makes films, but I'd be a terrible ingrate if I were dissatisfied for I've been very lucky.

"I think I've learned my craft, well, I must have. I say its ninety-nine percent luck, but there is that odd one percent that you must know what you're doing, and I think I know what I'm doing. I'm making an ass of myself, that's what I'm doing, and getting paid for it."

Returning for her second starring role in a Bond film (an unprecedented feat), Maud Adams was signed to play Octopussy, quelling early rumours that the front-runners would be either Faye Dunaway (once a contender for Domino in *Thunderball*) or voluptuous Sybil Danning, who even graced a magazine cover in an Octopussy-like wet suit.

Returning to direct — and deservedly so after the slam-bang success of *For Your Eyes Only* — was John Glen, who took his large production crew from the Brandenburg Gate in West Berlin, where principal photography commenced on August 16, 1982, to the jungles and crowded alleyways of central India. With ample funding supplied by MGM/UA (United Artists had been sold off by Transamerica Corporation following the disaster of *Heaven's Gate*), it truly looked as if Albert R. "Cubby" Broccoli was going to bring in another blockbuster.

POSTSCRIPT

THE END, BUT JAMES BOND WILL RETURN

Despite doubts and reservations, the continuing presence of Bond on the screen is a welcome one. For Bond fans, the thrill of hearing the opening James Bond theme and of watching Maurice Binder's 007 gunbarrel logo and Roger Moore's walk, kneel and fire are still ever present. A new John Barry score is always well worth waiting for and the exotic locations, tightly edited special effects and glamorous girls are still outstanding features of the films. If James Bond himself seems to be missing at times, for this author at least, the viewing of each Bond film provides an opportunity for nostalgia.

Remember *Dr. No* with Strangways and Quarrel and the beach at Crab Key – not to mention Ursula Andress in that white bikini. Remember Robert Shaw and Pedro Armendariz, both of whom are gone, and how much they contributed to *From Russia with Love*. Remember that *Goldfinger* Aston Martin. Memorable scenes from the Bond films of the Seventies are fewer in number but equally haunting: the Jimmy Dean character in *Diamonds Are Forever* for instance, evading a shot from Bruce Cabot, and then yelling out "You're fired!".

For many, the arrival of Roger Moore marked the beginning of a decline but this reaction is not altogether reasonable. Moore is tremendously likeable and often surprises us with his skill in pulling off even the silliest of sketches. As an actor, limited as his range may be, he has matured in the Bond role. A good example of Moore at his best occurs in *Moonraker*. Bond is being escorted around Hugo Drax's California space centre when the undercover CIA agent Holly Goodhead invites him to try the centrifuge trainer. Goodhead drifts away and Bond's spin is sabotaged by Drax's assistant, Chang. 007 is violently whirled around until he summons enough strength to unleash his dart gun and destroy the controls. The centrifuge machine comes to a halt and Bond stumbles out, avoiding the assistance of an astonished Holly Goodhead. He has been hurt and he does not want to talk about it. Instead of the predictable one liner, the silence following a moment of extreme danger is reminiscent of the finer moments of the earlier Bond films. Although *Octopussy* seems to be Roger Moore's swan song as Bond, he has finally managed to bring together many of the better elements of the earlier films.

Audiences have demonstrated that the appeal of the Bond series is more than strong enough to withstand the re-casting of its hero. There is no reason to assume that even Roger Moore will be the last of the line. James Bond will return . . .

INDEX

A

Adam, Ken, 9, 18, 20, 21, 39, 44-46, 59, 60, 66-68, 73, 75, 76, 83, 91, 99, 106, 114, 133, 141-145, 149 153, 156, 161, 168, 173
Adams, Maud, 130, 176, 177, 178
Ainley, Anthony, 79
Alba, Rose, 64
Allen, Irving, 9
Allen, Woody, 86
Anderson, David, 29
Anderson, Keith, 150
Andersson, Elga, 25
Andress, Ursula, 10, 12, 14, 15, 18-20, 176, 179
Armendariz, Pedro, 24, 31-33, 176, 179
Armstrong, Louis, 97
Aston Martin, 44-45, 64, 66
Auger, Claudine, 52, 54, 57, 63, 66, 67, 174

B

Bach, Barbara, 136, 137, 141, 142, 148, 149
Barbey, Alex, 93
Barr, Leonard, 107
Barry, John, vii, 21, 40, 62, 71, 76, , 85, 97, 159, 168, 179
Barwick, Anthony, 138-139
Basinger, Kim, 174, 180
Bassey, Shirley, 42
Bates, Cary, 138
Bennett, Bill, 119
Beswick, Martine, 24, 25, 33, 66, 67
Bianchi, Daniela, 25, 27-29, 31, 91
Binder, Maurice, 177
Blackman, Honor, 36, 43, 44, 46, 49
Blofeld, Ernst Stavro, 157, 173
Bogner, Willy, Jr., 93
Bond, Trevor, vii, 27
Boren, Evelyn, 66
Boren, Lamar, 59-60, 66, 68, 79, 143, 150, 151
Borienko, Uri, 88
Bouquet, Carole, 170, 175
Brandauer, Klaus-Maria, 173
Brennan, Michael, 66
Broccoli, Cubby, vii, 8-9, 12-14, 17, 18, 21, 23-25, 29, 31, 34, 37, 39, 40, 43, 48, 51, 54, 55, 59, 62, 63, 67, 72-74, 83, 84, 86, 88, 90, 96, 97, 100, 102, 105, 106, 111, 113, 125, 128, 135, 137-140,145-149,155-159, 160,162,165, 167, 168, 171, 172, 173, 174, 175, 178
Brolin, James, vii
Brosnan, John, 83
Brown, Earl Jolly, 115
Brown, Tony, 80
Browning, Ricou, 60

Brownjohn, Robert, vii, 27
Bryce, Ivar, 1, 3, 7, 51
Buccella, Maria, 63
Buckley, Jim, 136
Burgess, Anthony, 139
Burton, Norman, 103, 174

C

Cabot, Bruce, 108, 179
Cain, Syd, 18, 27-29, 33, 34, 90, 91, 95, 114
Campbell, Robert, 86
Carlisle, Tom, 48-49
Carrera, Barbara, 174
Carter, Reggie, 18
Cartlidge, William, 138, 155
Casey, Bernie, 174
Casino Royale, vii, 1-4, 8, 85-86, 171
CBS, 1-4
Celi, Adolfo, 58, 63
Ceylan, Hasan, 29
Chiles, Lois, 160
Chin, Tsai, 79
Chitwood, Joey, 116, 118, 130
Chomat, 80
Christian, Linda, 4
Christie, Julie, 62-63
Clery, Corinne, 157
Cleveland, Murray, 117-118
Columbia Pictures, 9, 51, 85
Comeaux, Jerry, 117, 118
Commander Jamaica, 2
Connell, Thelma, 75, 83
Connery, Sean, vii, 5, 13, 14, 16-20, 27-30, 33, 41-44, 46, 47, 54, 55, 57, 59, 62, 64-68, 70, 71, 73-74, 78, 79, 86, 91, 93, 97-103, 105, 106, 111, 112, 145, 146, 160, 162, 164, 165, 170, 171, 172, 173
Conti, Bill, 168, 173
Cooper, Jack, 33
Cornell, Phyllis, 45
Cousins, Frank, 66, 68
Coward, Noel, 20
Cracknell, Derek, 116, 130, 132-133
Cuneo, Ernst, 3

D

Dahl, Roald, 72, 73, 75, 78, 96, 138, 156, 175
Danning, Sybil, 178
Davis, Sammy, Jr., 108
Dawson, Anthony, 19, 20, 28
De Poitiers, Diane, 64
De Vries, Hans, 86
Dean, Jimmy, 105, 176
Dehn, Paul, 40, 48
Deighton, Len, 145
Deneuve, Catherine, 93
Derek, John, 10, 14, 18, 20
Diamonds Are Forever, 9, 88, 98-109, 111, 112, 157, 170, 173, 176, 179
Dr. No., vii, 3, 9-25, 28, 76, 80, 153, 158, 159, 176, 179

Doleman, Guy, 63
Dor, Karin, 75, 78, 79
Dunaway, Faye, 63, 178

E

Eaton, Shirley, 36, 42, 43
Ekland, Britt, 126, 130
Eon Productions, vii, 24, 25, 54, 55, 58, 59, 67, 68, 74, 86, 89, 90, 95, 112, 131, 143, 156, 174
Evans, Laurence, 3

F

Feldman, Charles K., 2, 8, 9, 51, 85, 171
Felton, Norman, 51, 53, 54
Fenn, Bob, 8
Ferzetti, Gabriele, 93
Fleming, Ian, 1-4, 6-8, 11, 12, 22-24, 26, 27, 32, 33, 44, 47, 51, 53-54, 66, 130, 156, 159, 165, 166, 171, 172, 174, 175, 177
Force Ten from Navarone, 161
For Your Eyes Only, 3, 165-175, 176, 178
Fox, Edward, 174
Fraser, George MacDonald, 171, 175, 178
Frobe, Gert, 40, 43, 44, 83, 101
From Russia with Love, vii, 2, 22, 24-35, 37, 40-42, 80, 137, 165, 167, 176, 179

G

Gardner, John, 165
Garrett, Donna, 105, 107
Gavin, John, 100
Gayson, Eunice, 12
Giddings, A1, 172
Gilbert, Lewis, 74, 78, 79, 83, 96, 139, 145, 148, 152, 155, 156, 158, 161, 168, 173
Gilliatt, Penelope, 24, 34
Glen, John, vii, 93, 96, 97, 136, 137, 165, 168, 173, 178
Glover, Julian, 167, 170
Goldfinger, 36-49, 51, 54, 55, 57-59, 62, 76, 80, 88, 101, 105, 133, 153, 157, 159, 167, 176, 179
Gotell, Walter, 28, 29, 174
Gray, Charles, 75, 105, 173
Great Train Robbery, The, 178
Green, Guy, 17
Greydon, Dicky, 94-95
Griffin, Don, 150
Gur, Aliza, 24, 33

H

Hall, Fergus, 113
Hama, Mie, 74, 81
Hamilton, Guy, 12, 17, 39, 40, 41, 43-48, 99, 104-106, 114-116, 123, 128, 130, 132, 139, 160, 162
Hamlisch, Marvin, 152